ArtScroll Series®

Rabbi Nosson Scherman / Rabbi Meir Zlotowitz
General Editors

CHOFETZ CHAIM-

Published by

Mesorah Publications, ltd

in conjunction with

THE
CHOFETZ CHAIM
HERITAGE
FOUNDATION

ספר שפת תמים • ספר שם עולם

LESSONS
TRUTH

DAILY STUDIES IN HONESTY
AND FUNDAMENTALS OF
JEWISH FAITH

TRANSLATION AND COMMENTARY BY
RABBI SHIMON FINKELMAN

FIRST EDITION
First Impression … September 2001

Published and Distributed by
MESORAH PUBLICATIONS, LTD.
4401 Second Avenue / Brooklyn, N.Y 11232

Distributed in Europe by
LEHMANNS
Unit E, Viking Industrial Park
Rolling Mill Road
Jarow, Tyne & Wear, NE32 3DP
England

Distributed in Australia and New Zealand by
GOLDS WORLDS OF JUDAICA
3-13 William Street
Balaclava, Melbourne 3183
Victoria, Australia

Distributed in Israel by
SIFRIATI / A. GITLER — BOOKS
6 Hayarkon Street
Bnei Brak 51127

Distributed in South Africa by
KOLLEL BOOKSHOP
Shop 8A Norwood Hypermarket
Norwood 2196, Johannesburg, South Africa

ARTSCROLL SERIES®
LESSONS IN TRUTH
© Copyright 2001, by MESORAH PUBLICATIONS, Ltd.
4401 Second Avenue / Brooklyn, N.Y. 11232 / (718) 921-9000 / www.artscroll.com

---

A project of
THE CHOFETZ CHAIM HERITAGE FOUNDATION
6 Melnick Drive / Monsey, N.Y. 10952 / (845) 352-3505

ISBN:
1-57819-596-9 (hard cover)
1-57819-597-7 (paperback)

Typography by CompuScribe at ArtScroll Studios, Ltd.

Printed in the United States of America by Noble Book Press Corp.
Bound by Sefercraft, Quality Bookbinders, Ltd., Brooklyn N.Y. 11232

מכתב ברכה מאת
הרב ר' שמואל קמנצקי שליט"א
ראש ישיבה, ישיבה דפילאדעלפיא

בס"ד

כ"ו מנחם אב תשס"א לפ"ק

עברתי על התרגום של ספר שפת תמים ממרן גאון עולם
רבינו ישראל מאיר הכהן זצוק"ל הידוע בשם החפץ חיים.

זכה שביעוד חייו נתקבל בכל קצוי תבל לצדיק הדור הפוסק
האחרון בחלק אורח חיים ובפרט בדיני והלכות שמירת
הלשון ומצוות בין אדם לחבירו.

כנראה שמן השמים זיכו והניחו לו מקום להתגדר ולזכות את
כלל ישראל בזהירות בין אדם לחברו. בטוח אני שהצלחת
האדם בתורה ויראת שמים תלוי' בהנהגת האדם בין אדם
לאדם.

יתן השי"ת שהתרגום יביא תועלת גדולה להכלל ובזכות זה
נזכה בקרוב לגאולה שלמה.

שמואל קמנצקי

RABBI YAAKOV PERLOW
1569 • 47TH STREET
BROOKLYN, NY 11219

יעקב פרלוב
ביהמ"ד עדת יעקב נאוואמינסק
ברוקלין נ.י.

בס"ד

עש"ק ה' אלול תשס"א

הראה לי הרב הנעלה והמחנך המצויין מו"ה שמעון
פינקעלמאן שליט"א תכריך גליונות מחיבור אשר הכין
בשפת המדינה מדבריו מוסרו של החפץ חיים זי"ע בספריו
הקדושים המלאים מוסר והדרכה ביראת שמים ותיקון
המידות. והדברים מסודרים בשפה ברורה ובאימרות
ומשלים קולעים אל הלב להבין כל אחד חובתו בעולמו
ולהתגבר על נסיונות החיים.

החיבור באמת אינו צריך להסכמה והמאמרים יעידו על
עצמם ואין ספק שיביא תועלת רבה לכל אשר יראת ה' היא
מבוקשו. ובאתי בדברים אלה רק לעשות רצונו של המחבר
היקר ולחזקו בברכה שיהא פרי עמלו נושא פירות ברחבי
הציבור לעורר הנפשות ולקרב את לבותיהם של ישראל
לאבינו שבשמים.

הכו"ח למען התורה והמצוה ובברכת הצלחה ונחת וכל
טוב סלה.

יעקב פרלוב

מכתב ברכה מאת
הרב ר' מתתי' סלומון, שליט"א
משגיח רוחני דישיבת בית מדרש גבוה דלייקוואוד

בס"ד
אור ליום ה' פרשת כי תצא תשס"א לפ"ק
פה לייקוד יצ"ו

הקדוש מרן רשכבה"ג בעל חפץ חיים זצוק"ל כתב בסוף הפתיחה להלכות לה"ר בזה"ל:

ואבקש לידידי הקורא שזאת הפתיחה יקרא ויחזור ויקרא, כי היא בודאי מועילה לענין זה על להבא יותר מן הכל כי היא מלקטת מאת הראשונים אשר דבריהם קדושים וטהורים בוערות כמראה הלפידים, ובודאי שמרו את עצמן ממדה הגרועה הזו עד תכליתה, על כן דבריהם פועלין מאד בלב קוראיהן עכ"ל. הרי שתלה החח"ם זצ"ל סוד ההצלחה וכח ההשפעה של ספרו על קדושת לשונם וטוהר לבבם אשר הוא רק כצינור אשר הראשונים כותבים דרך קולמוסו.

כן אנחנו היום זכינו לסופר מהיר כמוה"ר שמעון פינקעלמאן שליט"א מלקט מומחה אשר כבר זכה להציע לרבים דברי החח"ם זצ"ל בלשון המדוברת ובשפה ברורה ונעימה המושכת את הקורא ומשפיע על הלב, והוא בסוד הנ"ל כי הוא נשאר נאמן לדברי החח"ם זצ"ל ונאמן לרוחו עד שמרגישים כי דברי החח"ם זצ"ל בעצמם נמשכים דרך קולמוסו קדושים וטהורים ורישומם ניכר.

על כן נחזיקנא טיבותא להאי גברא רבה על שממשיך עוד בעבודת הקודש להוציא לאור ספר שפת תמים של האי סבא קדישא עם הערות וספורים משלים ודוגמאות כדי להקל על הקורא לקבל הדברים ולעשותם, וכן הביא מכמה כתבי החח"ם להאיר הדרך לתורה ולתפילה למדות ואמונה ובודאי גדול מעל שמים חסדו והש"י ישלם פעלו.

למען האמירע אשר ירחיב ה' את פעולו
ויזכה לגל טוב טלם
מאת' חיים סלומון
מתתי' חיים סלומון

THE CHOFETZ CHAIM HERITAGE FOUNDATION

*A not-for-profit foundation
dedicated to the teaching of
Jewish ethics & wisdom*

Dear Friend:

We are pleased and privileged to bring you this latest addition to our publications based on the works of the Chofetz Chaim, a Torah luminary whose wisdom continues to guide our generation.

The Chofetz Chaim Heritage Foundation is an organization devoted to disseminating the works of the Chofetz Chaim in order to move *Klal Yisrael* toward the Torah's vision of a united, holy nation. By spreading his teachings on human relations, personal integrity, ethical behavior and proper speech we hope to strengthen the connection of Jews to each other and to Hashem.

We invite you to join us in building a world worthy of Hashem's presence by spending some time each day learning from the Chofetz Chaim's works. If each of us can make his teachings part of our lives, together we can move our world forward toward Redemption.

Together, with your help, we can get there.

The Chofetz Chaim Heritage Foundation

6 Melnick Drive
Monsey, New York 10952
Tel 845 352-3505
Fax 845 352-3605

This sefer is lovingly dedicated to

Moreinu HaRav
Avraham Yaakov HaKohen Pam zt"l

Esteemed member of the Rabbinical Board of the
Chofetz Chaim Heritage Foundation

In our every interaction with him we were privileged to view
first-hand the heights to which the Torah can elevate those
who love it and live it wholeheartedly

ספר זה מוקדש

לזכר נשמת

גברא יקירא

ה"ה הר"ר חיים צבי בן שלמה ע"ה
וויינברגר

✍ *Table of Contents*

✒ Author's Acknowledgments

A number of years ago, my friend RABBI ASHER PAM suggested to me that I translate *Sefer Sefas Tamim*. I am grateful to R' Asher for his suggestion, which led to the publication of this volume.

As this book is being prepared for publication, *Klal Yisrael* mourns the passing of R' Asher's revered father, MOREINU HARAV AVRAHAM YAAKOV HAKOHEIN PAM, זצ״ל. I am grateful that on many occasions I had the *zechus* to seek the guidance and blessings of HaRav Pam, who was a symbol of *chesed* and *emes* in our generation. Many of HaRav Pam's thoughts, as recorded in *Sefer Atarah L'Melech* and in addresses published in *The Jewish Observer*, are found in this work. May HaRav Pam's shining example light the way for us and for future generations and may he be a *meilitz yosher* for his family, his *talmidim* and all of *Klal Yisrael*.

What finally convinced me to embark on this project was an address delivered by the *Mashgiach Ruchani* of Beth Medrash Govoha, HARAV MATISYAHU SALOMON, שליט״א, at Mesivta Torah Vodaath, on the *yahrtzeit* of another embodiment of *emes*, MOREINU HARAV YAAKOV KAMENETSKY, זצ״ל. HaRav Salomon read from the Chofetz Chaim's preface to *Sefas Tamim*, which states that this *sefer* follows naturally from *Sefer Chofetz Chaim*. HaRav Salomon suggested that our generation, in which the study and practice of *shemiras halashon* has become widespread, should now embrace the study of *Sefer Sefas Tamim* as well.

I am deeply grateful to HaRav Salomon and to the Novominsker *Rebbe*, HARAV YAAKOV PERLOW, שליט״א, for having taken of their precious time to read parts of the manuscript and grace this work with their *michtavei berachah*. I am grateful as well to the *Rosh Yeshivah* of the Yeshivah of Philadelphia, HARAV SHMUEL KAMENETSKY, שליט״א, who serves as Chairman of the Rabbinical Board of the Chofetz Chaim Heritage Foundation, for gracing this volume with his מכתב ברכה.

RABBI YISROEL REISMAN, distinguished *maggid shiur* and *rav*, took time from his busy schedule to review the manuscript in its entirety. I am grateful for this, as well as for his friendship.

The idea for this book was developed in collaboration with my dear friend, the indefatigable Director of the Chofetz Chaim Heritage Foundation, MICHAEL ROTHSCHILD. May he be granted continued *siyata diShmaya* in his efforts for *harbatzas Torah* and see much *nachas* from his family.

From the outset, RABBI MEIR ZLOTOWITZ recognized the importance of this project and gave it his encouragement and full support. Once again, RABBI NOSSON SCHERMAN has served as my mentor, advisor and friend from start to finish. I am deeply grateful to him for more than I can express in words. May Hashem grant ArtScroll/Mesorah's General Editors, as well as its graphics genius R' SHEA BRANDER, continued success להגדיל תורה ולהאדירה.

My thanks to ArtScroll's project coordinator R' AVROHOM BIDERMAN and his assistant, MRS. ZISSEL KELLER, as well the project coordinator for the Chofetz Chaim Heritage Foundation, MRS. SHAINDY APPELBAUM.

My thanks to the entire staff at ArtScroll/Mesorah, especially ELI KROEN for designing the pages, and paginators ESTY FRANKEL, TZINA HANOVER, and FRADY VORHAND.

My appreciation to Ben Gasner of Jerusalem for his striking cover design.

My siblings and myself are grateful to *Hashem Yisborach* for the continued *zechus* of learning from the ways and words of our father and mother שיחיו. May they be granted many more years together in good health.

My appreciation to my in-laws, שיחיו, for being who they are and for all that they have done for myself and my family. May Hashem grant them many more years together in good health.

My wife, TOVA, תחי', provides a home atmosphere which is conducive for *harbatzas Torah* and she assists me in all my endeavors. יהי רצון שימלא ה' משאלות לבה לטובה.

I thank Hashem for granting me the ability to undertake and complete this project. May *Klal Yisrael* merit the salvation which it so desperately needs, בביאת גואל צדק במהרה בימינו אמן.

Shimon Finkelman

Elul 5761

✑ Acknowledgments

Our gratitude to Hashem *Yisbarach* is inexpressible for His having permitted us to produce this *sefer* and continue to spread the teachings of the Chofetz Chaim.

Our success flows from the Torah leaders who map out our path:

The Manchester Rosh Yeshivah, HAGAON HARAV YEHUDAH ZEV SEGAL, *zt"l*, the founding Rabbinic Advisor of our organization, was one of the precious resources of our generation. His love and concern for every Jew can only be compared to that of the Chofetz Chaim himself.

HAGAON HARAV SHMUEL KAMENETSKY, *shlita*, is the Chairman of our Rabbinical Board. He is our source of inspiration and guidance, constantly taking time out of his busy schedule to answer our questions, to give us direction and advice and to attend all our board meetings. His *mesiras nefesh* for us is incredible and we are forever indebted to him.

HAGAON HARAV AVRAHAM PAM, *zt"l*, and יבל"ח, the Novominsker Rebbe, HAGAON HARAV YAAKOV PERLOW, *shlita*, have long provided us with their wisdom and advice as members of our Rabbinical Board of Advisors.

We are deeply grateful to the outstanding people of the Chofetz Chaim Heritage Foundation:

To our board of directors who have been a tremendous help in forging the path of our organization:

RAYMOND BEYDA, ABRAHAM BIDERMAN, ABA CLAMAN, NACHMAN FUTTERMAN, DAVID LOBEL, YITZCHOK MASHITZ, ARI PARNES, GEORGE ROHR, KURT ROTHSCHILD, DAVID SHWEKY, GEDALIAH WEINBERGER AND MOSHE ZAKHEIM.

If you have benefited from any of our programs, productions or publications, it is thanks to the selfless dedication of numerous talented individuals, our superb coordinators and our efficient office staff: GIORA CARMI, RABBI YAAKOV LOVE, ALAN PROCTOR, BLIMI BRAUNSTEIN, ETTI DEAN, CHANA MIRIAM BRESLER, GOLDIE GOTTESMAN, BASSIE GUGENHEIM, KAYLA HALPERN, GITTY KALIKSTEIN, DEVORAH LEIBA

KALMANOWITZ, ETTI KLEIN, SURI KNOBLOCH, ESTHER KOOT, BLIMIE
LESSER, FAIGY LIPSCHUTZ, CHAVA'LE LONDINSKI, CHUMI MANDELBAUM,
ESTHER MOR, CHANA NESTLEBAUM, JUDY OELBAUM, MIREL ORLOFSKY,
HEIDY ORT, RUCHIE PERLSTEIN, YAFFA ROSENTHAL, ROCHEL SCHNALL,
LEAH SEKULA, TZIPPORY STEINMETZ, CHAVIE TWERSKY AND BLIMIE
WINKLER.

The Chofetz Chaim Heritage Foundation is forever grateful to RABBI
MENDEL KESSIN, whose tapes inspired us to start our organization.

Our organization's success is due to friends around the world who
have brought our programs to their *shul,* school or community. To our
375 local coordinators—the *Rabbanim,* principals and lay people who
have put their time and energy into uplifting *Klal Yisrael*—thank you so
much.

To all of the above, as well as those who support us financially—the
major supporters who wish to remain anonymous, the main sponsors
of this book, the people who have dedicated a day in this *sefer* and the
many others that have supported us—may the great *z'chus* of the
Chofetz Chaim stand by you, your families and all of *Klal Yisrael.*

The Chofetz Chaim Heritage Foundation

Elul 5761

❧ Introduction

HONESTY AND FAITH:
Two Halves of a Whole

The Torah relates how the sons of Yaakov descended to Egypt during a famine and came before the land's viceroy who, unbeknownst to them, was their brother Yosef. When Yosef sent them back home with instructions to return with their youngest brother Binyamin, he gave them provisions for the road and grain for their father's house. Yosef also had his men take the money which his brothers had given as payment for the grain, and secretly return it to their sacks. What was the purpose of this?

The Torah's Standards

Rabbi Shimon Schwab, quoting the Brisker *Rav*, explained that this was Yosef's way of ensuring that the brothers would return to Egypt. He knew that as descendants of Avraham, Yitzchak and Yaakov, they would not be at peace with themselves as long as someone else's money was in their possession. Thus, they would feel forced to return to Egypt, if for no other reason than to return the money which was not their own.

The Torah tells of Avraham's abhorrence of dishonesty. When the shepherds of his nephew Lot allowed their flocks to graze in the property of others, Avraham asked Lot to move elsewhere, lest their neighbors think that it was Avraham's shepherds who were engaging in robbery.

Avraham, in turn, was well aware that the prohibition against robbery is among the Seven Noachide Laws [שֶׁבַע מִצְוֹת בְּנֵי נֹחַ] which are binding upon all of mankind, and that the sin of robbery had sealed the fate of the generation at the time of the *Mabul* (Deluge).

The sin of lying was also anathema to our forefathers and is underscored by the Torah's warning: *Distance yourself from falsehood (Shemos* 23:7). The Talmud teaches: "The seal of the Holy One, Blessed is He, is truth" (*Shabbos* 55a).[1] By contrast, habitual liars are among those who will not merit to greet the *Shechinah* (Divine Presence) in the World to Come (*Sanhedrin* 103a).

In Our Day   Unfortunately, we live in a world where dishonesty, in word and in deed, is all too commonplace and even acceptable — and this has had a negative influence on our own community. To quote Rabbi Yissocher Frand:

> In our day and age, the standard of truthfulness has sunk to new lows. That is really not surprising. It is generally agreed that we live in the predawn of the Messianic age,[2] and the

---

1. A comment of *Rashi* in his explanation of an incident recorded in the Talmud is enlightening:

    When Rav ascended to Eretz Yisrael, he arrived at the academy of his uncle, R' Chiya. R' Chiya asked him, "Is Aivu (Rav's father) still alive?" In fact, both of Rav's parents had already died, but to avoid reporting bad news outright, Rav responding by asking, "Is Ima (Rav's mother) alive?" R' Chiya then asked, "Is Ima, in fact, alive?" to which Rav responded, "Is Aivu alive?" In this way, R' Chiya understood that both Aivu and Ima were no longer alive (*Pesachim* 4a).

    Rashi cites an interpretation that in response to R' Chiya's questions, Rav responded with a statement. When R' Chiya asked about Rav's father, Rav replied, "My mother is alive," and when R' Chiya asked about his mother, Rav replied, "My father is alive." In this way, R' Chiya was to deduce that both had died.

    Rashi, however, rejects this interpretation: "It is incomprehensible to me that Rav would have uttered a falsehood [even if simply to avoid being the bearer of bad tidings]."

2. The Chofetz Chaim states this in *Shem Olam.* See Day 82 in this volume.

Mishnah (*Sotah* 49b) tells us that one of the hallmarks of our age is the disappearance of truth. And indeed, if we look around contemporary society, we are struck by the total bankruptcy of truth.

Lying has become endemic to society. The public has become accustomed to having the government lie and then cover it up... Lying is thoroughly pervasive in the business world, from the oft-repeated "the check is in the mail" to the guiding principle that determines policy by the likelihood of getting away with it.

Tragically, the disease of untruthfulness has infected the Jewish community as well. There was a time when the word of a Jew was sacrosanct. There was a time when people preferred to do business with observant Jews because they were assumed to be trustworthy. Is that still the case? Unfortunately, it is not.

(*Listen to Your Messages.* p. 91)

The oft-heard excuse, "But everyone does it," is unacceptable. Rabbi Yaakov Kamenetsky, when asked whether or not it is permissible to provide false information in order to be eligible for government programs, replied with an emphatic, "No!" When the petitioner countered, "But plenty of gentiles do it!" R' Yaakov responded, "But they did not stand at *Har Sinai* [when the Torah was given]."

The very last words of Moshe *Rabbeinu* (Our Teacher) to the Jewish people were: וְאַתָּה עַל בָּמוֹתֵימוֹ תִדְרוֹךְ, *You [Israel] will tread upon their [your foes'] high places* (*Devarim* 33:29). Rabbi Schwab interpreted this as symbolizing the exalted moral and ethical levels expected of our nation. When a Jew sets standards for himself, he should use the moral and ethical standards of the nations as a *starting* point; where their striving ends, ours should begin.

Within Our Reach

Attaining the level of integrity which the Torah expects of us is surely within our reach. In our days, many of our people have sanctified Hashem's Name by demonstrating exemplary behavior in this area.

The late Rabbi Avraham Pam, revered *Rosh Yeshivah* of Mesivta Torah Vodaath, was known for his passion for truth in both speech and action. His children learned this at a young age.

Once, he took the children on a city bus and handed the driver fare for everyone. The driver attempted to return one fare. "He rides for free," the driver said, motioning to the youngest boy who appeared to be under age. "No, he *is* of age," Rabbi Pam replied and he paid the fare.

On another occasion, Rabbi Pam and a son entered a taxi. After about a minute, the son realized that the meter was not running and he pointed this out to his father. Rabbi Pam mentioned this to the driver and was stunned by his reply. "Rabbi, this ride is for *me!*" meaning that he was purposely not running the meter so that he could pocket the entire fare. Rabbi Pam insisted that the meter be turned on and assured the driver that he would satisfy him. True to his word, he gave the man a very generous tip which left him very happy. To this *tzaddik*, the dividends of integrity far outweighed the extra money which he had spent.

Such behavior is not limited to the *tzaddikim* among us.

A student of Beth Medrash Govoha in Lakewood was pulled over on the highway and given a summons for speeding. The student was a responsible driver and was certain that he could not have been going more than a few miles above the speed limit. A hearing date was set.

At the hearing, the police officer who had issued the ticket called him aside and said, "I want you to get off easy so what you should do is plea-bargain. That means, admit to committing an offense, but not one as bad as speeding. Tell the judge that you weren't speeding, but that you *were* driving without wearing a seat belt. The fine will be a lot less and there won't be any points on your license."

The student's hearing was the last of the day. No one was in the room, save for himself, his father, the officer and the judge. The judge and the officer must have discussed the case beforehand, for the judge began the proceedings by telling the young man, "Listen, we want to let you off easy. Just plea-bargain and say that you weren't wearing a seat belt."

"But I *was* wearing a seat belt," the student replied.

The judge was annoyed by the young man's apparent naiveté. "Of course you were wearing one, but just say for the record that you weren't. That way we can give you a lighter fine."

"But it's a lie. I can't lie."

"We're not asking you to swear!" The judge was clearly upset by the student's stubbornness. "Just affirm that you were driving without being belted!"

But the student refused to cooperate and was fined for speeding. He, too, was motivated by the conviction that the importance of adhering to *emes*, truth, far outweighed the cost of the fine and the points on his license.

A Double Connotation

*A*t the time when they escort a person to *[his final] judgment [after death], they say to him, "Did you conduct your business dealings [בֶּאֱמוּנָה] in good faith?"*
(Shabbos 31a).

Rabbi Schwab commented on the above teaching:

The word אֱמוּנָה has two meanings: "Were your dealings done *in good faith*, that is, were they conducted honestly?" — and "When you were engaged in business, did you possess *faith in Hashem*?" In other words, did you believe that G-d "feeds and provides all" — that *hashgachah pratis* (Divine Providence) rules? — that there is Someone observing you? — listening to what you are saying and thinking, and that all that you do is being recorded for future reference?

Following these guidelines of accountability, one may conclude that if I merit to enjoy a livelihood that is free from all possible infractions, no *chillul* (desecration of) Shabbos, no *chillul Hashem* (desecration of Hashem's Name), no cheating, robbing, swindling or duplicity, and I am not lazy in my efforts to make a decent living, then I have every right to place my trust in Hashem that "He Who gives me life will give me sustenance." And if I succeed in my efforts, then I know it was not my know-how, not my intelligence, not my energy, not my hard work. Any success that I achieve is to be attributed to, "It is He Who grants you the prowess to amass a fortune" (*Devarim* 8:7).

And should I fail in spite of all this, I must accept the loss with *emunah*, faith, because all comes from Him. And throughout, I maintain the firm *bitachon* (trust) that He will not let me down, and that my financial difficulties are temporary; I have a right to pray and to remain confident that my trust in Hashem will not go unrewarded.

(from The Ethical Imperative)

Rabbi Pam noted that one who approaches his business dealings with firm אֱמוּנָה in Hashem will be inspired to conduct his business affairs even *beyond* the letter of the law. His higher sense of ethics and concern that he not be guilty of *chillul Hashem* will impel him to conduct his business in a way that will earn him the admiration and respect of all.

R' Pam would tell of a *tzaddik*, R' Avraham Hurvitz, who owned a bedding supplies store in the East New York section of Brooklyn. When someone would ask, "Do you have a nice mattress?" he would say, "Nice? I don't know. Maybe others have better merchandise. I can only show you what I have."

If he was in the back room of the store, and he overheard his wife showing a particular mattress to a purchaser, he would call out to her, "Did you show the customer the damage on that? Please show it." R' Hurvitz did this because he was wary of the Torah prohibitions against defrauding a customer or misleading him in any way.[3]

R' Yitzchak Silberstein, distinguished *Rav* of Ramat Elchonon in Bnei Brak, related the following story:

The Right Approach

In the days when Bnei Brak was still a small, developing community, a G-d-fearing man opened a publishing company there for the publication of *sefarim*. There was little competition in those days and his business prospered. After a few years, a second publishing firm opened only a block or two away. The children of the first publisher were incensed by this — but the publisher himself was not incensed at all. In fact, he made his way to the new publishing house, greeted the owner warmly and said:

"You are new in the neighborhood and you do not have any knowledge of whom to seek as customers. Let me share my customer list with you." And he proceeded to name a long list of customers.

"Are you familiar with the printing machinery?" he then asked. "If not, I will be more than happy to show you how everything works." The other man was new to the publishing business and he gratefully accepted the man's offer. For the next hour, the experienced publisher taught the tools of the trade to his competitor.

Later, the man's children asked him, "We can well understand why you did not take any action *against* him — but why did you have to help him?"

Their father replied, "You agree, of course, that whatever we are to earn is decreed in Heaven. One person cannot deprive another of *one cent* that has been decreed for him. Therefore, whatever I did

---

3. See *Atarah L'Melech*, pp. 107-108.

today to assist that man will not cause me any loss of income.

"We all know that this is true — but the trick is to *feel* that it is true and to live by it."[4]

The Purpose of This Volume

The great *mussar* (ethics) personality Rabbi Eliyahu Lopian would often quote a well-known verse:

וְיָדַעְתָּ הַיּוֹם וַהֲשֵׁבֹתָ אֶל לְבָבֶךָ, כִּי ה' הוּא הָאֱלֹקִים בַּשָּׁמַיִם מִמַּעַל וְעַל הָאָרֶץ מִתָּחַת, אֵין עוֹד.

You are to know this day and take to your heart that Hashem is the only G-d — in heaven above and on the earth below — there is none other (Devarim 4:39).

There is a great distance, said R' Lopian, between יְדִיעָה, intellectual knowledge of a Torah principle, and הַשָּׁבָה לַלֵּב, perceiving that truth in the depths of one's heart.

One can *know* that there is an omniscient Creator Who has given us a clear set of guidelines as to how we should conduct our business affairs, but unless we perceive in our hearts the imperative of living a life that is free of falsehood, we are in danger of failure.

The way to traverse the great distance from mind to heart is by studying and then pondering the truths upon which Torah life is based, as well as the importance of living a life of truth. This is the purpose of *Lessons in Truth*.

The first part of this volume is based on *Sefas Tamim*, the Chofetz Chaim's work on the subject of honesty in word and in practice. The second part is based on the second section of *Shem Olam*, which focuses on many fundamentals of Judaism: approaching one's service of Hashem with alacrity; reward and punishment in the World to Come; the imperative of Torah study; awareness of Hashem's Presence; the birthpangs of *Mashiach* and anticipating the redemption.

---

4. From *Tuvcha Yabi'u*, Vol. I. pp. 367-368.

Daily study of the Torah approach to honesty should help to strengthen one's commitment to these all-important principles. But there is another way to strengthen one's resolve in this area: by focusing on the true meaning of life. If one is constantly aware that he has been placed on this world for spiritual accomplishment, that ultimately he will stand judgment in the World to Come for how he lived his life on this world; and that his relatively mundane existence on this world is destined to change with the arrival of *Mashiach*, then his outlook on life will be decidedly spiritual. He will have traversed the great distance from יְדִיעָה, intellectual knowledge, to הַשָׁבָה לַלֵב, perceiving that truth in the depths of one's heart. He will live a life of *emunah*, faith in Hashem, and his monetary dealings will reflect his deep-rooted faith.

This is what joins *Sefer Sefas Tamim* to *Sefer Shem Olam*.

May we merit to absorb the Chofetz Chaim's teachings so that we may follow in his ways and live our lives with a genuine awareness of Hashem's Presence.

A Note to the Reader:

In each lesson, the bold italicized type
is a translation of the Chofetz Chaim's words.
This is usually followed by a commentary,
which appears in regular type.

Book I:

Sefer
Sefas Tamim

๙ *Who Wants Life?*

SEFER SEFAS TAMIM — Preface

ing David taught: "Which man desires life (chofetz chaim), who loves days of seeing good? Guard your tongue from evil and your lips from speaking deceit..." (Tehillim 34:13-14). Therefore, it is only natural that Sefer Chofetz Chaim, which teaches us how to guard our tongues from the evils of lashon hara, should be followed by "Sefas Tamim" ("Sincere Speech") which contrasts deceit and its punishments with honesty and its rewards. Sefas Tamim is drawn from many works, especially the classic ethical text Shaarei Teshuvah (Gates of Repentance) by Rabbeinu Yonah.

The Talmud relates (*Avodah Zara* 19b) that R' Alexandri once walked through the streets announcing, as would a peddler, "Who wants life, who wants life?" Everyone crowded around him and begged, "Give us life!" He quoted our verse, "Which man desires life... Guard your tongue from evil and your lips from speaking deceit..."

What did R' Alexandri tell the people that they did not already know from the verse? R' Eliyahu Meir Bloch explained that one might have thought that King David's words are intended only for those who aspire to a life of utter righteousness. To be a *tzaddik*, one must avoid gossip and deceit. But if one does not have such aspirations, then perhaps a bit of gossip or crookedness is to be expected! R' Alexandri taught that this is not so. David is telling *every* Jew that avoiding *lashon hara* and dishonesty is the key to a good life in this world and the Next.

R' Yissocher Frand relates the following story:

A man came to his *Rav* with a troubling question. "Rabbi, I don't understand. I come from a very distinguished religious family, I am quite learned and I am meticulous in observing every detail of *halachah*. Now, Mr. _____, as you well know, is a simple man from a simple family. He keeps what he knows, which is not very much.

"Yet I have not merited to see *nachas* from my children, while every one of Mr. _____'s children is a gem. Can you explain this?"

"Are you prepared to hear something painful?" asked the *rav*.

"Yes," the man replied.

"You entered the business world with nothing and worked very hard to be successful. But your approach was not at all straight; you would bend the rules to accomplish your goals, you could say one thing and mean another. That's what your children saw, that nothing really means anything.

"However, Mr. _____, as you said, is a simple man — simple and sincere. I am certain that he has never told a lie willfully. That is what his children saw and that is why they are the way they are."

Yes, honesty and sincerity are keys to a good life in both worlds.

Honesty and sincerity are keys to a good life in both worlds.

לע"נ יחיא-ל מיכל ז"ל בן ר' נחמן יבלחט"ט — **1 Tishrei**
Dedicated by Weiser, Yarmish, Nadell and Friedman families
1 Shevat — לזכות רפואה שלמה בילא לאה בת צירל בתושח"י
1 Sivan — Murray Niedober לע"נ מרדכי בן יצחק ז"ל
May today's learning be an עילוי for his נשמה. Dedicated by his wife, children and grandchildren

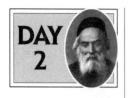

ב תשרי
2 TISHREI / CYCLE 1

September 19, 2001
September 8, 2002
September 28, 2003
September 17, 2004
October 5, 2005

ב שבט
2 SHEVAT / CYCLE 2

January 15, 2002
January 5, 2003
January 25, 2004
January 12, 2005
January 31, 2006

ב סיון
2 SIVAN / CYCLE 3

May 13, 2002
June 2, 2003
May 22, 2004
June 9, 2005
May 29, 2006

➳ *The Conniving Fellow*

SEFER SEFAS TAMIM — Chapter One:
Deceit vs. Truthfulness

irmah (deceit) refers to any statement that is intended to mislead someone. This includes misleading someone in business matters. It also includes statements which in themselves do not cause the listener harm, but which could lead to harm or loss. For example:

A conniving fellow sets his eyes on cheating a certain individual. In order to accomplish this, he first must earn the person's trust, so he "befriends" him. This in itself is mirmah and is a terrible sin.

People who are guilty of being אֶחָד בְּפֶה וְאֶחָד בְּלֵב, meaning that their words are not reflective of their true feelings, are classified among those who are "hated by G-d" (see Pesachim 113b).

As *Iyun Yaakov* (ibid.) explains, a person who is two-faced demonstrates that he lacks fear of Hashem. He befriends people while plotting behind their backs, ignoring — or denying — that the all-knowing G-d is aware of one's innermost thoughts and secrets.

The late Rabbi Shimon Schwab, revered *Rav* of the Washington Heights *kehillah*, made another observation: Those who resort to trickery, fraud or outright thievery to earn money show a basic lack of faith in Hashem. Do they truly believe that Hashem wants them to steal and cheat in order to make ends meet? Apparently they do not believe that each year on Rosh Hashanah, Hashem decrees our earnings for the coming year (*Beitzah* 16a), and that He has infinite means by which to ensure that we *will* earn whatever is meant for us.

But there are many Jews who do possess such faith.

Baruch Feldman (a fictitious name) owns a health-care facility on the east coast. A government audit revealed that he had overpaid $100,000 in taxes. A few weeks later he received a government check for that amount. Two weeks later, he received another check for the same amount. Mr. Feldman immediately called his accountant.

Upon looking into the matter, the accountant concluded that the second check had been issued in error. "Mr. Feldman," he said, "the decision is yours. Chances are very slim that anyone in the government will ever realize the error. So if you deposit the second check, you'll probably have no problem keeping it. Of course, you're not actually entitled to the money."

Mr. Feldman left the room and upon returning after a few minutes said, "I discussed the matter with my partner and we decided to return the money." The accountant was well aware that the only "partner" Mr. Feldman had was Hashem, and that he had left the room to ponder privately what Hashem would want him to do in such a situation. He concluded that without a doubt the right decision was to return the money.

Hashem has infinite means to ensure that we will earn whatever is meant for us.

2 Tishrei — Harold H. Winsten נ"י לזכות צבי בן אברהם
Dedicated by his family, with love and admiration, in honor of his 80th birthday.

2 Shevat — Max Herz ע"ה לע"נ מנחם בן החבר יוסף
Dedicated by his family

2 Sivan — Eugene Schrott ע"ה לע"נ איסר בן יעקב
Dedicated by his daughter Betsy

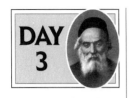

DAY 3

ג תשרי
3 TISHREI / CYCLE 1

September 20, 2001
September 9, 2002
September 29, 2003
September 18, 2004
October 6, 2005

ג שבט
3 SHEVAT / CYCLE 2

January 16, 2002
January 6, 2003
January 26, 2004
January 13, 2005
February 1, 2006

ג סיון
3 SIVAN / CYCLE 3

May 14, 2002
June 3, 2003
May 23, 2004
June 10, 2005
May 30, 2006

✦ Attacking the Root Cause

SEFER SEFAS TAMIM — Chapter One:
Deceit vs. Truthfulness (cont.)

*T*he terrible trait of אֶחָד בְּפֶה וְאֶחָד בְּלֵב, whereby one's kind words are contradicted by treacherous inner thoughts, was addressed by the prophet Yirmiyahu:

> with his mouth one speaks peace with his fellow, but inside of him he lays his ambush. "Shall I not punish for these things?" says Hashem. "From a people such as this, shall I not exact revenge?" (Yirmiyahu 9:8-9).

> Such behavior is sinful on two accounts: the harm that is caused and the lie itself. For aside from the harm that victims of two-facedness suffer, the falsehood is in itself despicable in Hashem's eyes: "False lips are an abomination to Hashem" (Mishlei 12:22).

The verse in *Mishlei* continues: "...but those who act faithfully are His desire." *Chevel Nachalah* explains that when a person becomes sick and feels pain in various parts of his body, one does not treat each organ separately. A good doctor will search for the root cause of all the symptoms and treat it; once that is cured, all the symptoms will disappear. Similarly, if someone is spiritually ill and is suffering from a variety of faults, he should first work on curing the root cause of all his maladies — שֶׁקֶר, *falsehood.*

The *Midrash* relates that once, a young man came before the Talmudic sage R' Shimon ben Shetach, bemoaning his sorry spiritual state. He felt himself trapped in the *yetzer hara's* snare and saw no way out. R' Shimon told him, "Do not weep, for I have a simple solution for your problems. Be extremely careful to avoid all forms of falsehood, whether in word or deed. This will be a cure for your maladies."

The young man took an oath to abide by these instructions.

Sometime thereafter, the young man noticed a neighbor leaving his home, and he was overcome by a tremendous urge to steal. He entered the house and filled a sack with all his neighbor's valuables, leaving nothing behind.

But as he left the house, a thought suddenly struck him: "Surely my neighbor will approach me and ask me if I know who might have broken into his house — and what will I tell him? If I lie and say that I know nothing about the robbery, I will have broken my oath."

The young man returned the items and repented of his sins (*Yalkut Me'am Loez* and other sources).[1]

Thus, *those who act faithfully* and avoid falsehood, will ultimately do *His desire.*

Hashem desires those who act faithfully.

---

1. The Chofetz Chaim mentions this incident at the close of Sefas Tamim.

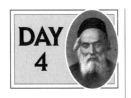

ד תשרי
4 TISHREI / CYCLE 1

September 21, 2001
September 10, 2002
September 30, 2003
September 19, 2004
October 7, 2005

ד שבט
4 SHEVAT / CYCLE 2

January 17, 2002
January 7, 2003
January 27, 2004
January 14, 2005
February 2, 2006

ד סיון
4 SIVAN / CYCLE 3

May 15, 2002
June 4, 2003
May 24, 2004
June 11, 2005
May 31, 2006

❧ *Banished from His Presence*

SEFER SEFAS TAMIM — Chapter One:
Deceit vs. Truthfulness (cont.)

If a person uses trickery to deprive some-one of some future gain, or to convince someone to grant him a gift which had been intended for someone else, then he, too, has been guilty of mirmah (deceit). In such situations, where the perpetrator has not stolen outright, he will suffer punishment primarily for falsehood, while his sin is compounded by the loss which he caused his fellow to suffer.

Mirmah is so disgraceful that it causes the sinner to be banished from Hashem's Presence, as it is written, "A perpetrator of deceit shall not dwell in My house" (Tehillim 101:7). Our Sages liken this to a king who issues a proclamation throughout his kingdom: "Whoever is not loyal to me must leave my kingdom, or else he will be executed!" In a similar way, Hashem declares: "Whoever pursues falsehood does not deserve to be in My world, for I have created the world with truth — otherwise, the world could not exist. And falsehood cannot coexist with truth."

The verse in *Tehillim* quoted by the Chofetz Chaim concludes, "One who tells lies shall not be established before My eyes."

The Book of *Melachim* tells of a prophetic vision where Hashem set into motion the events that would bring about the death of the wicked King Achav.

> Hashem said, "Who will entice Achav so that he will go up [to wage war] and fall at Ramos Gilad?" And the spirit came forth and stood before Hashem and said, "I will entice him." Hashem said to him, "How?" [The spirit] said, "I will go forth and be a lying spirit in the mouth of all [Achav's] prophets [and they will convince him that he will be victorious]." Hashem said, "You will entice and also prevail. Go out and do so"(*I Melachim* 22:20-22).

Those who engage in deceit are banished from Hashem's Presence.

The spirit was that of Navos *HaYizrae'li*, whom Achav's wicked wife Izevel had executed when he refused to sell Achav a vineyard which was adjacent to the king's palace. The Talmud relates (*Sanhedrin* 102b) that when Hashem told Navos' spirit, "Go out," the intention was, "Leave My presence!" for, "One who tells lies shall not be established before My eyes."

Yad Ramah explains: Although Hashem consented to allow the spirit to carry out its suggestion, He banished it from His presence. True, the task of being the spirit of untruth in the mouths of Achav's prophets had to be accomplished somehow, but one should not volunteer on his own to be the instrument of any act that involves lying. The fact that Navos' spirit was eager to carry out this mission indicated a character flaw, and therefore he was banished from Hashem's Presence.

4 Tishrei — Israel W. Kirshenbaum לע"נ ישראל זאב בן אליהו שמואל ז"ל
Dedicated in his loving memory by Les & Rochie Kirshenbaum and family

4 Shevat — Ralph S. Gindi לע"נ רפאל בן רחל ז"ל
Dedicated in loving memory by his wife and children

4 Sivan — In honor of our children: Aliza, Romema, Meira, Saadia, Aharon Yedidia and Yonina   Dedicated by Karen & Stan Fireman

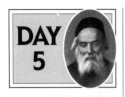

ה תשרי
5 TISHREI / CYCLE 1

September 22, 2001
September 11, 2002
October 1, 2003
September 20, 2004
October 8, 2005

ה שבט
5 SHEVAT / CYCLE 2

January 18, 2002
January 8, 2003
January 28, 2004
January 15, 2005
February 3, 2006

ה סיון
5 SIVAN / CYCLE 3

May 16, 2002
June 5, 2003
May 25, 2004
June 12, 2005
June 1, 2006

✑ *The Seal of Hashem*

SEFER SEFAS TAMIM — Chapter One:
Deceit vs. Truthfulness (cont.)

*O*ur Sages teach: "The seal of the Holy One, Blessed is He, is truth" (Shabbos 55a). Surely, if Hashem chose truth as His seal, then a person who regularly engages in falsehood is lowly and disgraceful.

Hashem has warned us in very strong terms concerning the importance of truth:

> "These are the things that you should do: Speak the truth with one another; and in your gates judge with truth, justice and peace. Do not think evil toward one another in your hearts and do not love false oaths, for all these are what I hate" — the word of Hashem (Zechariah 8:16-17).

The first, middle and last letters of the *aleph-beis* form the word אֱמֶת, *truth*, indicating that Torah is the ultimate, all-encompassing truth and that the more a person develops the quality of truth within himself, the more he can attach himself to Torah and merit to understand it in all its beauty and depth.

The Talmud (*Shabbos* 104a) finds significance in the shape of each letter of the *aleph-beis*, commenting: "Why do the letters ש-ק-ר *(falsehood)* each stand on [only] one foot, while the letters א-מ-ת *(truth)* each have a bricklike solidity? To teach that truth stands firm while falsehood cannot stand."

As *Rashi* explains, each letter of אמת stands on a solid foundation of two feet, but in the word שקר each letter has only one pointy foot to support it. [The ש of the Torah script comes to a point at the bottom.] In the words of *Tikunei Zohar* (475), "שֶׁקֶר אֵין לָה רַגְלַיִם, *Falsehood has no feet.*"

King David declared רֹאשׁ דְּבָרְךָ אֱמֶת, *The very beginning of Your word is truth* (*Tehillim* 119:160). The final letters of the Torah's first three words (when rearranged) — בְּרֵאשִׁית בָּרָא אֱלֹקִים — spell אֱמֶת. Alternatively, *Otzar HaChaim* explains that the "beginning of G-d's word" refers to the initial letters of the Ten Commandments [which were give at Sinai and which allude to all 613 *mitzvos*] and the Oral Law. The first word of the Ten Commandments is אָנֹכִי; the Mishnah begins with מֵאֵמָתַי; and the *Gemara* opens with תָּנָא. Together, the initials spell אֱמֶת.

A disciple of R' Eliyahu Lopian, a legendary *mussar* personality of recent times, wrote:

> Truth was the quality around which our teacher's service of Hashem revolved. He related to us that once, as a student in Kelm, he led the *davening* on Shabbos. When reciting the words וְטַהֵר לִבֵּנוּ לְעָבְדְּךָ בֶּאֱמֶת, *And purify our hearts to serve You in truth*, he stressed the words וְטַהֵר לִבֵּנוּ. When *davening* had ended, his mentor R' Hirsh Broide told him that he should rather stress the word בֶּאֱמֶת.

> We saw that his conduct was always guided by truth. In virtually every *mussar* (ethical) talk, he would cite the verse, יַעַן כִּי נִגַּשׁ הָעָם הַזֶּה, בְּפִיו וּבִשְׂפָתָיו וְלִבּוֹ רִחַק מִמֶּנִּי, *Inasmuch as*

(cont. on page 246)

The more one develops the quality of truth, the more he can attach himself to Torah.

לע"נ ר' אריה לייביש אפרים צבי הלוי ז"ל בן ר' יצחק מרדכי יבלחט"ו
5 Tishrei — Dr. Leibel Fink
Dedicated by his wife Suri and their children, Brooklyn, NY

לע"נ רב יחזקאל יהודה בן מרדכי ז"ל
5 Shevat — Herman Pasternak
Dedicated by his grandchildren, Los Angeles, CA

רפואה שלמה ליעקב בן פייגל נ"י
5 Sivan — John Boruchin
Dedicated by his son, Isak Boruchin

ו תשרי
6 TISHREI / CYCLE 1

September 23, 2001
September 12, 2002
October 2, 2003
September 21, 2004
October 9, 2005

ו שבט
6 SHEVAT / CYCLE 2

January 19, 2002
January 9, 2003
January 29, 2004
January 16, 2005
February 4, 2006

ו סיון
6 SIVAN / CYCLE 3

May 17, 2002
June 6, 2003
May 26, 2004
June 13, 2005
June 2, 2006

❧ *Everlasting Truth*

SEFER SEFAS TAMIM — Chapter One:
Deceit vs. Truthfulness (cont.)

*K*ing Shlomo said: "True speech will be established forever, but a false tongue is only for a moment" (Mishlei 12:19). Shlomo cautions us to be truthful at all times and to carefully avoid falsehood. When a person is truthful and is careful that his words are in consonance with emes (truth), then his words will accomplish and will be everlasting. People will believe what he has to say, for they know him as someone who always speaks the truth.

But when a person is known to speak falsehood, then his words will be reckoned with for but a moment's time. People may believe him at first, but when they examine his words and seek to corroborate them, they will realize that they are false. Therefore, Shlomo warns us that our words must be pure, unadulterated truth.

As a young man, Rabbi Shlomo Zalman Auerbach was informed that he was being considered for the position of *Rosh Yeshivah* at Yeshivah Kol Torah in Jerusalem and he was invited to deliver a *shiur* (Talmudic lecture) before the heads of the yeshivah.

Not long after the *shiur* had commenced, Rabbi Yonah Mertzbach, one of the founders of Kol Torah, interrupted with a question. After a few seconds of silence, R' Shlomo Zalman declared without hesitation, "*Ta'isi* (I'm mistaken)." He then began a new topic which was the focus of the remainder of his *shiur*. When he returned home and his Rebbeztin asked how he had fared, R' Shlomo Zalman replied, "Not so well. The *shiur* had hardly begun when I admitted to a mistake. Actually, I had three different answers to offer. But I felt that the question was closer to the truth than any of my answers."

R' Shlomo Zalman was informed that he had been accepted for the position. Years later, Rabbi Mertzbach told Rabbi Yehudah Addas, *Rosh Yeshivah* of Kol Yaakov, "Do you know why R' Shlomo Zalman was appointed to his position? When I asked him that question and he responded, 'I'm mistaken,' it was clear to me that with such a level of *emes* (truth), he should be our *Rosh Yeshivah*!"

It was not often that R' Shlomo Zalman retracted an explanation in favor of a student's opinion. But on those rare occasions that he found the student's reasoning superior to his own, he admitted this joyfully and without hesitation.

He once told a student, "I suspect that in the World to Come, I will not receive reward for the times when I admitted to the truth. What shall I do? — I *enjoy* letting someone know that he is right!"

Words of truth accomplish and are everlasting.

לזכות חנה רבקה בת דוד יחזק-ל שתחי' שתזכה להכנס לתורה לחופה ולמעשים טובים — **6 Tishrei**
Sponsored by David & Jo Anne Greene, Seattle, WA

6 Shevat — Rabbi Weinfeld הי"ד לע"נ הרב אברהם ז"ל בן ר' יחזקאל

6 Sivan — May today's learning be a זכות for our family and all of כלל ישראל.
Dedicated by Benyamin & Avigial Cweiber and family, Cleveland, OH

ז תשרי
7 TISHREI / CYCLE 1

September 24, 2001
September 13, 2002
October 3, 2003
September 22, 2004
October 10, 2005

ז שבט
7 SHEVAT / CYCLE 2

January 20, 2002
January 10, 2003
January 30, 2004
January 17, 2005
February 5, 2006

ז סיון
7 SIVAN / CYCLE 3

May 18, 2002
June 7, 2003
May 27, 2004
June 14, 2005
June 3, 2006

❧ *Truth of the Heart*

SEFER SEFAS TAMIM — Chapter One:
Deceit vs. Truthfulness (cont.)

*O*ur words must be free of falsehood — and even more so, they must be free of any form of mirmah (deceit). Hashem refers to those who engage in mirmah as רָע, evil, as the Sages state regarding the verse, "Deceit lurks in the heart of those who plot evil" (Mishlei 12:20). To such people, Tana D'Vei Eliyahu applies the verse: "May their way be dark and exceedingly slippery, with the angel of Hashem pursuing them" (Tehillim 35:6).

Therefore, one who is concerned for his own benefit should be sincere. Then he will merit to dwell in Hashem's presence, as it is written, "Hashem, who may dwell in Your tent? He who walks sincerely, does what is right and speaks truth in his heart" (Tehillim 15:2).

After opening the fifteenth chapter of *Tehillim* with: "Hashem, who may dwell in Your tent?" King David goes on to list eleven precious qualities in matters בֵּין אָדָם לַחֲבֵרוֹ, *between man and his fellow*. From this, says R' Samson Raphael Hirsch, we see that a person cannot truly be close to Hashem unless his service בֵּין אָדָם לַמָּקוֹם, *between man and Hashem*, is complemented by exemplary behavior בֵּין אָדָם לַחֲבֵרוֹ. People who deceive others are certainly not among those who are close to Hashem.

One of the eleven qualities extolled by David is דֹּבֵר אֱמֶת בִּלְבָבוֹ, one who speaks truth in his heart. The Talmudic sage R' Safra epitomized this quality. Once, R' Safra put an article up for sale. While he was reciting Shema, a man came to him and said, "Sell me that article for such and such an amount." R' Safra could not reply while reciting Shema, but the buyer misinterpreted his silence as a refusal to sell for so low a price. He offered a higher bid. When R' Safra completed Shema, he told the man, "Take the article for the first price which you offered, because at the time you made that offer, I decided in my mind that I would sell it for that price — and I cannot change my mind" (She'iltos D'R' Achai, Vayechi 36).

It is to one's own benefit to be sincere and avoid deceit.

R' Shraga Frank was one of the wealthiest Jews in Lithuania. He owned a leather factory, a leather goods store, and a great deal of real estate. More important, he was a *talmid chacham* and *tzaddik*, and he was held in high esteem by the founder of the *Mussar* Movement, R' Yisrael Salanter.

Once, a merchant came to purchase a large quantity of leather from R' Shraga. The man requested a reduction in the price, since he was making a large purchase.

R' Shraga replied that his profit margin was fixed, regardless of the size of the order, and therefore he could not offer a reduction. He told the man, "Feel free to purchase your leather from another dealer. In fact, I will give you a list of other dealers whom you can approach." And he handed the man such a list.

The man made the rounds of the leather dealers and found that R' Shraga's price was the cheapest. He

(cont. on page 246)

DAY
8

ח תשרי
8 TISHREI / CYCLE 1

September 25, 2001
September 14, 2002
October 4, 2003
September 23, 2004
October 11, 2005

ח שבט
8 SHEVAT / CYCLE 2

January 21, 2002
January 11, 2003
January 31, 2004
January 18, 2005
February 6, 2006

ח סיון
8 SIVAN / CYCLE 3

May 19, 2002
June 8, 2003
May 28, 2004
June 15, 2005
June 4, 2006

❧ *Truth will Prevail*

SEFER SEFAS TAMIM — Chapter Two:
The Severity of Deceit

*M*irmah (deceit) is so severe that it can cause a person's life to be cut short, **ר"ל**, as it is written, "Men of bloodshed and deceit shall not live out half their days" (Tehillim 55:24). And during his time on this earth, the deceitful person will ultimately be disgraced before all, for it is Hashem's way to publicize the deceit that lies hidden in the hearts of such men.

In Proverbs we learn: "He who walks with sincerity will walk securely, but he who walks crookedly will become known" (Mishlei 10:9). According to the Vilna Gaon, the latter half of this verse describes someone who is trying to harm his friend while concealing his evil intentions. He therefore walks a crooked path; in order to hide his schemes, he feigns friendship with his intended victim. But in the end, his crookedness will become known, for Hashem will publicize his treachery.

Midrash Shochar Tov states that Hashem does not punish a person until he publicizes the person's sinful deeds. And in the end, the harm which the man of deceit planned for his neighbor, will come upon him, as it is written, "One who seeks good for others seeks [G-d's] favor, but he who searches out evil [for others], it will come upon him" (Mishlei 11:27).

The Talmud relates that on his death bed, R' Yochanan ben Zakkai told his disciples: "May it be the will [of G-d] that the fear of Heaven be upon you like the fear of flesh of blood." His students reponded, "Thus far [and no more]?" It seemed incomprehensible to them that their fear of Hashem should not have to exceed their fear of mortal man. To this, R' Yochanan replied, "If only [your fear of Heaven were this much]! Know that when a person commits a sin in private, he says [to himself], 'O that a person not see me!' " (Berachos 28b).

The Chofetz Chaim teaches that the sins of treachery and deceit, no matter how well concealed, will ultimately become exposed. Taking this to heart should serve as a deterrent when one is tempted to mislead others.

Of course, the best deterrent to *mirmah* is to contemplate the severity of falsehood. In his *Lights Along the Way,* Rabbi Abraham Twersky tells of one man who had the proper outlook on falsehood.

The legendary *gaon* and hero of Holocaust rescue, Rabbi Michoel Ber Weismandel, once spent Succos in Yemen. On the day before the festival, a man entered the *shul* and emptied a large bag of *esrogim* onto a table. Each member of the congregation calmly selected an *esrog* for the *mitzvah* of *arba minim* and dropped a few coins into a charity box.

One who seeks good for others, seeks Hashem's favor.

(cont. on page 246)

רפואה שלמה לשמעון גדלי' בן פיגה זלדה בתושש"י — **8 Tishrei**
רפואה שלמה May today's learning be a זכות for his.

לע"נ ר' יצחק בן אברהם שפרן ז"ל — **8 Shevat** — May today's learning be a זכות for Yitzchok Safrin ז"ל
Dedicated by his wife, children and grandchildren

8 Sivan —

ט תשרי
9 TISHREI / CYCLE 1

September 26, 2001
September 15, 2002
October 5, 2003
September 24, 2004
October 12, 2005

ט שבט
9 SHEVAT / CYCLE 2

January 22, 2002
January 12, 2003
February 1, 2004
January 19, 2005
February 7, 2006

ט סיון
9 SIVAN / CYCLE 3

May 20, 2002
June 9, 2003
May 29, 2004
June 16, 2005
June 5, 2006

✌ *Sin upon Sin*

SEFER SEFAS TAMIM — Chapter Two:
The Severity of Deceit (cont.)

*T*he sin of mirmah (deceit) has the power to deprive a person of his possessions, and to bring punishment upon him in a variety of ways — in this world and in the Next. For mirmah usually encompasses a variety of transgressions, especially the dreadful sins of robbery, price fraud and lying. Furthermore, people who regularly engage in deceit, do so hundreds of times over the course of a lifetime; therefore, their end will be bitter.*

Rambam states:

> Do not say that *teshuvah* (repentance) is required only for sins which involve actions such as immorality and robbery. Rather, just as one must repent of these sins, so must he seek out and repent wicked traits within himself, such as anger, hatred, jealousy and mockery; a craving for money and honor; and a craving for food and other earthly pleasures. Of all such things one must repent.
>
> *These sins are worse than those which involve actions,* for when a person is sunk in them, it is difficult to separate from them. And so it is written [that one must repent of negative traits] (Yeshayah 55:7), "May the wicked one forsake his path and the deceitful man his thoughts" (*Hilchos Teshuvah* 7:3).

Mirmah, deceit, is in the category of this latter group of sins. It involves no action and one can easily delude himself into thinking that he is not actually deceiving the other person, or that the person deserves to be dealt with in a conniving way. Once a person has developed a habit for misleading people, it becomes second nature to him.

Lavan, father-in-law of our forefather Yaakov, was the classic conniver. He agreed to the marriage of Yaakov and his daughter Rachel, after Yaakov would work for seven years for the right to marry her. However, Lavan substituted Leah, Rachel's older sister, on the wedding night without Yaakov's knowledge. When Yaakov discovered the ruse and confronted Lavan, the latter justified his actions, "Such is not done in our place, to give the younger before the elder" (*Bereishis* 29:26). Ever the rogue, Lavan justified his wickedness by shifting responsibiilty. He portrayed himself as having been forced to do so, because the community or some vague influential body compelled him to act in this way (*R' David Zvi Hoffmann*).

Such an attitude is common to those who mislead others. Most unfortunate is that such people often come to actually believe their contrived excuses, so that they never feel remorse for what they have caused and never seek to undo the damage which they have brought about.

Once a person developes a habit for misleading people, it becomes second nature to him.

9 Tishrei — May today's learning be a זכות for a רפואה שלמה
for our daughter, granddaughter and niece.
9 Shevat — In loving memory of Jeffrey Bruce Becker ז"ל לע"נ זלמן דוב בן אליהו ז"ל
Dedicated by Tuvia & Rivka Meister
9 Sivan — May today's learning be a זכות for כלל ישראל.
Dedicated by Regina Walls

י תשרי
10 TISHREI / CYCLE 1

September 27, 2001
September 16, 2002
October 6, 2003
September 25, 2004
October 13, 2005

י שבט
10 SHEVAT / CYCLE 2

January 23, 2002
January 13, 2003
February 2, 2004
January 20, 2005
February 8, 2006

י סיון
10 SIVAN / CYCLE 3

May 21, 2002
June 10, 2003
May 30, 2004
June 17, 2005
June 6, 2006

✌ *Overindulgence*

SEFER SEFAS TAMIM — Chapter Four:
Chapter Two: The Severity of Deceit (cont.)

*T*ana D'Vei Eliyahu Zuta (Ch. 3) states:

The Holy One, Blessed is He, created everything in the world, except for false-hood and wrongdoing [meaning, that a person contrives falsehood and wrong-doing on his own without assistance from Above] as it is written, "The Rock! — perfect in His work, for all His paths are justice; a G-d of faith without wrong-doing, righteous and fair is He" (Devarim 32:4); "Hashem, the Righteous One, is within it; He does no wrong" (Tzephaniah 3:5); and "To do evil is sac-rilege to G-d, [as is] wrongdoing to the A-mighty! For He repays the deeds of man and brings upon him according to his conduct" (Iyov 34:10-11).

Heaven and earth bear witness that [to a large degree] people die or endure suffering because they, along with their wives and children, indulge in eating, drinking and making themselves happy [with materialism] until they leave this world.

And it is for this same reason that pro-duce of the field turns rotten, people suf-

fer disgrace, and their eyes grow dim while they are still in mid-life.

The yetzer hara (evil inclination) induces a person to lie and commit other wrongs, to steal, cheat and deceive, so that he and his household can enjoy the honor and materialistic pleasures of the rich. But this is not the way of Hashem; rather, every individual must live on a standard which his income allows — and not more. Those who choose the wrong path will suffer the consequences.

Every individual must live on a standard which his income allows — and not more.

Further in this work, the Chofetz Chaim elaborates upon the dangers of living a lifestyle which is above one's means. In fact, this subject was addressed two centuries earlier by R' Moshe Chaim Luzzato:

...Many worldly experiences are trials and temptations... If a person becomes so accustomed to good wine and tasty delicacies that he becomes dependent upon them, and they become necessities for him instead of dispensable luxuries... then should something happen whereby he cannot afford these, he may be driven to do things that are forbidden in order to satisfy his wants...

...it is clear that preoccupation with expensive garments, while not explicitly prohibited, can lead to arrogance, as well as to envy and lust. Furthermore, when expensive clothes become a necessity, one may exploit others to acquire them (*Mesilas Yesharim* Ch. 13).

(cont. on page 247)

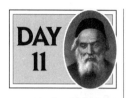

DAY 11

י"א תשרי
II TISHREI / CYCLE 1

September 28, 2001
September 17, 2002
October 7, 2003
September 26, 2004
October 14, 2005

י"א שבט
II SHEVAT / CYCLE 2

January 24, 2002
January 14, 2003
February 3, 2004
January 21, 2005
February 9, 2006

י"א סיון
II SIVAN / CYCLE 3

May 22, 2002
June 11, 2003
May 31, 2004
June 18, 2005
June 7, 2006

❧ *A Fateful Partnership*

SEFER SEFAS TAMIM — Chapter Two:
The Severity of Deceit (cont.)

*M*idrash Shochar Tov says by way of metaphor:

"Two by two they came to Noach in the Ark" (Bereishis 7:9). "Falsehood" came and wanted to enter the Ark. Noach told it, "You cannot enter unless you bring along a mate." Falsehood then met פְּחָתָא, Depletion [the capacity for man's possessions to become damaged or lost to him]. Depletion asked Falsehood, "Whence do you come?" Falsehood replied, "From the Ark, for I desired to enter it, but Noach would not permit this unless I bring along a mate. Will you be my mate?"

"And what will you give me in return?" Depletion asked.

"I will arrange with you," said Falsehood, "that whatever I prepare [for a person to acquire through dishonesty], you will take away."

The agreement was made, and together they entered the Ark. When they left the Ark, whatever a person acquired through Falsehood, Depletion took away. When Falsehood protested this, Depletion retorted, "Was it for naught that we made our agreement?" Falsehood had nothing to reply. This is what is meant by, "He is pregnant with evil schemes and gives birth to falsehood" (Tehillim 7:15).

There is a simple explanation as to why the Midrash associates the connection between falsehood and depletion with Noach and the Ark. Until the Flood, the attribute of אֶרֶךְ אַפַּיִם, slow to anger, was dominant as Hashem did not exact punishment from generations that were steeped in sin — including the sin of חָמָס, robbery, which usually involves much lying and deception. Wicked people saw that money which they had accumulated through dishonesty remained in their families over the course of generations. As a result of their apparent successes, they embraced the sin of robbery wholeheartedly, engaging in it throughout their lives, and the world became filled with it.

However, after the Flood, Hashem conducted the world differently. From then on, whatever would be earned through falsehood and deception would be lost through depletion, as it is written, "...one who amasses wealth unjustly, in the middle of his days it will leave him" (Yirmiyahu 17:11). People take note of this and learn a lesson.

Moreover, the money which a person earns through lying and deception will bring about the loss of the money which he had earned honestly. Masechta Derech Eretz Zuta states: "If you take what is not yours, then what is yours will be taken from you." All that one will be left with are the sins of lying and deception.

If you take what is not yours, then what is yours will be taken from you.

לע"נ חיים בן אליהו הלוי ז"ל — **11 Tishrei** — Hyman Siegel
Sponsored by the Siegel family
לע"נ דוד מרדכי בן אשר יעקב צבי ז"ל — **11 Shevat** — Dovid Mordechai Moskowitz
Dedicated by Mr. & Mrs. Moskowitz and family
11 Sivan — In honor of my אשת חיל, פרומה אסתר בת ר' יעקב שתחי' and her family
דוד פסח בן אברהם נ"י Dedicated by

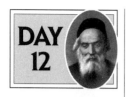
י"ב תשרי
12 TISHREI / CYCLE 1

September 29, 2001
September 18, 2002
October 8, 2003
September 27, 2004
October 15, 2005

י"ב שבט
12 SHEVAT / CYCLE 2

January 25, 2002
January 15, 2003
February 4, 2004
January 22, 2005
February 10, 2006

י"ב סיון
12 SIVAN / CYCLE 3

May 23, 2002
June 12, 2003
June 1, 2004
June 19, 2005
June 8, 2006

❧ *Chillul Hashem vs. Kiddush Hashem*

SEFER SEFAS TAMIM — Chapter Two:
The Severity of Deceit (cont.)

*T*o our great misfortune, lying and deception in matters of business have increased lately among some of our people, to the point that they see such behavior as permissible! They lie when negotiating a deal and say, "I paid such-and-such for this item," and sometimes they even swear to that effect. (According to Torah law, an oath in any language is binding.) They consider such shameful behavior mere "shrewdness" and contend that nowadays, anyone who does not engage in such practices will starve [for he will never succeed financially]. This has made us the object of scorn and derision among our neighbors, for they say that Jews are dishonest! Woe to us over this chillul Hashem (desecration of Hashem's Name)!

When a Jew conducts himself according to the Torah's high standards of honesty, he earns the respect and admiration of his gentile neighbors.

The late *Mashgiach* of the Kaminetz Yeshivah in Jerusalem, Rabbi Moshe Aharon Stern, often traveled abroad together with a distinguished acquaintance. Two months after R' Moshe Aharon passed away, his acquaintance found himself at the money-changer's desk at the Amsterdam train station. The clerk, a gentile woman, recognized the man and inquired about the rabbi who always accompanied him. Upon hearing that R' Moshe Aharon had passed away, she burst into tears. "It's thanks to him that I still have my job," she said tearfully. She explained:

Once, as he counted his money after changing some currency at her desk, R' Moshe Aharon realized that he had been given far too large a sum. He returned to the desk and asked the woman to recount the money. Assuming that he was claiming that she had given him too little, the woman snapped that she had already counted the money once and if he wanted to make a claim, he should have counted the money in her presence. "How can you leave the counter and then return to claim that I cheated you — everyone knows that you can't do that!"

After listening to her tirade in silence, R' Moshe Aharon said softly, "I think that you gave me *too much* money. Please do me a favor and count the money again." She did and was astonished to find that, indeed, he was correct. She told him gratefully, "Had you not returned the money, it would have been deducted from my salary. And since I am new at this job, I may very well have been fired for making such a mistake."

Later, she went to the station manager, related what had happened and told him, "I have never met such an upright person." The manager, equally amazed, announced over the station loudspeaker that a Jew from Israel had returned a large sum of money that had been given to him by mistake, and he praised R' Moshe Aharon's upright conduct (from *The Mashgiach of Kaminetz*).

A Jew who lives by the Torah's standards earns the admiration of his gentile neighbors.

12 Tishrei — רפואה שלמה לישראל מיכל נ"י בן רחל ע"ה
Dedicated by his nephew, Yisroel Meir Kenner

12 Shevat — Chaim Mizrahi לע"נ חיים בן חביבה ז"ל
Dedicated by his family

12 Sivan — Avrohom Waldinger לע"נ אברהם בן דוד ז"ל
Dedicated by his great-grandson, Avrohom Ben Emanuel Waldinger

י"ג תשרי
13 TISHREI / CYCLE 1

September 30, 2001
September 19, 2002
October 9, 2003
September 28, 2004
October 16, 2005

י"ג שבט
13 SHEVAT / CYCLE 2

January 26, 2002
January 16, 2003
February 5, 2004
January 23, 2005
February 11, 2006

י"ג סיון
13 SIVAN / CYCLE 3

May 24, 2002
June 13, 2003
June 2, 2004
June 20, 2005
June 9, 2006

❧ *The Wheel of Misfortune*

SEFER SEFAS TAMIM — Chapter Two:
The Severity of Deceit (cont.)

The sin of mirmah (deceit) has brought great material loss to the world. The wheel of misfortune is making its rounds and it is virtually unheard of that a man of wealth should retain his money his entire life. Rather, he retains it for half his life or for one-third, and sometimes for but a few short years. This is a phenomenon which was not seen in previous generations. It is the sin of mirmah that has caused all this, for as is well known, all Jews are responsible for one another [and therefore, the rich who are honest are affected by the sins of those Jews who are dishonest].

In our days, we have witnessed many who, all too suddenly, have gone from wealth to near poverty. As the Chofetz Chaim himself points out, this should not be taken as a sign that the individual was dishonest, for often the fortunes of the upright are affected by the sins of those who are dishonest.

Moreover, there can be many other reasons why Hashem chooses at any given time to bring financial hardship upon an individual. Life, as *Mesilas Yesharim* puts it, is like a battlefield where one is faced with challenge upon challenge. The man of pure faith recognizes this and accepts his lot as the will of Hashem. Rabbi Avraham Pam related the following:

> There was a Jew who, in spite of having lived his entire life in dire poverty, remained steadfast in his faith, and prayed with intense concentration. Someone once overheard this man reciting the morning blessing, "Blessed are You... Who has provided me my every need," with great joy.
>
> Asked the passerby, "Can you really say that your every need has been provided for? You are among the poorest of the poor!"
>
> The man replied, "Can one really know, on his own, what his particular needs are? If G-d has made me poor, then obviously this condition is necessary for me to fulfill my purpose in life. Poverty is what my soul needs, and I have been granted this in full measure!"

Life is like a battlefield where one is faced with challenge upon challenge.

We ask for "a life in which G-d fulfills our requests for the good," in the special blessing in advance of every new month. It would seem that the phrase "for the good" is superfluous; certainly a person would not request that which is bad for him! This, explained R' Pam, is precisely the point. We can never be sure that what we desire is ultimately to our benefit; this is known only to Hashem, Who "keeps watch and sees to the end of all generations" (*Mussaf* of Rosh Hashanah). We therefore ask that our requests be fulfilled, but only in a manner that will truly be for our good.

י״ד תשרי
14 TISHREI / CYCLE 1

October 1, 2001
September 20, 2002
October 10, 2003
September 29, 2004
October 17, 2005

י״ד שבט
14 SHEVAT / CYCLE 2

January 27, 2002
January 17, 2003
February 6, 2004
January 24, 2005
February 12, 2006

י״ד סיון
14 SIVAN / CYCLE 3

May 25, 2002
June 14, 2003
June 3, 2004
June 21, 2005
June 10, 2006

✑ *Crime Does Not Pay*

SEFER SEFAS TAMIM — Chapter Two:
The Severity of Deceit (cont.)

If you see someone who retains his wealth despite the fact that he is dishonest, know that ultimately this will lead to his downfall, as it is written, "And He repays His enemies in his lifetime to make him perish" (Devarim 7:10). His end in the World of Truth will be shameful; and in this world, "his teeth will be ground on gravel"[1] and his children will have to search for bread. For when dishonest earnings mix with honest earnings, the former come and destroy the latter, as mentioned above and as is seen in the story of Nakdimon ben Gurion's daughter (Kesubos 66b).

The Talmud relates that Rabban Yochanan ben Zakai was riding on a donkey exiting Jerusalem, when he saw a maiden gathering kernels of barley from between the excrement of animals belonging to Arabs. When the maiden noticed the sage, she covered her face and stood before him begging, "My master, feed me!"

Rabban Yochanan asked her, "My daughter, who are you?" and she replied, "I am the daughter of Nakdimon ben Gurion," an affluent man who lived in Jerusalem at the end of the Second Temple era. Rabban Yochanan asked her, "My daughter, where did the money of your father's house go?" She replied that her father's fortune had been forfeited because he was deficient regarding the giving of *tzedakah*.

Rabban Yochanan then asked her, "And where is the money of your father-in-law's house?" She replied that this money had been mingled with her father's money; when the latter was lost, the former was lost as well.

The Talmud proceeds to question this episode based on a tradition that when Nakdimon ben Gurion would walk to the study hall, fine woolen garments would be spread beneath him, and the poor were permitted to fold these up and keep them for themselves. This shows that Nakidimon did, in fact, give an abundance of charity. This, continues the Talmud, can be resolved in one of two ways: either Nakdimon gave *tzedakah* with wrong intent, that is, for his own honor; or, the amount of *tzedakah* he gave was not commensurate with his means.

Charity must come from money that is earned honestly.

In commenting on this passage, *Maharsha* bemoans the situation in his day, where people "accumulate wealth not in good faith, through *chillul Hashem* such as robbing gentile [customers and merchants]. Then they donate some of this money to charity so that they are honored each year and are the recipients of a *"Mi SheBeirach,"* which brings them fame and glory. In fact, this is a הַבָּאָה בַּעֲבֵירָה מִצְוָה, *a mitzvah which comes about through a sin*. Such wealth will not remain, as in the case here [of Nakdimon]."[2]

---

1. An expression borrowed from *Eichah* 3:16. There, the verse refers to the dismal state of the Jews at the time of the First Destruction, when they were forced to dig deep pits in which they would knead their dough. This caused the dough to become mixed with gravel, which damaged the teeth of those who partook of this bread.
2. See *Derashos Chasam Sofer*, part III, p. 87a, ד"ה ואמר.

ט"ו תשרי
15 TISHREI / CYCLE 1

October 2, 2001
September 21, 2002
October 11, 2003
September 30, 2004
October 18, 2005

ט"ו שבט
15 SHEVAT / CYCLE 2

January 28, 2002
January 18, 2003
February 7, 2004
January 25, 2005
February 13, 2006

ט"ו סיון
15 SIVAN / CYCLE 3

May 26, 2002
June 15, 2003
June 4, 2004
June 22, 2005
June 11, 2006

❧ *Trust in Hashem*

SEFER SEFAS TAMIM — Chapter Two:
The Severity of Deceit (cont.)

*I*t is virtually certain that the lies which many businessmen employ are not even necessary to accomplish their goals. For example, why must a person lie about the price he paid for an item, when he could simply state, "This is the price that I am asking; I cannot accept less"? What can He give you and what will you profit, O deceitful tongue?[1]

Even if he thinks that he will profit a lot from falsehood, he should distance himself from it, because in reality, he stands to lose more than he will gain. He who trusts in Hashem and conducts his business dealings honestly will be surrounded by kindness.[2] The blessing of Hashem will enrich him[3] and surely he will not lack for sustenance, for his bread will be earned honestly, with peace of mind and dignity.

Among his many works, the Chazon Ish, R' Avraham Yeshayah Karelitz, authored a slim, wondrous volume entitled *Emunah U'Vitachon* (Faith and Trust). In it he writes:

> *Emunah* and *bitachon* are a single entity, except that *emunah* involves a person's general world view while *bitachon* involves his

perspective on himself. *Emunah* is theoretical while *bitachon* is practical. It is simple to have *bitachon* when *bitachon* is *not* truly demanded — but it is not easy to have *bitachon* when *it is* truly demanded!

Only in the following way can a person prove whether his heart and lips are in tandem with regard to *bitachon*, or if his tongue is merely trained to mouth, *"Bitachon, bitachon!"* while his heart is lacking this trait:

When he meets a situation that demands *bitachon*, a situation where it is *bitachon* that must guide, restore and heal him, will he, at this difficult hour, turn toward *bitachon* and trust in Hashem? Or will he turn not to Hashem, but instead... to disdainful methods and worthless schemes?

He who trusts in Hashem will be surrounded by kindness.

Emunah and *bitachon* are the gateways to a serene and happy life. In his letters, the Chazon Ish wrote of the effects which happiness has on a person. Joy, according to the Chazon Ish, is the medium through which Heavenly wisdon flows. As for worry? "Worry is the greatest sin of all." Of despair: "Do not turn to despair — the cruel destroyer."

Those close to the Chazon Ish bore witness that his own meager livelihood was never any cause for worry. He subsisted on the income from the sale of his *sefarim* and firmly refused the many gifts offered him by those whom he helped. He would even discourage

(cont. on page 247)

---

1. *Tehillim* 120:3.
2. These phrases are from *Tehillim* 120:3.
3. Paraphrase of *Mishlei* 10:22.

DAY
16

ט"ז תשרי
16 TISHREI / CYCLE 1

October 3, 2001
September 22, 2002
October 12, 2003
October 1, 2004
October 19, 2005

ט"ז שבט
16 SHEVAT / CYCLE 2

January 29, 2002
January 19, 2003
February 8, 2004
January 26, 2005
February 14, 2006

ט"ז סיון
16 SIVAN / CYCLE 3

May 27, 2002
June 16, 2003
June 5, 2004
June 23, 2005
June 12, 2006

≈ *The Best of Both Worlds*

SEFER SEFAS TAMIM — Chapter Two:
The Severity of Deceit (cont.)

The meaning of the verse, "Which man desires life..." is now perfectly clear. Which man desires life in the World to Come and loves days to see good in this world? Guard your tongue from evil and your lips from speaking deceit... If one conducts his dealings deceitfully, then even if he will succeed at first, in the end his money will be lost, as we explained above. By contrast, if he will carefully avoid mirmah (deceit), then he will enjoy a pleasant old age on this world, and in the Next World an abundance of goodness will await him, as it is written, "He who goes in the path of sincerity will serve Me" (Tehillim 101:6).

The opposite of *mirmah*, deceit, is *temimus*, innocence and sincerity. This trait was epitomized by the *Mashgiach* of the Lomzer Yeshivah in Petach Tikvah, R' Elya Dushnitzer.

R' Elya's son, R' Asher, had owned an orange orchard which had been given to him as a dowry. The orchard, however, was not very productive and eventually was taken over by R' Elya, who wished to help his son by taking the property off his hands. It soon became apparent that the expense of maintaining the orchard exceeded its income and R' Elya fell into debt because of it. He put the orchard up for sale, but for a long time it remained unsold. This was probably due in large part to R' Elya's unusual honesty; when a prospective customer would come along, R' Elya would immediately point out every flaw and potential problem that he could find in the orchard.

It happened that an American businessman expressed great interest in the orchard. On the way to showing him the property, R' Elya pointed out all its deficiencies. The American was unperturbed; he very much wanted the property. As they began to make their way through the orchard, the American swallowed a few pills which he had taken from a small vial. "What is this?" asked R' Elya, who was quite concerned. "Oh, nothing," the American replied, "I have a minor heart condition, but these pills keep things under control."

Sincerity is the key to a good life.

"In that case," declared R' Elya, "I absolutely *will not* sell you this orchard! It will probably be a source of aggravation to you and may, G-d forbid, prove harmful to your health." Despite the American's protests, R' Elya would not budge. The orchard was not sold.

Some time later, R' Elya met his *talmid*, R' Sholom Schwadron, and asked him to remind the head of a certain *cheder* (elementary school) in Jerusalem to have the children recite some *Tehillim* after school hours, so that he would merit to finally sell the orchard. "But how does the *Mashgiach* know that the children have not already recited *Tehillim*?" asked R' Sholom.

"Oh, that is obvious," R' Elya responded. "I made this request a while ago. Had the children recited *Tehillim*, the orchard would surely have been sold by now."

Sure enough, R' Sholom later met the *cheder* dean who was dismayed at having forgotten about R' Elya's request. The children recited *Tehillim* that day and the orchard was sold a few days later.

DAY 17

י"ז תשרי

17 TISHREI / CYCLE 1

October 4, 2001
September 23, 2002
October 13, 2003
October 2, 2004
October 20, 2005

י"ז שבט

17 SHEVAT / CYCLE 2

January 30, 2002
January 20, 2003
February 9, 2004
January 27, 2005
February 15, 2006

י"ז סיון

17 SIVAN / CYCLE 3

May 28, 2002
June 17, 2003
June 6, 2004
June 24, 2005
June 13, 2006

✒ *Clean Hands*

SEFER SEFAS TAMIM — Chapter Three:
Mirmah — Its Root Causes

*T*here are many factors which lead a person to the sin of mirmah (deceit), to the point where he deceives people frequently and without any sense of guilt. We shall discuss the primary factors.

When gezel and sheker (theft and falsehood) are not viewed as sins and are practiced regularly, it is only natural that mirmah, which combines both these sins, will follow. Therefore, one who seeks to purify himself of the stain of mirmah must always ponder the severity of theft and falsehood. Then he will be saved from them.

The need to avoid all forms of theft is a mitzvah which logic dictates; had the Torah not commanded, "You shall not steal," (Vayikra 19:13), we would have deduced on our own that it is wrong. To refrain from theft is counted among the seven mitzvos regarding which Adam was commanded, known as the שֶׁבַע מִצְוֹת בְּנֵי נֹחַ, the seven Noachide laws.

A Jew's business dealings must be conducted in good faith, so that his hands remain clean of dishonest earnings. Then, he will merit to ascend the mountain of Hashem, as it is written, "Who may ascend the mountain of Hashem and who may stand in the place of His sanctity? One with clean hands and a pure heart..." (Tehillim: 24:3-4). From this verse we see that one whose hands are stained by dishonest earnings is distant from "the mountain of Hashem and the place of His sanctity." Our Sages have taught that whoever is guilty of theft will not be permitted within the confines of Hashem's Presence, as it is written, "No evil dwells with You" (Tehillim 5:5).

In his discourses, the Manchester Rosh Yeshivah, R' Yehudah Zev Segal, exhorted his talmidim to faithfully adhere to the Torah's requirements regarding honesty in word and in business:

> It is the *halachah* which determines what constitutes *gezel* (theft)... If the *halachah* requires one to pay and he does not, then he is a thief; if the *halachah* rules in his favor, then he is innocent.
>
> It is clear that without a thorough knowledge of *Choshen Mishpat*,[1] it is virtually impossible to conduct one's business in full consonance with Torah law.
>
> A *shochet* (ritual slaughterer) cannot practice without *kabbalah*, verification that he is skilled and well versed in the relevant laws. It would be proper if similar verification were required of those entering the business world...
> *(Inspiration and Insight, vol. I)*

To conduct one's business in accordance with Torah law, one must be well-versed in the relevant laws.

(cont. on page 247)

---

1. The section of *Shulchan Aruch* dealing with monetary matters.

✒ *The Severity of Theft*

SEFER SEFAS TAMIM — Chapter Three:
Mirmah — Its Root Causes (cont.)

Heavenly judgment for the sin of theft is extremely severe, so much so that even indirectly causing someone a financial loss, or even a lesser harm, is considered theft in the Heavenly realm. Our Sages teach:

> *Whoever robs his neighbor of even a perutah [i.e. a small coin] is considered as if he took his life, as it is written, "Such are the ways of all plunderers, they take the soul of its owners" (Mishlei 1:19); "They will consume your harvest and your bread; they will consume your sons and your daughters" (Yirmiyahu 5:17); "...because of the robbery of the children of Yehudah, for they shed innocent blood in their land" (Yoel: 4:19); and "Hashem said: 'It is for Shaul and for the House of Blood; for his having killed the Gibeonites' " (II Shmuel 21:1).*
>
> *Why are all these verses necessary [to adduce this teaching]? For if you will contend that this [the severity of robbery] applies only when money is not paid [for the item that was seized], but when money is paid, then there is no [sin*

of robbery], then the verse "...because of the robbery of the children of Yehudah" [where the word חָמָס *refers to seizing an item by force and paying for it] refutes that. If you will contend that robbery is akin to taking the owner's life, but not the lives of his offspring, then the verse, "...they will consume your sons and your daughters" refutes that.*

If you will contend that this is only where he actually robs, but where he causes an indirect loss it is not akin to taking a life, then the verse, "...It is for Shaul and for the House of Blood; for his having killed the Gibeonites" refutes that. For where do we find that Shaul killed the Gibeonites? Rather, because Shaul killed the inhabitants of Nov, the city of Kohanim, to whom the Gibeonites would provide food and drink [and as a result, the Gibeonites' livelihood was lost], it was considered as if he killed them.

(Bava Kamma 119a)

From this we see that if one indirectly causes someone a loss, then he is liable to be punished severely.

If this is so, then what shall we say of men of mirmah, who commit actual robbery with frightening regularlity? One shudders to think of what lies in store for them.

Heavenly judgment for the sin of theft is extremely severe.

(cont. on page 248)

18 Tishrei — לזכות רפואה שלמה רוחמא גולדא בת חנה בתושח"י

18 Shevat — In honor of Phil & Marilyn Shapiro
Dedicated by their children and grandchildren

18 Sivan — Chaim Nochum Feit לע"נ חיים נחום בן יהודה דוד ז"ל
Dedicated by his grandchildren: Feit, Finkelstein, Fishberg, Klien, Nebenzahl and Shechter families

✌ *When an Advocate Becomes an Accuser*

SEFER SEFAS TAMIM — Chapter Three:
Mirmah — Its Root Causes (cont.)

*B*ecause gezel (theft) is so severe, Heaven is quick to hear the cry of the victim. Our Sages teach: There are three offenses for which the "curtain of Heaven" does not close — ona'ah (wronging someone), theft and idol worship (Bava Metzia 59a).

If a thief uses his loot to offer an olah sacrifice (which is entirely burnt upon the Altar) or for some other mitzvah, it will find no favor before Hashem, Who declares: "For I am Hashem, Who loves justice, Who hates robbery in an olah offering" (Yeshayah 61:8). Our Sages offer a parable:

> An armed bandit would hide at the crossroads robbing everyone who crossed his path. One day, the king's tax officer passed by and the bandit robbed him of everything he had. Eventually, the bandit was caught and thrown into prison.
>
> The tax officer paid the bandit a visit and said, "If you return everything that you took from me, I will intercede on your behalf before the king." The bandit replied, "I have nothing left except for

this one royal garment which I took from you. Here, take it!"

"Fine," replied the officer. "Now, tomorrow when you are taken out to be judged, the king will ask if you have anyone to speak on your behalf. Ask the king to summon me!"

The next day, the officer was summoned to the king's court. "Do you know this man?" asked the king. "Yes," the officer replied, "he attacked me on the road and robbed me of everything I had. He returned this garment to me yesterday, so you can see that what I have said is true!"

"Woe to this robber!" the spectators exclaimed. "The very item which he returned and which should grant him some leniency, is actually the main evidence to indict him!"

Similarly, a person takes a lulav on Succos to gain merit for himself. But if the lulav is stolen, then it goes before Hashem, as it were, and exclaims, "I am stolen!" And the Heavenly angels declare, "Woe to this man, for what should have been his source of merit is actually a source of indictment" (Yalkut Shimoni 504).

A mitzvah that is a product of theft will find no favor before Hashem.

(cont. on page 248)

19 Tishrei — May today's learning be a זכות for נ"י אבי שמעון and נתלי שמחה שתחי׳.
Dedicated by Eric and Marilyn Levy

19 Shevat — Abraham Baker לע"נ אברהם יצחק בן יוסף ז"ל
Jeanette Jarashow לע"נ שיינא בת שמיאי צבי ע"ה

19 Sivan — Reuven Pollack לע"נ ראובן זצ"ל בן יעקב יבלח"ט
Dedicated in loving memory by the Kaufman family, St. Louis, MO

❧ Sin-Free Mitzvos

SEFER SEFAS TAMIM — Chapter Three:
Mirmah — Its Root Causes (cont.)

In foretelling the Future Redemption, the prophet states: "Establish yourself through tzedakah (charity)..." (Yeshayahu 54:14). This means that the Redemption will be in the merit of tzedakah. It is well known that the mitzvah of tzedakah brings a tremendous flow of Heavenly mercy, for the donor and for the entire Jewish people. Therefore, tzedakah will release the Jewish people from the bonds of exile forever.

However, the prophet continues with some advice: "... distance yourself from cheating, for then you need not fear..." In other words: When will the mitzvah of tzedakah protect you so that you need not fear any indictment? When you distance yourself from cheating and theft. But if, Heaven forfend, you do not distance yourself from cheating and theft, then these sins will indict more than all other sins, as the Sages teach: "When a measure is filled with sins, which sin indicts more than any other? Thievery" (Vayikra Rabbah 33:3). This is what happened with the generation of the Flood, which was destroyed when their fate was sealed on account of thievery.

When someone is in the habit of lying and cheating, his mitzvos are tainted by these sins [for the money he uses to accomplish his mitzvos is earned dishonestly]. Thus, his mitzvos lack the power to awaken Heavenly mercy. To the contrary, they will arouse judgment against him.

As Zohar states regarding the verse: "Surely you should break your bread for the hungry" (Yeshayahu 58:7) — לַחְמֶךָ, your bread, and not the bread of cheating and theft.

In 1938, the legendary Torah giant R' Elchonon Wasserman journeyed to America in order to rescue his yeshivah in Baranovich, Poland, from financial disaster. World ecomonic depression had brought his yeshivah to a a point where the *talmidim* were literally going hungry.

During his year-long stay on these shores, R' Elchonon always inquired about the source of the money that was donated to his yeshivah. When he learned that elements of a planned fund-raising event contradicted *halachah*, he tore the admission tickets to pieces one by one, asking with pleading eyes, "Is it possible to build Torah this way?"

On another occasion, he entered the home of a generous contributor to charitable causes and found a card game in progress. The participants suggested that the winnings be given to the Baranovich Yeshivah. "I don't need such money," R' Elchonon told them.

(cont. on page 248)

The mitzvah of tzedakah brings a flow of Heavenly mercy only when it is achieved through honest earnings.

20 Tishrei — לע"נ נתן בן אשר הלוי ז"ל ומלכה רבקה בת יצחק חיים ע"ה
May today's learning be a זכות for our dear parents and grandparents.
20 Shevat — יום נישואין של שמואל יואב מיכאל ודינה אסתר היילפרין
כ' שבט תש"ס   January 27, 2000
20 Sivan — לע"נ יצחק בן אבא ז"ל

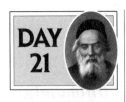

DAY 21

כ"א תשרי
21 TISHREI / CYCLE 1

October 8, 2001
September 27, 2002
October 17, 2003
October 6, 2004
October 24, 2005

כ"א שבט
21 SHEVAT / CYCLE 2

February 3, 2002
January 24, 2003
February 13, 2004
January 31, 2005
February 19, 2006

כ"א סיון
21 SIVAN / CYCLE 3

June 1, 2002
June 21, 2003
June 10, 2004
June 28, 2005
June 17, 2006

✎ *Easy Come, Easy Go*

SEFER SEFAS TAMIM — Chapter Three:
Mirmah — Its Root Causes (cont.)

One who acquires his money dishonestly will ultimately lose everything in this world, for Hashem will send someone even more wicked his way, to serve as His rod of punishment and deprive him of his possessions. As our Sages teach: "A person who robs and coerces on this world will not depart it without seeing others plunder his possessions."

His plunderer, who considers himself invincible, will have his possessions taken when his Heavenly account has reached an appropriate level. As the Mishnah teaches: "He [Hillel the Elder] also saw a skull floating on the water. He said to it, 'Because you drowned others, they drowned you; and eventually those who drowned you will be drowned.' " (Avos 2:7).

The *Baal Shem Tov* captured the essence of Hillel's words with a haunting parable:

An impoverished woman, who lived in a hovel on the outskirts of town, spent her days going from door to door asking for charity. Upon receiving some coins, she would always tell her benefactor, "Everything man does he does not for others, but for himself." People became accustomed to her strange response.

Once, she decided to approach the royal palace and seek assistance. The queen presented her with a generous contribution and the woman responded as usual, "Everything man does he does not for others, but for himself."

The woman became a regular visitor to the palace and the queen always gave her a tidy sum — and the poor woman would respond as always. After a while, the queen became incensed at the woman's apparent lack of gratitude. After all, having being shown such generosity by the royal household, could this wretched soul think of nothing more to say other than her silly maxim —which was absolutely false?

The queen would not tolerate such insolence any longer. In anticipation of the woman's next visit, the queen prepared a loaf of bread laced with deadly poison. The poor woman was delighted to receive the bread, in addition to the queen's usual monetary gift. She took the bread home, but before partaking of it she placed it on her table where she could enjoy gazing upon it and smelling its delicious aroma.

Meanwhile, the prince was on a hunting expedition in the woods near the poor woman's shack. Famished and exhausted after a day of hunting, the prince knocked on the woman's door and asked for something to eat. Recognizing the prince from her visits to the palace, the woman welcomed him inside and after offering him a seat, cut him a generous slice of bread from the queen's loaf. A few minutes later, the prince fell onto the floor of the shack and died.

Immediately, the woman dashed to the palace and reported the tragic news to the queen, who collapsed in a faint. After being revived, the queen told the woman, "I now understand the truth of your refrain: *'Everything man does he does not for others, but for himself.'* "

> **Ultimately, one will have to answer for his actions.**

(cont. on page 249)

21 Tishrei — Rosalind Lipschitz לע"נ רייזל בת משה ע"ה
Dedicated in loving memory by her daughter מרים בת אברהם אהרן שתחי'

21 Shevat — Stephen Levitz לע"נ שלום גאזיק בן חונה ז"ל
Dedicated by Jason Bronstein

21 Sivan — Mrs. Rymer Frankel לע"נ רייזנה בת ר' יצחק ע"ה
Dedicated by her children and grandchildren

כ"ב תשרי
22 TISHREI / CYCLE 1

October 9, 2001
September 28, 2002
October 18, 2003
October 7, 2004
October 25, 2005

כ"ב שבט
22 SHEVAT / CYCLE 2

February 4, 2002
January 25, 2003
February 14, 2004
February 1, 2005
February 20, 2006

כ"ב סיון
22 SIVAN / CYCLE 3

June 2, 2002
June 22, 2003
June 11, 2004
June 29, 2005
June 18, 2006

✑ *Secular Courts*

SEFER SEFAS TAMIM — Chapter Three:
Mirmah — Its Root Causes (cont.)

*T*he sin of theft has the power to awaken Heavenly judgment against the sinner and to seal his fate, more than any other sin. As the Talmud states (Sanhedrin 108a):

> R' Yochanan said: Take note of how great is the power of theft, for the generation of the Flood transgressed everything, yet the decree of their punishment was not sealed until they stretched their hands forth in theft, as it is written, "For the earth is filled with theft on account of them, and I am prepared to destroy them from the earth" (Bereishis 6:13).

This is one of the factors which today causes Jewish money to be lost, so that the wealthy hold on to their wealth for but a short time. To our great misfortune, theft and coercion have increased through those who go to secular courts to inform on their fellow Jew and thereby extract money from them. They are fully confident that this is "kosher money" for, after all, the courts have awarded it to them! In truth, however, this is actual theft, since the Torah, in which the will of Hashem is expressed, does not endorse this.

Therefore, if one is aware that according to Torah law he has no claim against his adversary, but that he could extract money from him in secular court, then he should flee from such money as from a fire, for such money will consume even that which he has earned previously, as mentioned above.

It is impossible to see matters objectively when one's own interests are involved.

The Torah states: "And these are the laws that you shall place before them"(*Shemos* 21:1). *Rashi* (citing *Midrash Tanchuma*) comments: "Before them [i.e. Jewish courts that will rule according to Torah law], and not before gentile [courts]." For Jews to bring their case before a secular court — even if such laws concur with halachah in a particular instance — is a desecration of Hashem's Name because it is tantamount to a public declaration that their system of justice is superior to that of the Torah.

Shulchan Aruch states:

> It is prohibited to litigate before non-Jewish judges, and in their court... Whoever does so is an evildoer, and it is as if he blasphemed and raised a hand against the Torah of Moshe, Our Teacher (*Choshen Mishpat* 26:1).

There are exceptions to this rule (see, for example, *Choshen Mishpat* 26:2). Generally speaking, however, to bring one's case against a fellow Jew before a secular court is a great *chillul Hashem*.

Sometimes, a person is tempted to take his case before a secular court because he feels that the *beis*

(cont. on page 249)

22 Tishrei — Arlie Sachs Rubovits לע"נ יעל בת ראובן דוב ויהודית ע"ה
Dedicated in loving memory by her family

22 Shevat — The Manchester Rosh Yeshiva
לע"נ הגאון הצדיק הרב יהודא זאב בן הרב משה יצחק הלוי סג"ל זצוק"ל
הוצנח ע"י משפחת דיוויס

22 Sivan — Libby Gross Chavkin לע"נ ליבא בת צבי אשר הכהן ע"ה
Dedicated by Yerachmiel Chavkin, Dvorah & Yeshaya Stone, Yoel Chavkin and families

כ"ג תשרי
23 TISHREI / CYCLE 1

October 10, 2001
September 29, 2002
October 19, 2003
October 8, 2004
October 26, 2005

כ"ג שבט
23 SHEVAT / CYCLE 2

February 5, 2002
January 26, 2003
February 15, 2004
February 2, 2005
February 21, 2006

כ"ג סיון
23 SIVAN / CYCLE 3

June 3, 2002
June 23, 2003
June 12, 2004
June 30, 2005
June 19, 2006

☙ *Murky Prayers*

SEFER SEFAS TAMIM — Chapter Three:
Mirmah — Its Root Causes (cont.)

*O*ne's prayers will not be accepted by Hashem as long as he is in possession of money which he acquired dishonestly. Such a prayer is considered "murky," as our Sages explain regarding the words, "And my prayer is pure" (Iyov 16:17): "Is there such a thing as a 'murky' prayer?" The meaning is: A prayer from someone who is innocent of theft is deemed a "pure prayer," while a prayer offered by someone guilty of theft is a "murky prayer" (Shemos Rabbah 22:44).

This can be likened to a barrel whose wine is murky with sediment. As long as the sediment remains mixed with the wine, the wine is unfit to drink even to a lowly person — and certainly it is unacceptable as a gift to a king. So it is with theft. It "mixes" with every word of prayer and prevents it from ascending and being accepted by Hashem — until the person surrenders what he has stolen.

Scholars of earlier generations have noted something incredible, which forces us to ponder the severity of cheating and theft:

We all know that Yom Kippur is the high point of the year, an awesome day when our sins are forgiven. The climax of Yom Kippur is the Ne'ilah prayer. And what do we ask for in this prayer?

וַתְּלַמְּדֵנוּ ה׳ אֱלֹקֵינוּ לְהִתְוַדּוֹת לְפָנֶיךָ עַל כָּל עֲוֹנוֹתֵינוּ, לְמַעַן נֶחְדַּל מֵעשֶׁק יָדֵינוּ . . .

You have taught us, Hashem, our G-d, to confess before You regarding all our sins so that we can withdraw our hands from cheating...

This should inspire us to protect ourselves from gezel (theft) with all our might, all the days of our lives.

In commenting on the *Ne'ilah* prayer, *Yesod V'Shoresh Ha'Avodah* (11:11) writes that when saying "...so that we can withdraw our hands from cheating..." one should ponder whether, Heaven forfend, he has any semblance of *gezel* in his possession. If he does, he should repent fully and accept upon himself at that moment to correct this sin immediately following the fast's conclusion by either returning what he has stolen or by appeasing the one whom he wronged [if returning the item is not feasible].

Earlier (10:2), the author writes: "It is found in sacred works that that there is no sin which prevents one's prayers from ascending Heavenward like the sin of *gezel*, may the Compassionate One save us from it. Ponder the matter and consider how crucial it is to distance onself from this grievous sin."

The sin of theft prevents one's prayers from gaining acceptance before Hashem.

כ״ד תשרי
24 TISHREI / CYCLE 1

October 11, 2001
September 30, 2002
October 20, 2003
October 9, 2004
October 27, 2005

כ״ד שבט
24 SHEVAT / CYCLE 2

February 6, 2002
January 27, 2003
February 16, 2004
February 3, 2005
February 22, 2006

כ״ד סיון
24 SIVAN / CYCLE 3

June 4, 2002
June 24, 2003
June 13, 2004
July 1, 2005
June 20, 2006

No Escape

SEFER SEFAS TAMIM — Chapter Four:
Retribution in the Next World for Theft

*I*n the preceding chapters, we have detailed some of the punishments which are visited upon a person in this world for the sins of gezel and chamas (theft and purchasing through coercion). In this chapter, we will discuss some of the great punishments for these sins in the World to Come — unless the sinner will rectify his misdeeds in his lifetime, by either returning that which he acquired wrongfully, or by seeking and receiving his victim's forgiveness.

It is well known that for the sin of gezel, or any other sin between man and his fellow, Yom Kippur does not atone until one appeases his fellow man. Even death will not atone for this, as our Sages teach regarding the verse, "[Remember your Creator in the days of your youth, before...] the pitcher is broken at the fountain" (Koheles 12:6): This refers to the stomach which digested food acquired through dishonest earnings. After death, the stomach will split open, as if to return the food to the mouth and say, "Here, take back what you stole because of your cravings and gave to me!"

Elsewhere, our Sages state that the soul of the thief will be fed "fine sand" and when it will not want to eat, Hashem will say, "Why were stolen items sweet in your mouth in the other world?"

And after all the punishments in the Next World, the sin of gezel will still not be rectified until the soul returns in a gilgul (transmigration) to this world to return what it stole. This is stated in many sources, including the Vilna Gaon's commentary to the verse, "A truthful witness saves souls" (Mishlei 14:25): A truthful witness who causes a thief to return what he stole, saves the thief's soul from having to return to this world.

Restitution must be made for the thief to gain atonement.

It is in this vein that I explained the Midrash to the verse, "Rejoice, young man, in your childhood, let your heart cheer you in the days of your youth... but be aware that for all these things G-d will call you to account" (Koheles 11:9). Midrash likens this to one who, after being convicted, fled from the king's executioner. The executioner chased the convict as others shouted at him, "Don't run too far, for the further you run, the further you will have to walk back!" This is a puzzling Midrash which is easily explained by what we have said above.

Koheles is teaching us the secret of gilgul (transmigration). He is telling us: "True, it is your choice on this world to do whatever you please; if you choose, you can steal, coerce and cheat; you can ignore any mitzvah that you please — but remember one fact: The

(cont. on page 249)

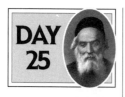

DAY 25

כ״ה תשרי
25 TISHREI / CYCLE 1

October 12, 2001
October 1, 2002
October 21, 2003
October 10, 2004
October 28, 2005

כ״ה שבט
25 SHEVAT / CYCLE 2

February 7, 2002
January 28, 2003
February 17, 2004
February 4, 2005
February 23, 2006

כ״ה סיון
25 SIVAN / CYCLE 3

June 5, 2002
June 25, 2003
June 14, 2004
July 2, 2005
June 21, 2006

❧ A Difficult Form of Return

SEFER SEFAS TAMIM — Chapter Four:
Retribution in the Next World for Theft (cont.)

he concept of gilul which we have discussed above can be likened to a teacher who tells his wayward student: "Why must you run away from school and be punished for this while accomplishing nothing? For in the end, you will have to return and learn as I insist. You would be better off remaining here and obeying me, and be considered a good student!" Similarly, it is far better for a person to rectify his misdeeds while he is still on this world, than to die and then be forced to return to this world again.

I have read in sefarim an amazing fact, that in earlier generations, a soul was reincarnated as a horse and it worked with all its might to pay back what it owed; this is a most difficult form of gilgul.

R' Yosef Chaim Sonnenfeld, legendary *Rav* of Jerusalem in the early part of the twentieth century, related the following story which he heard from his *rebbi*, R' Yehoshua Leib Diskin:

When R' Yehoshua Leib was *Rav* in Kovno, Lithuania, a resident there experienced a terrifying dream. His father, who had died the previous year, appeared to him and told him that he had been reincarnated in a black bull which was owned by a certain gentile some distance from Kovno. In the dream, the man's father ordered him to go and buy the bull, adding that the owner would ask eighty rubles for the animal but that he would settle for forty. After buying the animal, the son was to bring it back to Kovno and have it slaughtered by a G-d-fearing *shochet* in the presence of the *Rav*, R' Yehoshua Leib, who would answer "*Amen*" to the slaughterer's blessing. The *Rav* was to eat some of the meat and the rest was to be distributed among other Jews. Only then would the father's soul find eternal peace.

Although this dream was repeated on three consecutive nights, the man paid no attention to it. Some time later, however, the man was praying in *shul* when he collapsed in a faint. After being revived, he explained that he had seen a vision of his father who had again commanded him to go purchase the bull and have it slaughtered.

The people in the *shul* accompanied the man to the *Rav's* house. R' Yehoshua Leib held a private conversation with the man in which he related the entire episode. The man was impoverished, so R' Yehoshua Leib asked the people if they would provide the money for the purchase of the animal, and they readily agreed.

R' Yehoshua Leib instructed the man to purchase the bull, on condition that its description, price, location and owner all tallied exactly with the dream. The man took the money, went to the specified town and found the gentile. The gentile said that he did have a bull which fit the description but that it was extreme-

Far better for a person to rectify his misdeeds while he is still on this world.

(cont. on page 249)

25 Tishrei — לע״נ חסי״ה פרומיט בת שמואל יבלחט״ט
Dedicated by Mrs. Shana Kramer

25 Shevat — Pessi Goldman לע״נ ברכה פעשע בת יעקב יצחק ע״ה
Dedicated by Shai & Aliza Goldman

25 Sivan — לע״נ אהרן דוד בן שלמה דוב הכהן ז״ל
Dedicated by Pearl Cohen

DAY 26

כ"ו תשרי
26 TISHREI / CYCLE 1

October 13, 2001
October 2, 2002
October 22, 2003
October 11, 2004
October 29, 2005

כ"ו שבט
26 SHEVAT / CYCLE 2

February 8, 2002
January 29, 2003
February 18, 2004
February 5, 2005
February 24, 2006

כ"ו סיון
26 SIVAN / CYCLE 3

June 6, 2002
June 26, 2003
June 15, 2004
July 3, 2005
June 22, 2006

✧ *A Voyage for Naught*

SEFER SEFAS TAMIM — Chapter Four:
Retribution in the Next World for Theft (cont.)

*O*ne may be wondering: It is obvious that to be reincarnated as an ammial is a horrible form of punishment. But what could be so bad about returning to this world in human form?

This can be explained by way of a parable:

A man was unable to provide for his wife and children and so, with a heavy heart, he left them and traveled to a faraway island in the hope of succeeding in business. It was many years before he finally began to see some success; eventually, he became a very wealthy man. How happy he was when he sent word to his family that he had amassed a fortune and that he could finally plan his voyage home, which was to take several months.

When his message arrived at his home, there was great rejoicing and everyone began to anticipate the emotional day of reunion.

As the man was about to set out on his journey, he was met by a friend who advised him, "Before you leave, make sure that your earnings are entirely yours and that you don't owe anyone any money. It would be very unfortunate if you had to return here because of a small amount that you owed someone." This advice, however, fell on deaf ears. The wealthy man simply laughed it off and sent word to his family that he was on his way home.

On the day when he was to finally arrive, the man's wife and children went out to the city gates to greet him. After hours of anxious waiting, they spotted the ship in the distance. Their excitement grew as the boat docked and they watched as the passengers disembarked.

But their joy quickly turned to dismay as the city gates suddenly swung shut and they heard the man arguing with officials, who had just received a disturbing message from the island whence he had come. He had embezzled someone ten years earlier and had never returned what he had stolen. The island had no postal service and there was no way for him to send the payment through a messenger. He would have to return there immediately.

The man pleaded for mercy. "Please, I'll pay the man back ten times what I stole! Just let me remain here with my family, whom I have not seen for ten years! Let me at least stay here for a month, a week, a day!"

The officials, however, would not budge. "It's your own fault," they told the distraught

"Make sure that your earnings are entirely yours and that you don't owe anyone any money!"

(cont. on page 250)

26 Tishrei — לע"נ פערל ע"ה בת ר' משה יוסף יבלח"ט
Dedicated by the Ginsburg family

26 Shevat — Naftali Jaroslawicz לע"נ נפתלי בן מנחם מענדל ז"ל
Dedicated by Yitzchok & Tzivie Eisenstein and family

26 Sivan — Sabina Friedman לע"נ שיינדל יוכבד ע"ה בת ר' יעקב הלוי יבלח"ט
Dedicated by her husband, Nathan Friedman and her children, Steven & Helene, Francine, Rafe & Lori and her grandchildren

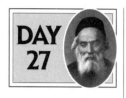

כ"ז תשרי
27 TISHREI / CYCLE 1

October 14, 2001
October 3, 2002
October 23, 2003
October 12, 2004
October 30, 2005

כ"ז שבט
27 SHEVAT / CYCLE 2

February 9, 2002
January 30, 2003
February 19, 2004
February 6, 2005
February 25, 2006

כ"ז סיון
27 SIVAN / CYCLE 3

June 7, 2002
June 27, 2003
June 16, 2004
July 4, 2005
June 23, 2006

✎ *A Clean Slate*

SEFER SEFAS TAMIM — Chapter Four:
Retribution in the Next World for Theft (cont.)

Our primary purpose in this world is to accrue Torah and mitzvos, and thereby bask in the radiance of the Next World. Therefore, we should see ourselves as a foreigner who has traveled to a distant land for the sole purpose of engaging in business pursuits. We, too, should be concerning ourselves with nothing else but our spiritual pursuits.

But reality is often not this way. From their youth, people become distracted by their earthly desires and by other factors, and they forget their real purpose in life. Then, as old age approaches, they turn their attention to gathering their "merchandise" — Torah and mitzvos — and embarking on their journey to the World of Truth.

Zohar states that one must endure seven judgments before coming to his eternal place in Gan Eden... but if after all the judgments have passed one's soul is found to be stained by the sin of gezel (theft) in any of its various forms, then it will be denied entrance to Gan Eden. At most, if the person has some great source of merit, he will be permitted to see his place in Heaven from a distance without gaining entry. His soul will weep bitterly, for he will be forced to descend again to this lowly world with all its difficulties — and who knows whether or not he will succeed this time?

The following story was related by the Manchester *Rosh Yeshivah*, R' Yehudah Zev Segal. It was transmitted by R' Chaim Volozhiner to R' Zundel of Salant, who passed it on to R' Yisrael Salanter, the *rebbi* of the *Alter* of Kelm. The *Alter* related it to R' Zvi Hirsh Broide, who told it to R' Eliyahu Lopian, from whom R' Segal heard it.

In the early years of the Volozhiner Yeshivah, one of its students suddenly fell seriously ill. It was decided that the boy should be sent home where his family would attend to him. Another student was designated to accompany the boy on his journey home.

On the way, the two stopped off at an inn. When they perpared to leave and were presented with the bill, the ill student, who had accepted responsibility for the payment, realized that he was short the necessary money. The innkeeper kindly said that he fully trusted the boy to pay the bill at some future date.

When they arrived at their destination, the ill student asked his parents for money to pay the innkeeper and handed it to his friend, who would be passing the inn on his return trip to Volozhin. However, the student completely forgot about this and returned to Volozhin without paying the debt. The ill student succumbed to his illness and departed this world.

(cont. on page 250)

From their youth, people become distracted by earthly desires.

27 Tishrei — Irving Deutsch לע"נ רפאל ישראל חיים בן יעקב יהודה ז"ל
Dedicated by his children and grandchildren

27 Shevat — In honor of our dear parents, Mrs. Anita Shulman and Rabbi & Mrs. Sladowsky
Dedicated by your loving children

27 Sivan — Harry Gurwitz לע"נ צבי בן אברהם ז"ל
Sponsored by the Gurwitz family

DAY 28

כ"ח תשרי
28 TISHREI / CYCLE 1

October 15, 2001
October 4, 2002
October 24, 2003
October 13, 2004
October 31, 2005

כ"ח שבט
28 SHEVAT / CYCLE 2

February 10, 2002
January 31, 2003
February 20, 2004
February 7, 2005
February 26, 2006

כ"ח סיון
28 SIVAN / CYCLE 3

June 8, 2002
June 28, 2003
June 17, 2004
July 5, 2005
June 24, 2006

✒ *Justice Prevails*

SEFER SEFAS TAMIM — Chapter Four:
Retribution in the Next World for Theft (cont.)

*S*omeone who steals from or cheats others will be held accountable not only for the actual theft, but also for all the emotional pain and anxiety that he caused his victims. He will be punished for this measure for measure.

Koheles states: "And I returned and contemplated all the acts of cheating that are committed beneath the sun: Behold! Tears of those who are cheated with none to comfort them, and from the hand of those who cheat them, power [is taken] — with none to comfort them" (Koheles 4:1).

Picture the following scenario:

A poor man borrows a thousand dollars which he hopes to use for business so that he can earn some profit and provide for his family. On the way to the market, he is held up by bandits. The poor man begs for mercy, but his pleading falls on deaf ears, as the bandits beat him mercilessly and rob him of every penny. The poor man cries out in anguish, but there is no one to comfort him, and finally he falls to the ground in a faint.

Some passersby find him and after much effort they manage to revive him. Hearing his tragic tale, they wonder to one another:

"What did this poor man do to deserve such pain and distress? How will this unfortunate soul provide for himself?"

This is how the passersby, men of flesh and blood, see the situation. We, however, know that Hashem's ways are perfect and that any suffering which a person endures is decreed by Heaven in precise measure. In all probability, the poor man in our story had, earlier in life or in a previous gilgul (transmigration), been guilty of the same sins. He, too, had attacked someone and robbed him; he, too, had left some unfortunate soul dazed and penniless. And now, Heaven has punished him measure for measure.

This is the intent of the above-mentioned verse: "Behold! Tears of those who are cheated with none to comfort them..." Koheles [i.e. King Shlomo] saw victims of robbery crying out in pain with no one to comfort them and he perceived through Ruach HaKodesh (Divine Inspiration) that ultimately, those who robbed them would suffer the same fate — "and from the hand of those who cheat them, power [is taken] — with none to comfort them." Hashem showed Koheles that the sin of gezel, and all the pain that comes along with it, is never ignored or forgotten in Heaven. It may take years or even lifetimes, but ultimately, justice will prevail.

Any suffering which a person endures is decreed by Heaven in precise measure.

רפואה שלמה לפריידל אדל בת סימא בתושח"י — **28 Tishrei**

28 Shevat — Shmuel Horowitz ר' שמואל בן ר' יחיאל דוד הלוי ז"ל לע"נ בעלי היקר,
Dedicated in loving memory by his wife and children

28 Sivan — י"נ לרפו"ש שבח בן יענטה
ולרפו"ש גולדה בת שרה שתחי', בתושח"י

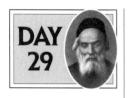

כ"ט תשרי
29 TISHREI / CYCLE 1

October 16, 2001
October 5, 2002
October 25, 2003
October 14, 2004
November 1, 2005

כ"ט שבט
29 SHEVAT / CYCLE 2

February 11, 2002
February 1, 2003
February 21, 2004
February 8, 2005
February 27, 2006

כ"ט סיון
29 SIVAN / CYCLE 3

June 9, 2002
June 29, 2003
June 18, 2004
July 6, 2005
June 25, 2006

✑ *Warped Standards*

SEFER SEFAS TAMIM — Chapter Five:
Why People Steal

*W*hatever guidance we have offered thus far is for someone who is not in the habit of stealing and cheating, and therefore can easily be cured of such maladies, relatively speaking. However, if someone is in the habit of stealing and cheating, Heaven forfend, and he finds it difficult to stop, then he must search within himself to discover how he developed this sickness. While there are many possible causes, two are obvious to all.

The first cause is the high standard of living which many have accepted as the norm, to our misfortune. Expensive wardrobes and other unnecessary expenditures have brought troubles and distress in our times, both within and without. When a person first accustoms himself to this sort of living, he does not realize where it will lead.

The yetzer hara deals with people in this regard like a hunter who places food in a bird trap. The bird craves the food and with its limited understanding, does not even notice the trap. It snatches the food and suddenly, it is caught and ready for slaughter. This is exactly how it is with many people. Hashem, in His infinite kindness, provides a person with an income that will supply him with all his basic needs and allow him to meet his spiritual obligations: to give tzedakah (charity), to perform chesed (lovingkindness), to support Torah, etc. But then, the yetzer hara comes along and convinces the person that he should purchase clothing and other material items which are actually above his means. The simple person wants to live like the prominent one, and the prominent one is satisfied only if he can live like the very wealthy, so that he should appear distinguished and deserving of honor in the eyes of his friends.

Pursuit of materialism has brought troubles and distress in our times.

The individual follows his desires, accustoming himself to this higher standard until, with the passage of time, he feels compelled to live this way. Then, when for a year or two, he is unable to earn enough to satisfy what, for him, has now become necessity, the yetzer hara convinces him to steal, to cheat, and to be "a wicked one [who] borrows and does not pay" (Tehillim 37:21). This way, he can live luxuriously, as he is accustomed, and he will not feel ashamed before his peers.

And so, from someone who once was basically honest, the person has become a thief and a cheat, who cares for no one but himself.

In an address to women, R' Yehudah Zev Segal decried a trend among Orthodox women to dress "in

(cont. on page 251)

29 Tishrei — May today's learning be a זכות for the Kluger & Danto families.
Dedicated by Akiva, Jeni and Ronit Liba Danto

29 Shevat — In memory of Irving Graff ז"ל לע"נ יצחק בן ישראל ז"ל
Dedicated by his appreciative children

29 Sivan — Moshe Reisman לע"נ משה פסחי ז"ל בן אברהם הלוי יבלח"ט
Dedicated by the Fixler family

ל תשרי
30 TISHREI / CYCLE 1

October 17, 2001
October 6, 2002
October 26, 2003
October 15, 2004
November 2, 2005

ל שבט
30 SHEVAT / CYCLE 2

February 12, 2002
February 2, 2003
February 22, 2004
February 9, 2005
February 28, 2006

ל סיון
30 SIVAN / CYCLE 3

June 10, 2002
June 30, 2003
June 19, 2004
July 7, 2005
June 26, 2006

✑ The Distress of Overextension

SEFER SEFAS TAMIM — Chapter Five:
Why People Steal (cont.)

Often, a person who lives above his means suffers enormous stress which can cause illness and endanger his life. This can happen when he reaches a point where he can no longer maintain his high standard of living. In place of the "honor" which the yetzer hara had convinced him to pursue and which to his mind he had attained, he now receives a double measure of scorn and ridicule from those who are steeped in materialism and are capable of maintaining their standard. This is his punishment in this world, aside from what he will suffer in the World to Come for the sin of gezel (theft).

Aside from the scorn one may be subjected to when his pursuit of wealth ends in failure, he must also contend with the distress and sadness which such failure usually brings with it. By contrast, "Who is [truly] rich? One who is happy with his lot" (*Avos* 4:1).

King Shlomo captured this contrast when he wrote: "All the days of the pauper are bad, but the good-hearted constantly celebrate" (*Mishlei* 15:15). One who suffers pangs of hunger for material wealth is like a pauper who never has enough. Those who are satisfied with their lot, however, enjoy life and find it a constant celebration (Rabbeinu Yonah).

"One who has one hundred wants two hundred" (Koheles Rabbah 1:34). Someone who covets money never has enough, while one who has an inner sense of contentment is truly wealthy.

The Chofetz Chaim had a number of comments and observations on the meaning of true wealth and the importance of being happy with one's lot:

He once encouraged a wealthy acquaintance to spend more time in prayer and Torah study. The gentleman replied, "I would like to but I have no time." Said the Chofetz Chaim, "If you have no free time, you are not a rich man, but a pitiful pauper. There is no greater poverty than yours."

He once offered a parable: A carpenter must use a large saw. If his saw was taken from him and replaced with a fine diamond saw, he would be out of business, even though the diamond saw is far more expensive than the large one; for his work, the carpenter needs the right tools. Similarly, a person's lot in life provides him with the particular means to accomplish his mission on this earth. Some are granted financial wealth and then are tested as to how they will use their money, while others need poverty in order to achieve spiritual perfection by overcoming adversity. Only Hashem knows who needs which tool.

The Steipler *Gaon* wrote: בִּטְחוֹנִי בְּצוּרִי הִיא אוֹצָרִי, *My faith in my Creator — that is my treasure*. A person's faith in Hashem is the treasure that allows him to be satisfied with his lot.

Who is truly rich? One who is happy with his lot.

א חשון
1 CHESHVAN / CYCLE

October 18, 2001
October 7, 2002
October 27, 2003
October 16, 2004
November 3, 2005

א אדר*
*1 ADAR / CYCLE 2

February 13, 2002
February 3, 2003
February 23, 2004
February 10, 2005
March 1, 2006

א תמוז
1 TAMMUZ / CYCLE 3

June 11, 2002
July 1, 2003
June 20, 2004
July 8, 2005
June 27, 2006

During Hebrew leap years a thirteenth month called Adar Sheni (the second Adar) is added to the calendar. For those years, two sets of corresponding dates are given, the first for Adar, and the second for Adar Sheni.

א אדר ב
1 ADAR SHENI

March 5, 2003
March 12, 2005

✑ The Right Way to Live

SEFER SEFAS TAMIM — Chapter Five:
Why People Steal (cont.)

*O*ur Sages have taught: "Who is a wise man? One who foresees future happenings" (Tamid 32a). Even when a person is experiencing great financial success, he should bear in mind that with time, situations can reverse themselves, as is often the case. Therefore, even if he is presently wealthy, he should live a lifestyle that is considered average for a man of his stature in his place of residence. Even if Hashem has blessed him with great wealth, he should not wear very expensive, princely clothing. To do so is to harm oneself, for expensive dress inspires arrogance and also incites the yetzer hara upon oneself.*

Such behavior also causes others who cannot afford this to seek to emulate such a lifestyle. In the end, they will resort to borrowing and not repaying, to stealing and cheating.

The Chofetz Chaim cites four reasons why a person should avoid expensive living, particularly with regard to dress, even though he can currently afford it. The first reason, that his financial status may change, and the last reason, that his lifestyle will have a detrimental effect on others, are directly related to the discussion of what can lead a person to rob and cheat.

The other two reasons relate to the negative effect

which lavish living and expensive dress can have on the individual's own personality. In a discourse to women, R' Yehudah Zev Segal focused on the dangers of being fashion conscious:

> Let us think for a moment: Who are the designers of these fashions and what guidelines do they use in originating their designs? The designers are secularists and, more often than not, are immoral. Their goal is to design a style that will attract the attention of men. In other words, these styles are a direct contradiction to the attribute of *tznius* (modesty) that is the hallmark of Jewish daughters (*Inspiration and Insight*, vol. I).

Even the wealthy should pursue a modest lifestyle.

With regard to young men who show excessive concern over their appearance, R' Segal cited a *Midrash*:

> R' Ami said: The *yetzer hara* (evil inclination) does not walk on the "side streets" [among the humble and modest who are not overly concerned with their outward appearance — *Maharzu*]; rather, he walks down the "main thoroughfares" [after those who are concerned with their appearance]. When he sees someone fingering his eyes, fixing his hair, and adjusting his step, he says, "This one is mine!" (*Bereishis Rabbah* 22:6).

R' Segal concluded that certainly a student of Torah must have a neat and clean appearance. But to be overly concerned with one's outward appearance is to incite the evil inclination upon oneself, as the *Midrash* teaches.

1 Cheshvon — Mordechai Rosenberg לע"נ מרדכי ארי' בן ר' משה ז"ל
Dedicated by his children

1 Adar — Edward Weiss לע"נ מרדכי בן מענדל ז"ל
Sponsored by Mark Weiss

1 Tammuz — May today's learning be a זכות for our משפחה.
Dedicated by Mr. & Mrs. Ha-Cohen Rinde

ב חשון

2 CHESHVAN / CYCLE 1

October 19, 2001
October 8, 2002
October 28, 2003
October 17, 2004
November 4, 2005

ב אדר*

*2 ADAR / CYCLE 2

February 14, 2002
February 4, 2003
February 24, 2004
February 11, 2005
March 2, 2006

ב תמוז

2 TAMMUZ / CYCLE 3

June 12, 2002
July 2, 2003
June 21, 2004
July 9, 2005
June 28, 2006

During Hebrew leap years a thirteenth month called Adar Sheni (the second Adar) is added to the calendar. For those years, two sets of corresponding dates are given, the first for Adar, and the second for Adar Sheni.

◈ *Domino Effect*

SEFER SEFAS TAMIM — Chapter Five:
Why People Steal (cont.)

*B*ecause of excesses in lifestyle, the price of outfitting a family for a wedding has skyrocketed. Those brides who cannot afford this feel shamed, while their fathers and mothers weep with no one to help them. These are only some of the many misfortunes which have befallen the poor. What is the cause of all this, if not the excess spending for clothing and other material items which, to our misfortune, has become the norm in our day? Those who are guilty of such excesses harm themselves in this world and the Next, and they cause harm to others as well.

A number of years ago, a New York yeshivah student from an affluent home became bar mitzvah. The celebration was held in a *shul's* basement catering hall; plastic and paper goods were used. It was the plainest of affairs. Toward the end of the meal, the father spoke. The gist of his message was: "I could well afford a more elaborate affair, but I felt it unnecessary. Instead, I calculated the difference, and will now present a check in that amount to the dean of my son's yeshivah."

Later, when the boy's *rebbi* expressed his admiration to the father, he responded, "I was very uncomfortable making that speech. It seemed as if I was patting myself on the back. But I felt it had to be said."

At another bar mitzvah celebration of a boy from an affluent home, the guests were similarly impressed by the affair's simplicity. There were about sixty guests aside from the boy's classmates. The highlight of the celebration was the boy's completion of all six orders of the Mishnah. The father wept tears of joy. It was a beautiful evening. Most important was the lasting impression which the evening surely had on the bar mitzvah boy.

Sometimes, it is a feeling for the plight of one's fellow Jews which can impel a person to tone down what otherwise might have been a lavish affair.

Mr. Avraham Meyers was a supporter of Beth Medrash Govoha of Lakewood during that Torah citadel's formative years. Mr. Meyers' son became engaged at the height of the Second World War when word of the Nazi's policy of genocide had already reached the West. Mr. Meyers asked the legendary *Rosh Yeshivah*, R' Aharon Kotler, "How can I spend money on a wedding when Jewish blood is being spilled on the other side of the ocean?" Mr. Meyers said that if the *Rosh Yeshivah* would allow his son's wedding to take place on the lawn of the yeshivah, he would donate all the money saved to *tzedakah*.

After R' Aharon gave his consent, Mr. Meyers consulted a caterer and figured out to the penny what the wedding would have normally cost. He then gave the total — $7500 — to *tzedakah*.

> *Those who pursue an excessive lifestyle cause pain and shame to others.*

ג חשון
3 CHESHVAN / CYCLE 1

October 20, 2001
October 9, 2002
October 29, 2003
October 18, 2004
November 5, 2005

ג אדר*
*3 ADAR / CYCLE 2

February 15, 2002
February 5, 2003
February 25, 2004
February 12, 2005
March 3, 2006

ג תמוז
3 TAMMUZ / CYCLE 3

June 13, 2002
July 3, 2003
June 22, 2004
July 10, 2005
June 29, 2006

*During Hebrew leap years a thirteenth month called Adar Sheni (the second Adar) is added to the calendar. For those years, two sets of corresponding dates are given, the first for Adar, and the second for Adar Sheni.

❧ *Parameters of Gezel*

SEFER SEFAS TAMIM — Chapter Five:
Why People Steal (cont.)

*T*he second major factor which may cause an observant Jew to engage in acts of gezel (theft) is ignorance of certain basic truths in this area of Jewish law. There are those who actually believe that the sin of gezel is committed only when one physically takes something from someone else's possession. This, of course, is a gross error, for to deprive someone of an item in a secretive way is also gezel. And gezel encompasses much more: using a deposit or collateral, or borrowing an item without the owner's permission; withholding a rental fee or a worker's wages; or lending an item and accepting more than its worth in return. Aside from the sin of gezel, these last two cases also involve the prohibitions against withholding a worker's wage and charging interest, respectively.

In summation: Whenever a person wrongfully possesses even a penny that is someone else's, he is guilty of gezel.

Regarding withholding a worker's wage, I offer the following advice. Whenever hiring a worker to perform some chore, the wage should be established in advance. Otherwise, one is liable to sin, unless he will be extremely generous with his money, so as to be innocent of any hint of gezel. This is why:

Over the course of a year, a person is likely to engage scores of workers for various chores in his home. It is common that after a job has been completed, the householder and worker argue over the price and each one walks away feeling that he has been cheated. Each decides to reluctantly accept the other's final offer, but in his heart, he is not completely forgiving. Sometimes, this can lead to an open feud.

According to halachah, such wages should be determined by prevailing rates in that locale. If the householder withholds even one cent to which the worker is entitled, then he is guilty of gezel and of the specific prohibition against depriving a worker of his rightful earnings.

In reality, it is difficult to know the exact rate in a given locale for each specific chore. Thus, if no agreement was made in advance and the householder wishes to guarantee that he has fulfilled his obligation, he would have no choice but to give the worker whatever he asks for — and this, of course, is no simple matter.

Therefore, anyone who seeks to fulfill his halachic obligations should agree to a fee with the worker before the work begins. The householder will gain in that the worker will reduce his fee, for he knows that at that

The sin of gezel encompasses much more than just outright thievery.

(cont. on page 251)

3 Cheshvon — In memory of Miriam Chaya לע"נ מרים חי' בת שמואל יוסף ע"ה
Dedicated by her children   נלב"ע ג' חשון תשמ"ב

3 Adar — לע"נ עוזר בן ישראל ז"ל
Dedicated by his family

3 Tammuz — Joseph Gittleman לע"נ יוסף בן אלטר איסר ז"ל
May today's learning be a זכות for his נשמה. Dedicated by his wife and children

ד חשון
4 CHESHVAN / CYCLE 1

October 21, 2001
October 10, 2002
October 30, 2003
October 19, 2004
November 6, 2005

ד אדר*
*4 ADAR / CYCLE 2

February 16, 2002
February 6, 2003
February 26, 2004
February 13, 2005
March 4, 2006

ד תמוז
4 TAMMUZ / CYCLE 3

June 14, 2002
July 4, 2003
June 23, 2004
July 11, 2005
June 30, 2006

*During Hebrew leap years a thirteenth month called Adar Sheni (the second Adar) is added to the calendar. For those years, two sets of corresponding dates are given, the first for Adar, and the second for Adar Sheni.

❧ Fooling Oneself

SEFER SEFAS TAMIM — Chapter Five:
Why People Steal (cont.)

*T*he Torah states: אַל תּוֹנוּ אִישׁ אֶת אָחִיו, *Do not wrong one another (Vayikra 25:14). This refers to what our Sages call ona'ah, price fraud. Though the buyer pays the high price of his own volition, the seller still transgresses this sin. Sadly, many people totally ignore the prohibition of ona'ah; instead, they consider misleading consumers or other fraudulent behavior as "shrewd business tactics."*

Remember: It is absolutely forbidden to exaggerate or fabricate an item's quality, or to claim that the item was purchased from the wholesaler for a high price when in fact it was not. Obviously, it is forbidden to disguise an item or to place it among items of better quality, so as to mislead the consumer.

Our Sages speak harshly of one who transgresses the sin of using faulty weights or measures (see Vayikra 19:35). He is, in the Sages' words, a perverter of justice, and he is deemed "hateful, repulsive and an abomination" (Rashi, ad loc. citing Toras Kohanim). The ultimate punishment for this sin is worse than the punishment for immorality (Yevamos 21a). While the actual sin of immorality is worse, it is possible to achieve complete repentance for it. However, one who uses false weights and measures steals from the public and will find it almost impossible to return all that he has stolen (see Rashi ad loc. and Rashbam to Bava Basra 88b).

When *Sefer Chofetz Chaim* was being printed, the Chofetz Chaim spent weeks on end in the printing shop in Warsaw to make sure that there were no errors in the printing or binding; he was literally frightened that someone might purchase a faulty copy and that this would constitute *gezel*.

In 1906, when the Chofetz Chaim was publishing his *Mishnah Berurah*, he asked his son R' Leib, who had moved to Warsaw, to oversee the *sefer's* production. Later, someone who purchased a set of *Mishnah Berurah* discovered that one section was printed incorrectly. The man sent a letter of complaint to the Chofetz Chaim, who immediately dispatched an anguished letter to his son: "What have you done to me, my son? All my days I was concerned that I should be saved from even the remotest possibility of *gezel*! Never did I dream that I would be guilty of outright *gezel*! And now, I have fallen into the snare of this sin!"

He instructed his son to print a number of extra, error-free copies of this section, out of concern that other copies contained the same error. He then placed an advertisement in the Jewish newspaper: "Whoever purchased a copy of the *Mishnah Berurah* containing a misplaced section should please write to me, and I will send you a corrected copy."

"All my days I was concerned that I should be saved from the remotest hint of gezel."

DAY 35

ה חשון
5 CHESHVAN / CYCLE 1

October 22, 2001
October 11, 2002
October 31, 2003
October 20, 2004
November 7, 2005

ה אדר*
*5 ADAR / CYCLE 2

February 17, 2002
February 7, 2003
February 27, 2004
February 14, 2005
March 5, 2006

ה תמוז
5 TAMMUZ / CYCLE 3

June 15, 2002
July 5, 2003
June 24, 2004
July 12, 2005
July 1, 2006

*During Hebrew leap years a thirteenth month called Adar Sheni (the second Adar) is added to the calendar. For those years, two sets of corresponding dates are given, the first for Adar, and the second for Adar Sheni.

❧ The First Question

SEFER SEFAS TAMIM — Chapter Five:
Why People Steal (cont.)

The Torah expressly states that one may not even own innacurate measures, as it is written (Devarim 25:14), "You shall not have in your house a measure and a measure — a large one and a small one" (see Bava Basra 89b and Rambam, Hilchos Geneivah 7:3). Every moment that a person possesses faulty measures, he transgresses this sin; even while he sleeps, his sin is multiplying — in contrast to other Torah prohibitions. This sin will surely not lead to success; an unfortunate, disgraceful end awaits him on this world, aside from the punishment that he will receive in the World to Come.

As is well known, when a soul is judged after departing this world, the first question asked is, "Did you conduct your business affairs in good faith?" (Shabbos 31a).

The Talmud states that the first two questions which the soul is asked are: "נָשָׂאתָ וְנָתַתָּ בֶּאֱמוּנָה, *Did you conduct your business affairs in good faith?*" and "עִתִּים לַתּוֹרָה קָבַעְתָּ, *Did you set aside fixed times for Torah study?*" Elsewhere, however, the Talmud (*Kiddushin* 40b and *Sanhedrin* 7a) states that a person is first judged with regard to Torah. *Tosafos* explains that regarding judgment, business conduct takes precedence over Torah study, while retribution is in the opposite sequence: punishment for neglecting Torah study comes first.

70   ☐   LESSONS IN TRUTH

This is because a Jew's misconduct in business is usually due to a lack of proper Torah knowledge and a lack of loyalty to its teachings. Punishment, therefore, begins at the source — laxity in Torah study.

A *shochet* (ritual slaughterer) once informed R' Yisrael Salanter that he was giving up his practice, for he found the responsibility of slaughtering properly an unbearable pressure. "If I make but one mistake, imagine how many people would be eating unkosher meat because of me!"

"And what will you do instead?" asked R' Yisrael.

"I will open a small businesss," came the reply.

R' Yisrael replied adamantly, "Do you really think that is preferable? *Shechitah* involves one prohibition, 'You shall not eat from that which was improperly slaughtered' (*Devarim* 14:21) and this you find too much to handle! Well, virtually any business transaction is governed by a host of positive and negative commandments — these laws are more difficult to observe than the laws of *shechitah*!"

R' Yehudah Zev Segal said: "A *shochet* cannot practice slaughtering without *kaballah*, verification that he is skilled and well-versed in the relevant laws. It would be proper if similar verification were required of those entering the business world."

He would frequently quote the Chassidic master R' Mendel of Rimanov, who observed that many Jewish children, as they grow older, seem to lose the special charm which they possessed in their youth. R' Mendel attributed this to the טִמְטוּם הַלֵב, *numbness of the heart*, which results from their being fed forbidden foods — that is, foods which were purchased with dishonest earnings.

Virtually any business transaction is governed by a host of positive and negative commandments.

שלמה יהודה בן דינה נ"י, שיזכה לרפואה שלמה בקרוב בתושח"י — **5 Cheshvan**
Dedicated by his family

5 Adar — Elimelech Rauzman לע"נ אבינו מורינו ר' אלימלך בן ר' אלכסנדר ז"ל
Dedicated by his wife, Lani and his children,
Alex Rauzman, Arthur Rauzman, Edie Gross and families

5 Tammuz — Chaim Meir Lipman לע"נ ר' חיים מאיר בן ר' מנחם מנדל ז"ל
Dedicated by his family

ו חשון
6 CHESHVAN / CYCLE 1

October 23, 2001
October 12, 2002
November 1, 2003
October 21, 2004
November 8, 2005

ו אדר
6 ADAR / CYCLE 2

February 18, 2002
February 8, 2003
February 28, 2004
February 15, 2005
March 6, 2006

ו תמוז
6 TAMMUZ / CYCLE 3

June 16, 2002
July 6, 2003
June 25, 2004
July 13, 2005
July 2, 2006

*During Hebrew leap years a thirteenth month called Adar Sheni (the second Adar) is added to the calendar. For those years, two sets of corresponding dates are given, the first for Adar, and the second for Adar Sheni.

ו אדר ב
6 ADAR SHENI

March 10, 2003
March 17, 2005

❧ Within Everyone's Power

SEFER SEFAS TAMIM — Chapter Five:
Why People Steal (cont.)

Temptation for money can blind even a wise, decent person and convince him that what is actually forbidden is permitted. Nevertheless, our Sages tell us that one of the ways to discern a person's true character is by observing the way in which he conducts his business dealings (Eruvin 65b). It is within everyone's power to prevail over temptation and follow his intellect in doing what is right. It is at such times that one must remember: better to live a life of poverty than to be considered wicked in the eyes of Hashem. And in truth, "Those who seek Hashem will not lack any good" (Tehillim 34:11); and "He who walks with sincerity will walk securely" (Mishlei 10:9). Hashem provides for those who place their trust in Him.

Regarding anything towards which a person feels a natural temptation — especially money, for which the yetzer hara is especially powerful — one should follow this rule: "Do not rely on your own understanding" (Mishlei 3:5). Seek the counsel of a Torah authority and do exactly as he says. This is how a G-d-fearing Jew should conduct himself.

Those who will follow what we have said above, to refrain from living a life of luxury, and to acquire knowledge of the halachos (laws) relating to money matters, will be able to avoid the dreadful sin of gezel.

Hashem provides for those who place their trust in Him.

In an address on business ethics, Rabbi Shimon Schwab stressed that according to the *Shulchan Aruch* (Code of Jewish Law), *gezel akum*, stealing from a gentile, is clearly forbidden. As for *ta'us akum*, taking advantage of a gentile's mistakes, *Be'er HaGolah* (Ch. 266) states that returning such money is praiseworthy, for then non-Jews will come to admire Jews for their integrity. This was written in the Middle Ages, when many non-Jews were illiterate and could not calculate properly, and it was very easy to take advantage of them. In this context, *Be'er HaGolah* writes in an uncharacteristic manner:

I am writing this down for future generations, for I have seen many who have become wealthy through errors that gentiles have made. But I have also seen how they have lost their money again, and have left nothing for their heirs, as is recorded in *Sefer Chassidim*. Those who sanctified Hashem's Name by returning gains made through the errors of others became wealthy and left much of their riches to their children.

R' Schwab added:

I feel duty-bound to mention that, thank G-d, there are a great many cases of *kiddush*

(cont. on page 252)

6 Cheshvan — David M. Kasten לע"נ הרב דוד יחיאל מיכאל בן ר' יהושע חיים ז"ל
Dedicated in loving memory by his children

6 Adar — Joan Fried ע"ה לע"נ שיינע פרומע בת שלום מרדכי ע"ה
Dedicated in loving memory by her husband, children and grandchildren

6 Tammuz — In loving memory of a great tzadekes לע"נ בינה מחלה בת יהודה ע"ה
Dedicated through the Bina Machla David Tzedakah Fund

During Hebrew leap years a thirteenth month called Adar Sheni (the second Adar) is added to the calendar. For those years, two sets of corresponding dates are given, the first for Adar, and the second for Adar Sheni.

⚜ *A Lesson from Yaakov*

SEFER SEFAS TAMIM — Chapter Five:
Why People Steal (cont.)

*" **I**f you know not where to graze, o fairest of nations, follow the footsteps of the sheep" (Shir HaShirim 1:8). When the Jewish people need spiritual direction, they ponder the ways of their forefathers and follow their footsteps (Rashi ad loc.). When considering what sort of lifestyle is the way of Torah, and what material standards one should seek, a lesson can be learned from the way of our forefather Yaakov.*

Yaakov was from a house of great wealth; the Torah tells us that the wealth of his father Yitzchak far exceeded that of the Philistine king Avimelech. Yet when Yaakov beseeched Hashem for his needs, all he asked for was "bread to eat and clothes to wear" (Bereishis 28:20). It would seem that Yaakov could have simply said "bread and clothes"; the words "to eat" and "to wear" seem superfluous. We can explain this as follows:

It is the way of rich people to provide themselves with much more than they actually need. At their meals, much more food is served than what is actually eaten. Their closets hold wardrobes with many outfits for any type of occasion. Our forefather Yaakov was not like this, despite his having lived all his life amid great wealth. Therefore, he asked Hashem only for necessities: "Bread to eat and clothes to wear."

In our days, no one should be in a rush to attain wealth. We can understand why by way of a parable:

There once was a wealthy man who lived a life of indulgence. At every meal, he would stuff himself with delicacies, as musicians entertained him and his guests. His wealth caused him to become very arrogant, to the point that eventually, he rebelled against the king. The man was brought to trial and handed an unusual sentence: For a year's time, the government would serve him the same delicacies and provide him with the same music to which he was accustomed — as he stood precariously on the edge of a high rooftop! Could he derive any pleasure from the good food, drink and musical renditions, when at any given moment he might lose his balance and fall to his death? Surely he would have much preferred to have both feet on the ground and to be served bread and water instead.

This is what it is like to be rich in our times. To our misfortune, the turmoil of the period in which we live can bring about drastic changes in one's financial status, causing the rich to suddenly be reduced to poverty. The pain which a once-wealthy man experiences upon such misfortune is far greater than the joy which he felt in good times.

Whoever will ponder this thought will not be anxious to attain wealth, even through

When in need of spiritual direction, ponder the ways of our forefathers.

(cont. on page 252)

7 Cheshvan — Mary Brendzel לע״נ מרים בת סקלה ע״ה

7 Adar — לרפואה שלמה יהושע בן חי־ה נ״י בתושח״י

7 Tammuz — Burton Kleinman לע״נ ברוך בן נתן ז״ל
Dedicated in loving memory by his children, Michael & Susie Rosen

ח חשון
8 CHESHVAN / CYCLE 1

October 25, 2001
October 14, 2002
November 3, 2003
October 23, 2004
November 10, 2005

ח אדר*
*8 ADAR / CYCLE 2

February 20, 2002
February 10, 2003
March 1, 2004
February 17, 2005
March 8, 2006

ח תמוז
8 TAMMUZ / CYCLE 3

June 18, 2002
July 8, 2003
June 27, 2004
July 15, 2005
July 4, 2006

*During Hebrew leap years a thirteenth month called Adar Sheni (the second Adar) is added to the calendar. For those years, two sets of corresponding dates are given, the first for Adar, and the second for Adar Sheni.

❧ *Exaggerated Tales*

SEFER SEFAS TAMIM — Chapter Six:
The Lowliness of Lying

*L*et us return to a point which we have already mentioned. Anyone who seeks to avoid the sin of mirmah (deceit) must constantly be cognizant of how terrible is the sin of speaking sheker (falsehood). By avoiding sheker, one will naturally avoid mirmah.

How careful one should be to avoid all forms of falsehood! To speak untruths is an extremely shameful trait, even when there is no deceit concealed in one's words. Furthermore, by uttering untruths, the speaker profanes his mouth, the precious vessel which has been granted to him by Hashem to utter His praises and study His holy Torah. This thought alone should be enough to deter anyone from speaking sheker. (See Sefer Shmiras HaLashon, Shaar HaZechirah, Ch. 10).

There are many levels of falsehood, a few of which we will now discuss, beginning with the worst level.

Sometimes, a person who has heard interesting information will intentionally alter some of the facts when relating it to others. He does this not to achieve any gain, nor does he cause anyone else a loss. He does this simply because he enjoys telling exaggerated tales. At times, he may even fabricate an entire story for the sake of making conversation, or so that he will appear wise and well informed. For such brazenness and love of falsehood, this person will be liable to incur great punishment. It is concerning such people that it is written, "False lips are an abomination to Hashem" (Mishlei 12:22) and "Your lips speak falsehood, your tongue utters wickedness" (Yeshayahu 59:3).

Our Sages list shakranim, liars, among the four groups who will not merit to bask in the Divine Presence.

By speaking untruths, the person profanes his mouth — a precious vessel for serving Hashem.

The Talmud (*Sotah* 42a) states:

> R' Yirmiyah bar Abba said: Four classes [of sinners] will not merit to greet the Divine Presence: scoffers, flatterers, liars, and those who speak *lashon hara*... The class of liars — as it is written, "One who tells lies shall not be established before My eyes" (*Tehillim* 101:7).

Malbim explains: The place where Hashem's Presence dwells is permeated with righteousness and truth — qualities which contradict the liar's very nature. It follows, then, that a liar will be unable to greet the *Shechinah*.

The four classes which the Talmud lists are mentioned in ascending order of severity: The least severe is the class of scoffers, followed by the class of flatterers, followed by the class of liars, followed by the most severe — those who speak *lashon hara* (*Ben Yehoyada* citing *Arizal*).

DAY 39

ט חשון
9 CHESHVAN / CYCLE 1

October 26, 2001
October 15, 2002
November 4, 2003
October 24, 2004
November 11, 2005

ט אדר*
*9 ADAR / CYCLE 2

February 21, 2002
February 11, 2003
March 2, 2004
February 18, 2005
March 9, 2006

ט תמוז
9 TAMMUZ / CYCLE 3

June 19, 2002
July 9, 2003
June 28, 2004
July 16, 2005
July 5, 2006

*During Hebrew leap years a thirteenth month called Adar Sheni (the second Adar) is added to the calendar. For those years, two sets of corresponding dates are given, the first for Adar, and the second for Adar Sheni.

ט אדר ב
9 ADAR SHENI

March 13, 2003
March 20, 2005

◈ *Careless Untruths*

SEFER SEFAS TAMIM — Chapter Six:
The Lowliness of Lying (cont.)

In the second level of falsehood are those who relate information inaccurately, not with real intent to distort the truth, but simply because they do not bother to listen carefully and ascertain the facts about what they have heard. Obviously, such people do not view the sin of speaking falsehood very seriously; therefore it does not disturb them to relate information which may contain half-truths or outright misrepresentations. This is a רָעָה מִדָּה, wicked trait, for with the passage of time, such people become accustomed to lying until it becomes natural to them. These are the people whom our Sages classify as בַּדָּאִים, fabricators, whose word cannot be trusted. "This is the punishment of a fabricator, that even when he speaks truth, no one believes him." Everyone knows this man's weakness, that he simply cannot utter anything that it absolutely free of falsehood. It is about such people that the prophet cries out, "They train their tongues to speak falsehood, striving to be sinful" (Yirmiyahu 9:4).

In his *Emunah U'Vitachon*, the Chazon Ish writes:

One's manner of speech should be based upon a firm adherence to truth and a firm abhorrence of falsehood. Our Sages were unforgiving in their condemnation of falsehood. Its corrosiveness is powerful and its destructiveness is all too prevalent.

The Chazon Ish would stress that to alter facts even slightly when recounting an incident of no consequence is falsehood.

Once, in response to a question posed to him, the Chazon Ish said that in a certain *sefer* which he owned, he had written this very question in the margin of a certain page. He instructed the person to go to his study and bring him the *sefer*. The person returned a few minutes later and reported, "I looked for the *sefer* but it is not there." The Chazon Ish corrected him, "Do not say, 'The *sefer* is not there,' for in fact it is there. Instead say, 'I could not find it. ' " Sure enough, the Chazon Ish's brother-in-law, the Steipler *Gaon*, went and found the *sefer*.

Once, the Chazon Ish dispatched an emissary to another Torah luminary, with his decision on a certain matter. The message contained approximately ten words. The Chazon Ish had the emissary repeat the ruling to him three times, until he was certain that the message would be given over verbatim.

He once said, "It is possible to go through life without uttering a single falsehood. Heaven will assist those who sincerely desire to speak nothing but the truth."[1]

Heaven will assist those who sincerely desire to speak nothing but the truth.

---

1. In this context, he pointed out that when our forefather Yaakov told his father, "I am Eisav, your firstborn" (*Bereishis* 27:19), he did so only because of the Divinely ordained nature of his mission. As is clear from *Targum Onkelos*, Rivkah, who instructed Yaakov to pose as Eisav, was guided by prophecy in this episode (ibid. v. 13). And though Yaakov had no choice but to state that he was Eisav, he strove to stay as close to the truth as possible (see *Rashi* to v. 19).

י חשון
10 CHESHVAN / CYCLE 1

October 27, 2001
October 16, 2002
November 5, 2003
October 25, 2004
November 12, 2005

י אדר*
*10 ADAR / CYCLE 2

February 22, 2002
February 12, 2003
March 3, 2004
February 19, 2005
March 10, 2006

י תמוז
10 TAMMUZ / CYCLE 3

June 20, 2002
July 10, 2003
June 29, 2004
July 17, 2005
July 6, 2006

*During Hebrew leap years a thirteenth month called Adar Sheni (the second Adar) is added to the calendar. For those years, two sets of corresponding dates are given, the first for Adar, and the second for Adar Sheni.

✑ *Variations of Falsehood*

SEFER SEFAS TAMIM — Chapter Six:
The Lowliness of Lying (cont.)

here are other situations which fall under the category of sheker, falsehood. For example:

A person gives a friend his word that he will give him something as a gift — but in his heart he knows that he has no intention of doing so. This is considered being אֶחָד בְּפֶה וְאֶחָד בְּלֵב, *meaning that one's words are not reflective of his true feelings and, as we have already discussed, this is mirmah, deceit, which King David warned us to avoid.*

Then there is a person who at the time he utters his assurance does intend to benefit his friend, but later reneges on his word. This is not the way of a G-d-fearing Jew, as the prophet declares: "The remnants of Israel will not do wrong, they will not speak falsehood and a deceitful tongue will not be found in their mouth" (Tzephaniah 3:13).

Sometimes, a person deceives his friend by saying, "I did that favor for you," or, "I put in a good word for you," when in fact this is not so. Our Sages categorize such deceit as geneivas da'as (lit. intellectual thievery) and declare it to be forbidden (Chulin 94a). The same applies to someone who boasts of qualities which he knows that he does not possess. Of such people King Shlomo said, "Lofty speech is unbecoming in a degraded person; and surely lying speech in a noble person" (Mishlei 17:7): A person of low character should not boast of his distinguished ancestry, while a noble person should not claim qualities which are not his own. For example, he should not say, "I have given such-and-such to charity," when in fact this is not so. While such behavior is shameful for anyone, it is especially so for a person of stature.

A man of truth always honors his word.

Each day, a *minyan* met in the Chazon Ish's home for the daily prayers. *Minchah* was recited in the early afternoon. Assembling the required ten men at that time of day often presented a problem. One day, a long time passed before a tenth man was finally found. As the man walked in, Rabbi Shmuel Greineman turned to his brother-in-law the Chazon Ish and asked, "What shall I do? I have an appointment with someone at my house at this hour. Shall I *daven* and make him wait for me or should I leave now in order to be on time?"

Said the Chazon Ish, "For a man who cleaves to the attribute of truth, there can be no question as to what to do." Rabbi Greineman left and the search for a tenth man began anew.

Their brother-in-law, the Steipler *Gaon*, had a similar passion for truth. In 1984, a few days after he delivered his annual *shiur* (Torah lecture) in honor of

(cont. on page 252)

10 Cheshvan — Jacob Levinson ז"ל לע"נ יעקב בן צבי דוב ז"ל
Dedicated by Miriam Levinson, Harry Levinson, Lee Ann Levinson, Daniel Levinson, Sarah Bernard and families

10 Adar —

10 Tammuz — Yechiel Scheiner ז"ל לע"נ אלטער יחיאל בן אלטער יחיאל ז"ל
Dedicated by Isaac S. Sheiner, Esq.

DAY 41

רי"א חשון
II CHESHVAN / CYCLE 1

October 28, 2001
October 17, 2002
November 6, 2003
October 26, 2004
November 13, 2005

רי"א אדר*
*11 ADAR / CYCLE 2

February 23, 2002
February 13, 2003
March 4, 2004
February 20, 2005
March 11, 2006

רי"א תמוז
II TAMMUZ / CYCLE 3

June 21, 2002
July 11, 2003
June 30, 2004
July 18, 2005
July 7, 2006

*During Hebrew leap years a thirteenth month called Adar Sheni (the second Adar) is added to the calendar. For those years, two sets of corresponding dates are given, the first for Adar, and the second for Adar Sheni.

רי"א אדר ב
II ADAR SHENI

March 15, 2003
March 22, 2005

⁓ Maintain Your Distance

SEFER SEFAS TAMIM — Chapter Six:
The Lowliness of Lying (cont.)

*T*here are people who do not suffer from the sickness called "falsehood" in the way in which we have described above, but they are not entirely free from it. They are not habitual liars, but they do not take care to distance themselves from untruths; if they see a need to lie, they will do so. Often, they will lie in jest, without any harm intended. However, the wisest of men has taught us that this is not the way of Hashem and His righteous servants: "A righteous person hates something false" (Mishlei 13:5).

The Torah teaches us: "Distance yourself from falsehood" (Shemos 23:7). Regarding no other sin does the Torah make such a statement. This demonstrates that falsehood is a most serious sin and that we must stay as far from it as we possibly can. This includes not only avoiding speaking falsehood, but also refraining from any situation which may result in a false impression, as our Sages discuss at length (Shavuos 31a).

Truth is one of the foundations upon which this world exists (Avos 1:18). When a person speaks falsehood, it is as if he is *destroying a foundation of the world. Conversely, when a person carefully adheres to truth, it is as if he is upholding one of the world's foundations.*

Aside from all of the above, a person who suffers from the terrible trait of speaking falsehood usually becomes an object of scorn and disgrace. Ultimately, his lies become known and he acquires a bad name and a reputation for being untrustworthy. However, one who always speaks the truth acquires for himself a good name; and although at times he alters the truth for the sake of peace, his words are respected and accepted.

Truth is one of the foundations upon which the world exists.

On a journey from Manchester to the city of Bournemouth, R' Yehudah Zev Segal stopped off in London to attend a gathering to which he had been personally invited. In his remarks, the chairman thanked the *Rosh Yeshivah* for having made a special trip to attend the gathering. Later in the evening when the chairman mentioned this a second time, Rabbi Segal's passion for truth did not allow him to remain silent. He called out from his seat that, in fact, he had only stopped off on his way to another destination.

That we are permitted to alter the truth for the sake of peace is derived from the episode where the angels, disguised as wayfarers, came to inform Avraham and Sarah that they would be granted a son.

(cont. on page 252)

11 Cheshvan — May today's learning be a זכות for our משפחה.
Dedicated by Ron Greenberg and family, Chicago, IL

11 Adar — Pearl Atlas ע"ה לע"נ פערל בת שמואל ע"ה
Dedicated in memory of our beloved mother and Bubby, by the Atlas family

11 Tammuz — May today's learning be a זכות for all חולים in כלל ישראל.
Sponsored by the Barkhorder family

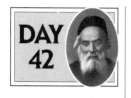

DAY 42

י"ב חשון
12 CHESHVAN / CYCLE 1

October 29, 2001
October 18, 2002
November 7, 2003
October 27, 2004
November 14, 2005

י"ב אדר*
*12 ADAR / CYCLE 2

February 24, 2002
February 14, 2003
March 5, 2004
February 21, 2005
March 12, 2006

י"ב תמוז
12 TAMMUZ / CYCLE 3

June 22, 2002
July 12, 2003
July 1, 2004
July 19, 2005
July 8, 2006

During Hebrew leap years a thirteenth month called Adar Sheni (the second Adar) is added to the calendar. For those years, two sets of corresponding dates are given, the first for Adar, and the second for Adar Sheni.

✒ *Training Our Youth*

SEFER SEFAS TAMIM — Chapter Six:
The Lowliness of Lying (cont.)

*I*t is a mitzvah to regularly remind one's children — even young children — to distance themselves from speaking untruths. "Train the youth according to his way" (Mishlei 22:6). Our Sages have already taught (Succah 46b):

> A person should not say to a child, "I will give you something," and then not give it to him, because he thereby teaches him to lie, as it is written (Yirmiyahu 9:4), "They train their tongue to speak falsehood."

When children see that parents honor their own word, they learn the importance of truth and they will follow this example. Parents must also stand watch constantly that their children should not lie. They should teach their young ones that to lie is to commit a grave sin, so that the children will take the matter very seriously and will be extremely careful to avoid it. Through such training, it will become natural for our young ones to speak nothing but the truth.

One who carefully avoids all falsehood will not tell a person who requests something, "Come back tomorrow," when he knows that *he has no intention of giving him anything. If one cannot give, he should say so. A wise man will ensure that all his words and deeds conform with truth.*

May Hashem, Whose seal is truth and Whose Torah is truth, guide us along the path of truth.

Rabbi Yaakov Kamenetsky would stress that children should be taught the way of truth in all instances.[1]

Rabbi Shmuel Shain was once asked by some children from Monsey to take them to Lakewood the next time he would be visiting their area. On a subsequent visit to Monsey, he told one of the children that he could take them to Lakewood the next morning. That same night, a *talmid chacham* who had arrived from Eretz Yisrael asked Rabbi Shain for a ride to Lakewood. Rabbi Shain assumed that the right thing was to take the scholar, but he felt bad about disappointing the children. When Rabbi Shain mentioned this to R' Yaakov the next morning, the sage told him, "*Chas v'shalom* (Heaven forfend) to do such a thing. You will be teaching the children to be liars. They are too young to understand that an older person comes first. You promised them; you must take them."

When children see that parents honor their word, they learn the importance of truth.

---

1. R' Yaakov's own passion for truth is discussed in Day 45.

12 Cheshvan — Rae Abramowitz ע"ה לע"נ רחל בת פנחס ע"ה
Dedicated in memory of our mother and grandmother, by the Kimmel and Kagan families

12 Adar — Yoshe Nussen ז"ל לע"נ יוסף דוד בן צבי מנחם ז"ל
Dedicated by the Nussen families of Briarwood, NY and Lakewood, NJ

12 Tammuz — ז"ל לע"נ ר' אברהם חנוך בן ר' טובי' אלעזר ז"ל
Dedicated by Yitzchok & Rivka Mashitz

DAY 43

י"ג חשון
13 CHESHVAN / CYCLE 1

October 30, 2001
October 19, 2002
November 8, 2003
October 28, 2004
November 15, 2005

י"ג אדר*
*13 ADAR / CYCLE 2

February 25, 2002
February 15, 2003
March 6, 2004
February 22, 2005
March 13, 2006

י"ג תמוז
13 TAMMUZ / CYCLE 3

June 23, 2002
July 13, 2003
July 2, 2004
July 20, 2005
July 9, 2006

*During Hebrew leap years a thirteenth month called Adar Sheni (the second Adar) is added to the calendar. For those years, two sets of corresponding dates are given, the first for Adar, and the second for Adar Sheni.

❧ The Quality of Temimus

SEFER SEFAS TAMIM — Chapter Seven:
The Rewards of Sincerity and Truth

We have discussed the severity of *mirmah* (deceit) and the terrible punishment which it can bring about. We will conclude this work by discussing the great reward of *temimus* (sincerity).

Sefer Ma'alos HaMidos writes:

> Know, my son, that temimus is a great, precious quality. When a person possesses temimus, then Hashem takes pleasure in him and in his service, as it is written, "He who walks the way of sincerity — he shall serve Me" (Tehillim 101:6). The Torah states: "You shall be sincere with Hashem" (Devarim 18:13).
>
> Temimus is precious, for whoever acts with temimus in all instances will merit to bask in Hashem's Presence, as it is written, "Hashem, who may dwell in Your tent? ...He who walks with sincerity..." (Tehillim 15:1-2). Our forefather Yaakov possessed this quality, as the Torah states: "And Yaakov was a sincere person..." (Bereishis 25:27). King David praises this quality: "Praiseworthy are those whose way is sincere..." (Tehillim 119:1).

What is temimus? It is to speak and conduct one's business without any sort of deception, and to ensure that one's words express his true inner feelings. A person who is אֶחָד בְּפֶה וְאֶחָד בְּלֵב, meaning that his words are not reflective of his true feelings, cannot be considered a תָּם, sincere person. Rather, he is a flatterer and deceiver, as it is written, "Deceit lurks in the hearts of those who plot evil" (Mishlei 12:20).

When a person conducts himself with temimus, Hashem helps him in his activities, and ensures the perfection of his ways, as the prophet states: "With the devout You deal devoutly" (II Shmuel 22:26). Our Sages have also taught, "One who seeks to purify himself will be granted assistance from Hashem." It is such people whom Hashem truly desires and seeks: "His desire is for those whose way is sincere" (Mishlei 11:20). Furthermore, the quality of temimus leads a person in the right direction, as it is written, "The righteousness of one who is sincere straightens his path" (Ibid. v. 5).

When a person conducts himself with temimus, Hashem protects him from all forms of sin, as it is written, "I was sincere with Him, and I was vigilant against my sin" (Tehillim 18:24); and "And I, because of my sincerity You have sup-

When a person conducts himself with sincerity, Hashem helps him in his activities.

(cont. on page 252)

---

13 Cheshvan — L'zichron Olam, our father Henry Gleitman ז"ל — לע"נ דוד ארי' בן יחזקא-ל ז"ל
Dedicated in loving memory by the Gleitman family

13 Adar — Morris Rozenek ז"ל — לע"נ משה בן שמואל יהודה ז"ל
Dedicated in loving memory by Ralph and Frieda Elefant and family

13 Tammuz — Israel Khasak ז"ל — לע"נ ישראל בן חיים ז"ל
Dedicated in memory of my uncle by David Khasak

DAY 44

יי"ד חשון
14 CHESHVAN / CYCLE1

October 31, 2001
October 20, 2002
November 9, 2003
October 29, 2004
November 16, 2005

יי"ד אדר*
*14 ADAR / CYCLE 2

February 26, 2002
February 16, 2003
March 7, 2004
February 23, 2005
March 14, 2006

יי"ד תמוז
14 TAMMUZ / CYCLE 3

June 24, 2002
July 14, 2003
July 3, 2004
July 21, 2005
July 10, 2006

During Hebrew leap years a thirteenth month called Adar Sheni (the second Adar) is added to the calendar. For those years, two sets of corresponding dates are given, the first for Adar, and the second for Adar Sheni.

ᴥ *Nonsensical Claims*

SEFER SEFAS TAMIM — Chapter Seven:
The Rewards of Sincerity and Truth (cont.)

*S*efer Pele Yoetz states:

It is well known that the first question which every soul is asked when it ascends to the Next World for judgment is, "Did you conduct your business affairs in good faith?" (Shabbos 31a). To our misfortune, in our days there are those who put forth claims which are nonsense, that in these times of economic difficulty, anyone who will conduct his dealings with uprightness and good faith will not be able to put even bread and salt on his table. Such arguments are designed as a permit for all sorts of wrongdoings: to lie, cheat, steal, encroach on someone else's business domain, and many other wicked practices — aside from bitul Torah and bitul tefillah b'tzibur (disruption of Torah study and of praying with a minyan), desecration of Shabbos, etc.

And no one takes these matters to heart to seek to mend his ways! Woe to these people on their day of judgment! It is for good reason that the World to Come was created with the [small] letter י, yud, symbolizing that the righteous who will enjoy its pleasures [in the fullest sense] are few.

All of Torah is based upon emunah (faith), as it is written, "And a righteous person lives by his faith" (Chavakuk 2:4). A person's true character can be perceived from "his wallet" (Eruvin 65b), for a person who truly believes that it is Hashem Who grants success, and that He decrees on Rosh Hashanah what a person will earn for the coming year, cannot possibly believe that he will succeed in business by contravening Hashem's will — Heaven forfend to even suggest this!

If a person will succeed in amassing wealth through dishonesty, this will ultimately lead to his undoing — aside from the punishment that awaits him in the Next World. Conversely, if one sees an honest, G-d-fearing fellow struggling to make ends meet, do not think that, G-d forbid, his righteousness is the cause of his difficulties. Shall the Judge of all the earth not do fair justice?[1] The ways of Hashem are hidden from us and true men of faith firmly believe that "The Rock! — perfect is His work, for all His paths are justice" (Devarim 32:4). "Whatever the Merciful does, He does for the good" (Berachos 60b), so that He will reward him in the World that is entirely good.

True, all Jews are ma'aminim b'nei ma'aminim, believers who are descendants of believers, but most important is not faith itself, but actions which point to one's faith.

"And a righteous person lives by his faith."

---

1. From *Bereishis* 18:25.

ט"ו חשון
15 CHESHVAN / CYCLE 1

November 1, 2001
October 21, 2002
November 10, 2003
October 30, 2004
November 17, 2005

ט"ו אדר*
*15 ADAR / CYCLE 2

February 27, 2002
February 17, 2003
March 8, 2004
February 24, 2005
March 15, 2006

ט"ו תמוז
15 TAMMUZ / CYCLE 3

June 25, 2002
July 15, 2003
July 4, 2004
July 22, 2005
July 11, 2006

*During Hebrew leap years a thirteenth month called Adar Sheni (the second Adar) is added to the calendar. For those years, two sets of corresponding dates are given, the first for Adar, and the second for Adar Sheni.

ט"ו אדר ב
15 ADAR SHENI

March 19, 2003
March 26, 2005

❧ Source of Life

SEFER SEFAS TAMIM — Chapter Seven:
The Rewards of Sincerity and Truth (cont.)

When a person strengthens himself in matters of truth, it is considered as if he upholds the world (Avos 1:18) and he brings blessing to it. As Yalkut Shimoni states to the words "Truth will sprout from the earth" (Tehillim 85:12): When there is truth among people, Hashem responds by generating a flow of righteousness and kindness from Heaven, and saves the world from calamity. By striving for truth, one also fulfills the mitzvah, "And you shall walk in His ways" (see Sifrei to Devarim 10:12).

By clinging steadfastly to the quality of truth, one can save himself and his offspring from premature death. The Talmud relates that a certain Torah scholar once declared that for all the money in the world, he would never veer from the truth. His attitude was the result of an episode which he related:

> *Once, he visited a certain town by the name of Kushta (Aramaic for Truth), whose inhabitants would not tell a lie, and no one there died before his time. He married a woman from among them and she bore him two sons. One day, his wife was sitting washing her hair, when*

a neighbor came knocking on the door and asked to speak to her. Thinking that it would not be proper [to tell the neighbor what his wife was doing at the time], he said, "She is not here." Later, his two sons died.

The people of the town came to him and asked, "What is the reason for this?" He told them what had happened. They said to him, "We beg you, leave our town and do not incite death against us" (Sanhedrin 97a).

The message of this story is that whoever clings steadfastly to the quality of truth attaches himself to Hashem, the Source of all truth, and therefore, the Angel of Death has no power over him. Only when he is aged and has lived a full life will he die, because of the decree of death caused by the sin of Adam and Chavah.

When there is truth among people, Hashem responds with blessing and compassion from Above.

Our forefather Yaakov symbolized the *midah* (character trait) of *emes* (truth). Rabbi Yaakov Kamenetsky, who felt a special identity between himself and Yaakov *Avinu*, was renowned as a man of truth. Rabbi Yitzchak Hutner, late *Rosh Yeshivah* of Mesivta Rabbi Chaim Berlin, once remarked, "R' Yaakov's *midah* of *emes* is a throwback to past generations."

R' Yaakov lived to age ninety-five. When in his nineties, he was asked in what merit he had lived so long. "I never said a lie," was his reply.

(cont. on page 253)

15 Cheshvan — לע"נ יוסף בן דוד הכהן ז"ל
Dedicated by his family

15 Adar — In loving memory of Anna Sennitzky Gordon לע"נ חנה בת יהודה לייב ע"ה
Dedicated by her son, Milton Gordon and by her grandchildren,
Judy Israel, Daniel Gordon and Eve Goren

15 Tammuz —

DAY 46

ט"ז חשון
16 CHESHVAN / CYCLE 1

November 2, 2001
October 22, 2002
November 11, 2003
October 31, 2004
November 18, 2005

ט"ז אדר*
*16 ADAR / CYCLE 2

February 28, 2002
February 18, 2003
March 9, 2004
February 25, 2005
March 16, 2006

ט"ז תמוז
16 TAMMUZ / CYCLE 3

June 26, 2002
July 16, 2003
July 5, 2004
July 23, 2005
July 12, 2006

*During Hebrew leap years a thirteenth month called Adar Sheni (the second Adar) is added to the calendar. For those years, two sets of corresponding dates are given, the first for Adar, and the second for Adar Sheni.

ט"ז אדר ב
16 ADAR SHENI

March 20, 2003
March 27, 2005

❧ In Conclusion

SEFER SEFAS TAMIM — Chapter Seven:
The Rewards of Sincerity and Truth (cont.)

*I*n conclusion: One must train himself to speak as truthfully as possible in all situations. He should admit the truth at all times whether for good or for bad — except for the sake of peace and for three specific situations mentioned in the Talmud (see Bava Metzia 23b).

This quality will bring the person to do good and to refrain from evil. The story is told of someone who trangressed virtually every sin, until he came before a Torah scholar and asked that he be guided along the path of teshuvah (repentance). The scholar told him to distance himself from falsehood to the furthest degree possible. By following this advice, he became a complete baal teshuvah, for he could not sin and then conceal his misdeed by lying.

Truth is the foundation of life; whoever lives by it will find favor in the eyes of Hashem and man. Be extremely careful regarding truth, for it is the source of all admirable qualities.

May Hashem help us, through His kindness and compassion, to succeed in acquiring the precious quality of emes, truth.

Maharal explains that peace is a form of truth while strife is a form of falsehood. In a similar sense, if by speaking the truth we hurt another's feelings unnecessarily, then this too is a form of falsehood, for it conflicts with the Torah's requirements in this regard.

As mentioned above, in our generation the quality of *emes* (truth) was personified by Rabbi Yaakov Kamenetsky. R' Yaakov's passion for speaking the truth did not conflict with his unusual concern for the feelings of others.

If he was unable to come to the phone, he would never allow someone to tell the caller that he was not home, a clear falsehood. However, R' Yaakov would not allow the person to say, "He's busy now. Can you call back later?" for this might cause the caller to feel a sense of rejection. Instead, R' Yaakov always tried to take the phone personally to explain that he was unable to talk at that time. In situations where that was impossible, he would ask whoever answered the phone to say that the *Rosh Yeshivah* would be home at a certain hour, without any reference as to whether he was then home. In this way, no untruth was said and no feelings were hurt.

For R' Yaakov, no lie, no matter how small, was justified by the result. A former *talmid* had planned to take a vacation day from work on Purim. His company, however, was particularly busy at that time and no days off were being granted. He asked R' Yaakov if it was permissible for him to feign illness, or to claim that the discomfort which he was feeling on *Ta'anis Esther* because of fasting would extend to the following day.

Those who live by truth will find favor in the eyes of Hashem and man.

(cont. on page 253)

---

16 Cheshvan — Maier Cahan לע"נ ר' מאיר בן ר' משולם פייביש הכהן ז"ל
Sponsored by the Cahan family

16 Adar — Today's learning has been dedicated as a זכות for the Kirshner family, Kingston, PA.

לע"נ צבי זאב בן משה ז"ל — **16 Tammuz**

Book II:

Sefer
Shem Olam
Part II

As discussed in the Introduction, the level of one's honesty in word and deed is very much dependent on his level of faith. The following section is based on the Chofetz Chaim's thoughts in Sefer Shem Olam, which discusses a number of fundamental concepts of Jewish faith.

While the Chofetz Chaim published the following as the second part of Shem Olam, it can be studied independently and in fact, has its own sub-title: Sha'ar Hizchazkus (The Gate of Strengthening [Oneself in Service of G-d]), based on the verse: קַוֵּה אֶל ה׳ חֲזַק וְיַאֲמֵץ לִבֶּךָ וְקַוֵּה אֶל ה׳, *Hope to Hashem; strengthen yourself and He will give you courage, and hope to Hashem (Tehillim 27:14).*

** י״ז חשון**
17 CHESHVAN / CYCLE 1

November 3, 2001
October 23, 2002
November 12, 2003
November 1, 2004
November 19, 2005

** י״ז אדר***
*17 ADAR / CYCLE 2

March 1, 2002
February 19, 2003
March 10, 2004
February 26, 2005
March 17, 2006

** י״ז תמוז**
17 TAMMUZ / CYCLE 3

June 27, 2002
July 17, 2003
July 6, 2004
July 24, 2005
July 13, 2006

*During Hebrew leap years a thirteenth month called Adar Sheni (the second Adar) is added to the calendar. For those years, two sets of corresponding dates are given, the first for Adar, and the second for Adar Sheni.

✑ Strengthening Each Other

SEFER SHEM OLAM — Chapter One:
Strengthening Oneself in Service of G-d

*O*ur Sages teach: "Four things need strengthening [i.e. constant renewal of effort in order to succeed]: Torah study, performance of good deeds, prayer and earning a livelihood" (Berachos 32b). This statement was made in Talmudic times, when the Jewish people were on a spiritual level far beyond anything we can imagine. How much more so is this true in our day, when the world is filled with worry and distress which cause a weakening of our already diminished spirit. Furthermore, in Talmudic times, virtually all Jews were observant of Torah and believed firmly in all basic tenets of Jewish belief. In our days, however, we who observe the Torah are in the minority, while various groups and movements spread false teachings and philosophies which distort and contradict Torah truth.

In our times, it is a mitzvah for G-d-fearing Jews to assemble from time to time to lend strength to one another in service of Hashem. Rest assured that the words spoken at such gatherings are recorded in Heaven before G-d's Throne, as it is written, "Then those who fear Hashem spoke to one another, and Hashem listened and heard, and a *book of remembrance was written before Him for those who fear Hashem and give thought to His Name" (Malachi 3:16).*

Always one to practice what he exhorted others to do, the Chofetz Chaim pushed himself to the limits of his physical strength to attend the First *Knessiah Gedolah* (World Conference) of Agudath Israel in 1923. He was then age eighty-five and his state of health was fragile, yet he undertook the difficult journey by wagon and train from Radin, Poland to Vienna, Austria. The gathering was covered by both secular and religious newspapers from around the world. A religious newspaper reported:

It is a mitzvah for G-d-fearing Jews to assemble to lend spiritual strength to one another.

> When the cry is heard, "The Chofetz Chaim is coming!" excitement breaks out in the assembly hall. All spring up from their places, and everyone's gaze focuses on him...
>
> The Chofetz Chaim never wanted to be a leader, and he has no wish to be one now. He has only pleaded all his life: *Jews! Be good Jews, be G-d-fearing Jews, be peaceful Jews, be honest Jews.* He is distant from all the politics of parties, and when the *tzaddik* was told that his coming to Vienna would help strengthen *Yiddishkeit* (Judaism), he got up and came...

A secular writer had this to say:

> When you see this tiny eighty-five year-old man for the first time, it makes a singular impression upon you. You feel a quiver of awe

(cont. on page 253)

17 Cheshvan — Chaim Yitzchak Sattelmeier ז"ל לע"נ חיים יצחק בן אברהם ז"ל
Dedicated by his children, Aryeh & Faige Scheiner

17 Adar — Miriam Kalmuk ע"ה לע"נ מרים בת מנחם מענדל ע"ה whose love and dedication to Yiddishkeit was inspirational. Dedicated by Dr. and Mrs. Reuven & Rochel Shanik

17 Tammuz — לע"נ הרה"ג ר' שמואל יעקב בן הרב יצחק מתתיהו ווינברג ז"ל
Dedicated by Rabbi & Mrs. Simcha Weinberg

י״ח חשון
18 CHESHVAN / CYCLE 1

November 4, 2001
October 24, 2002
November 13, 2003
November 2, 2004
November 20, 2005

י״ח אדר*
*18 ADAR / CYCLE 2

March 2, 2002
February 20, 2003
March 11, 2004
February 27, 2005
March 18, 2006

י״ח תמוז
18 TAMMUZ / CYCLE 3

June 28, 2002
July 18, 2003
July 7, 2004
July 25, 2005
July 14, 2006

*During Hebrew leap years a thirteenth month called Adar Sheni (the second Adar) is added to the calendar. For those years, two sets of corresponding dates are given, the first for Adar, and the second for Adar Sheni.

❧ *"I Am a Wall"*

SEFER SHEM OLAM — Chapter One:
Strengthening Oneself in Service of G-d (cont.)

*W*hen we speak of chizuk, strengthening of spirit, we mean not only intellectually, but more important, in practice. A Jew must constantly be on the alert to ensure that his actions and those of his family members are in accordance with Torah and that negative outside influences should not pervade the confines of his home or the minds of his loved ones. A Jew needs to muster every ounce of his spiritual strength to counteract these destructive winds. This is alluded to in the following verses:

"We have a little sister... if she will be a wall, we will build upon her a turret of silver, but if she will be a door, we will enclose her with cedar panel." [And the sister responds] "I am a wall... Then, I am in His eyes like one who found peace" (Shir HaShirim 8:8-10).

"We" in the opening verse are the Heavenly angels who serve G-d in the Upper Worlds, and their "sister" refers to the Jewish people who serve Him on earth. The angels ask, "What will become of our sister at the time of the War of Gog and Magog?" the climactic war which will herald the future Redemption through the coming of Mashiach. They respond: If the Jewish people

will be firm in their faith and in their performance of mitzvos like a solid wall, which
no wind in the world can budge, then in that
merit the "turret of silver" — the Holy City of
Jerusalem and the Beis HaMikdash — will be
rebuilt. But if they will waver like a "door"
which swings on its hinges, then that door
will be enclosed with "cedar" which rots with
the passage of time.

A Jew needs to muster all his spiritual strength to counteract destructive influences.

The Jewish people respond, "I am a wall,
for I will remain steadfast in my faith and
service of Hashem come what may." And it is
this response that makes our people beloved
to Hashem.

To the words אָחוֹת לָנוּ קְטַנָּה, *We have a little sister*,
the *Midrash* comments: "This refers to [our forefather]
Avraham, who stitched [מְאַחֶה — a play on the word
אָחוֹת, *sister*] a tear" (*Shir HaShirim Rabbah* 10:1).
Alshich explains:

Brother and sister, by virtue of their being of the
same parents, feel a natural closeness towards one
another. This is not the case with body and soul,
which come from opposite origins. The body is drawn
to that which has a connection to the earth from
which it was fashioned, while the soul is drawn to the
Heavens whence it came. Man's mission on this
world is to achieve *shleimus*, spiritual perfection,
whereby the body is the soul's tool in serving its
Creator through Torah and *mitzvos*.

For ten generations, from Noach until Avraham,
mankind angered its Creator as it pursued its earthly

(cont. on page 254)

(cont. on page 254)

18 Cheshvan — Dr. Henry C. Rhein ז"ל לע"נ חיים בן אביגדור ז"ל
Dedicated by his wife, children and grandchildren

18 Adar — Meyer A. Shatz ז"ל לע"נ מאיר בן ר' שרגא דוד ז"ל
Dedicated in loving memory by Henry & Golda Reena Rothman and family

18 Tammuz — R' Moshe Feldman זצ"ל לע"נ ר' משה בן ר' יוסף ארי' זצ"ל
נלב"ע כ"ה תמוז תשנ"ז הונצח באהבה ע"י רעיתו ובנותיו

DAY 49

י"ט חשון
19 CHESHVAN / CYCLE 1

November 5, 2001
October 25, 2002
November 14, 2003
November 3, 2004
November 21, 2005

י"ט אדר*
*19 ADAR / CYCLE 2

March 3, 2002
February 21, 2003
March 12, 2004
February 28, 2005
March 19, 2006

י"ט תמוז
19 TAMMUZ / CYCLE 3

June 29, 2002
July 19, 2003
July 8, 2004
July 26, 2005
July 15, 2006

During Hebrew leap years a thirteenth month called Adar Sheni (the second Adar) is added to the calendar. For those years, two sets of corresponding dates are given, the first for Adar, and the second for Adar Sheni.

❧ *Winning the War*

SEFER SHEM OLAM — Chapter Two:
Strengthening Oneself in Service of G-d — II

In our times, it is more crucial than ever that those who are immersed in the study of Torah should strengthen themselves in their service of Hashem.

The workings of the Heavenly kingdom are, in certain ways, similar to the ways of kingdoms on earth. Earthly kings rely on dependable, loyal officers in whom they place their trust and through whom the stability of their kingdom is ensured. If such an officer were to betray the king, the king would, undoubtedly, be extremely upset. The king would be furious if such a betrayal would happen during wartime, with the once-loyal officer providing help to the enemy. His fury would be compounded if the traitor is a high-ranking officer, whose betrayal affects scores of soldiers serving under him and also causes great embarrassment to the king.

And so it is with the Heavenly kingdom. The talmidei chachamim (Torah scholars) of each generation are the loyal, dependable servants of the king; the greater their knowledge, the higher their rank. At the end of the galus (exile), the period in which we now find ourselves, a fierce war is being waged between the forces of *kedushah* (sanctity) and *tumah* (impurity). The forces of *tumah* shoot lethal arrows in all directions. Some are wounded in the foot or hand, others in a vital organ such as the brain or heart, and some in the mouth. Few emerge from this war unscathed. The *talmidei chachamim* of the generation, who serve Hashem faithfully and influence others to do so, are capable of remaining unaffected by the spiritual dangers which lurk everywhere. The King of kings relies upon them to light the way for others in this great struggle.

In our times, when to our misfortune, so many falsify the Torah and wage war against it, it is more crucial than ever that those who are truly knowledgeable in Torah live faithfully by its teachings and influence others to do so. If they falter in their Divine service and thereby lend strength to the "other side," they are likely to provoke Divine wrath on a large scale. However, if they succeed in their mission, they will earn Hashem's special love and will be among those who will bask in Hashem's Presence when the glorious days of Redemption will arrive.

Hashem relies on the Torah scholars of each generation to light the way for others.

The Chofetz Chaim writes of the fierce war which the forces of impurity wage in the period before the Final Redemption. He wrote this about a century ago.

(cont. on page 254)

---

19 Cheshvan — Sarah Bat Flora ע"ה לע"נ שרה בת פלורה ע"ה
קמו בניה וישרוה בעלה ויהללה Dedicated by Sasson Shalam & family
19 Adar — Sandor Fleischmann ז"ל לע"נ שמואל בן יעקב ז"ל
Dedicated by his children
19 Tammuz —

כ חשון
20 CHESHVAN / CYCLE 1

November 6, 2001
October 26, 2002
November 15, 2003
November 4, 2004
November 22, 2005

כ אדר*
*20 ADAR / CYCLE 2

March 4, 2002
February 22, 2003
March 13, 2004
March 1, 2005
March 20, 2006

כ תמוז
20 TAMMUZ / CYCLE 3

June 30, 2002
July 20, 2003
July 9, 2004
July 27, 2005
July 16, 2006

During Hebrew leap years a thirteenth month called Adar Sheni (the second Adar) is added to the calendar. For those years, two sets of corresponding dates are given, the first for Adar, and the second for Adar Sheni.

כ אדר ב
20 ADAR SHENI

March 24, 2003
March 31, 2005

❧ *Priceless Commodities*

SEFER SHEM OLAM — Chapter Three:
Approaching Mitzvos with Alacrity

"*Someone who is wise of heart will seize mitzvos, but one of foolish lips will become weary*" (Mishlei 10:8). We can explain this with a parable:

In the ledger of a small retail business, an entry may represent either a profit or loss of just a few dollars. But for a large wholesaler, recording small profits or gains would be a waste of time and energy. The entries in a wholesaler's ledgers represent hundreds, perhaps thousands, of dollars either lost or gained. Any knowledgeable businessman who studied such figures would understand their significance.

The owner of a huge corporation uses a different standard. In his ledger, each notation represents net gains or losses in the hundreds of thousands, perhaps millions of dollars. Nothing less has much significance to him.

The same is true of Hashem's "ledger" — our holy Torah. Each "entry" — any of the 613 mitzvos — represents something of priceless value, something that no amount of money can buy. A wise person understands this, so he seizes every opportunity to perform a mitzvah. A fool, however, does not

*fathom the greatness of Torah and the ines-
timable value of its mitzvos. Therefore, he
approaches mitzvos with laziness and allows
countless opportunities to pass him by.*

A classic servant of Hashem, the Manchester *Rosh
Yeshivah*, Rabbi Yehudah Zev Segal, evaluated any
given situation to determine which *mitzvos* were
inherent in it. For example, he saw helping a parent as
an opportunity to fulfill both the *mitzvah* of honoring
parents as well as that of performing an act of kindness. A visit to a sick person was also a fulfillment of
the *mitzvah* to love one's fellow Jew.

His love for every *mitzvah* was readily apparent. He
would run to his *succah* on the first night of Succos
with the excitement of a young child. One Succos, he
was visited by a *talmid*. When the *talmid* rose to leave,
Rabbi Segal escorted him to the door of the *succah*
and stopped. "Please forgive me — I would love to
escort you further," he said, "but it would mean too
great a loss — each moment that one is in the *succah*
he fulfills a *mitzvah*."

Rabbi Segal spared no effort to fulfill a *mitzvah*.
One summer, cloudy weather made it impossible to
recite *Kiddush Levanah* (Blessing of the New Moon).
As the middle of the month approached (after which
the *mitzvah* cannot be performed), someone drove
Rabbi Segal around as they searched for a spot where
the moon was visible. After a long time, their search
was successful, and with great excitement they performed the *mitzvah*.

Before Pesach, Rabbi Segal would spend an entire
day at a *matzah* bakery accompanied by a group of

*A wise
person
appreci-
ates the
value of a
mitzvah
and will
seize every
opportuni-
ty to
perform it.*

(cont. on page 254)

DAY 51

כ"א חשון
21 CHESHVAN / CYCLE 1

November 7, 2001
October 27, 2002
November 16, 2003
November 5, 2004
November 23, 2005

כ"א אדר*
*21 ADAR / CYCLE 2

March 5, 2002
February 23, 2003
March 14, 2004
March 2, 2005
March 21, 2006

כ"א תמוז
21 TAMMUZ / CYCLE 3

July 1, 2002
July 21, 2003
July 10, 2004
July 28, 2005
July 17, 2006

*During Hebrew leap years a thirteenth month called Adar Sheni (the second Adar) is added to the calendar. For those years, two sets of corresponding dates are given, the first for Adar, and the second for Adar Sheni.

❧ Optical Illusions

SEFER SHEM OLAM — Chapter Three:
Approaching Mitzvos with Alacrity (cont.)

*T*o our misfortune, we are often witness to a disheartening phenomenon:

A person embarks on a business venture with great energy and planning. He rejoices as his efforts bear fruit and his initial success spurs him on to yet greater attempts at achievement. Yet the very same person goes about his mitzvah performance as if by habit, without any energy or apparent pleasure in fulfilling the will of his Creator. Even worse, when he engages in what is clearly a sin, he shows no sign of laziness or regret over his inability to overcome his yetzer hara (evil inclination).

Our Sages reveal the source of such behavior:

> *R' Shimon ben Lakish said: A person's yetzer hara threatens to overpower him every day and seeks to destroy him, as it is written, "The wicked one looks out for the righteous person and seeks to slay him" (Tehillim 37:32). And if not for Hashem Who assists him, he would be unable to withstand it, as it is written (ibid. v. 33), "Hashem will not forsake him to his hand, nor condemn him in His judgment."*

> *(Succah 52b)*

The above verse refers to the yetzer hara as a tzopheh, a lookout. When a lookout stands atop a watchtower scouting the terrain, he uses a variety of optical aids, such as field glasses. Some of the lenses he uses magnify, while others minimize. The yetzer hara, which is extremely clever, operates in a similar way. When the yetzer tov (positive inclination) encourages a person to perform a good deed, the yetzer hara discourages it. If he is not successful at this, then he tries to at least mimimize its importance, so that the person will approach the mitzvah as if in a slumber, without any joy at all.

With a sin, the yetzer hara uses an opposite approach. When the yetzer tov attempts to convince the person to refrain from sinning, the yetzer hara comes along and minimizes the act's inherent evil. Sometimes, the yetzer hara dispatches its trusted "emissaries" — passion, lust, anger and the like — to convince the person that what he is about to do is not a sin at all! Moreover, the sinner is encouraged to go about his business with alacrity, before he has a chance to contemplate the true nature of his behavior.

Sometimes, when the person is tempted to speak lashon hara, the yetzer hara, rather than use his "reducing lens" to mimimize the sin of lashon hara, instead magnifies the

The yetzer hara is expert at distorting the true value of a mitzvah or the destructiveness of a sin.

(cont. on page 255)

21 Cheshvan — Leon Lief לע״נ אריה בן יעקב שלום הלוי ז״ל
Dedicated in loving memory by his daughter, Deborah Lief-Dienstag

21 Adar — Paul Hegeman לע״נ שאול ז״ל בן אברהם יבלח״ט
Dedicated by his parents, Kathryn & Andrew Hegeman

21 Tammuz — לע״נ חיים אלקנה ז״ל בן ארי ליב יבלח״ט
May today's learning be a זכות for his נשמה.
Dedicated by Rabbi Yaakov & Faigy Goldstein and family

כ"ב חשון
22 CHESHVAN / CYCLE 1

November 8, 2001
October 28, 2002
November 17, 2003
November 6, 2004
November 24, 2005

כ"ב אדר*
*22 ADAR / CYCLE 2

March 6, 2002
February 24, 2003
March 15, 2004
March 3, 2005
March 22, 2006

כ"ב תמוז
22 TAMMUZ / CYCLE 3

July 2, 2002
July 22, 2003
July 11, 2004
July 29, 2005
July 18, 2006

*During Hebrew leap years a thirteenth month called Adar Sheni (the second Adar) is added to the calendar. For those years, two sets of corresponding dates are given, the first for Adar, and the second for Adar Sheni.

❧ A Proper Perspective

SEFER SHEM OLAM — Chapter Three:
Approaching Mitzvos with Alacrity (cont.)

*I*t happens often that when a person does some small, good deed, the yetzer hara magnifies it in his eyes, so that his heart will become swelled with pride over his own righteousness. In fact, a person should minimize his own accomplishments so that he does not fall prey to the terrible trait of ga'avah (arrogance).

If a person will take an honest look at his own good deeds, he will find them lacking in many ways; either their details were left incomplete or his intent when performing them was to achieve honor and recognition. Even if some of his good deeds were carried out to perfection, without ulterior motives, of what value are they in comparison to all the good with which Hashem has blessed him throughout his lifetime?

Midrash Rabbah comments on the words, "All man's toil is for his mouth" (Koheles 6:7): All of a person's mitzvos and Torah learning are not sufficient to repay Hashem for the breath which he inhales over a lifetime. Furthermore, if a person will contemplate all the sins which he committed throughout his life and for which he has yet to fully repent, he will find that they far outweigh whatever good he has accomplished.

Arrogance is a most detestable character flaw, while humility is a most admirable trait. Nevertheless, Rabbi Yehudah Zev Segal would note that humility does not preclude accepting a compliment for a job well done. For example, complimenting a speaker for his having delivered an excellent address will encourage him to speak well in the future. This sort of feeling is healthy and productive, as long as one bears in mind that without *siyata diShmaya* (Divine assistance) one can accomplish nothing at all in this world, and that inborn talents are a gift from Above, not something in which to take pride.

Similarly, after performing a *mitzvah*, it is important to feel joy at having merited to serve Hashem through yet another good deed. For example, if someone has recited the *Shemoneh Esrei* with proper concentration or has studied Torah for an appreciable amount of time without interruption, it is proper and productive to feel gratified at this accomplishment. Nevertheless, it would be wrong to think, "I'm really special — not many people are capable of doing what I've just done." As the Chofetz Chaim pointed out, one can never be absolutely certain that his deeds are without flaw. Secondly, without Hashem's help we can accomplish nothing. This is why we begin *Shemoneh Esrei* with the verse, "Hashem, open my lips, so that my mouth may declare Your praise" (*Tehillim* 51:17).

The Chazon Ish added another point:

> People are mistaken in thinking that humility means to think of oneself as an ignorant boor, even when such is surely not the case. Humility means that one realizes his true worth... but he must not seek honor and glory

If a person will take an honest look at his own good deeds, he will find them lacking in many ways.

(cont. on page 255)

22 Cheshvan — Murray Akawie לע"נ משה העשיל הכהן בן אברהם ז"ל
Joseph Brownstein לע"נ יונה גרשון בן יצחק דוב ז"ל

22 Adar — Dovid Dachs לע"נ ר' דוד בן חיים יצחק ז"ל
Dedicated in loving memory by his grandchildren Shloime & Libby Dachs and family

22 Tammuz — לזכות משה ארי' בן דבורה נ"י
ולזכות שמשון מרדכי בן דבורה נ"י

DAY 53

כ"ג חשון
23 CHESHVAN / CYCLE 1

November 9, 2001
October 29, 2002
November 18, 2003
November 7, 2004
November 25, 2005

כ"ג אדר*
*23 ADAR / CYCLE 2

March 7, 2002
February 25, 2003
March 16, 2004
March 4, 2005
March 23, 2006

כ"ג תמוז
23 TAMMUZ / CYCLE 3

July 3, 2002
July 23, 2003
July 12, 2004
July 30, 2005
July 19, 2006

*During Hebrew leap years a thirteenth month called Adar Sheni (the second Adar) is added to the calendar. For those years, two sets of corresponding dates are given, the first for Adar, and the second for Adar Sheni.

✒ Avoid Arrogance

SEFER SHEM OLAM — Chapter Three:
Approaching Mitzvos with Alacrity (cont.)

*T*he early commentators have already pointed out that the Torah cautions a Jew against viewing himself as a tzaddik, as it is written, "Do not say in your heart... Because of my righteousness did Hashem bring me to possess this Land... Remember, do not forget, that you provoked Hashem, your G-d, in the Wilderness" (Devarim 9:4,7). This applies to all Jews in every generation; we should bear in mind our failings so that we will not become arrogant. As the prophet Yirmiyahu said, "How can you say, 'I have not become contaminated...'? See your pathway in the valley and recognize what you have done" (Yirmiyahu 2:23). King David said, "And my sin is before me always" (Tehillim 51:5).

King David said, "For I recognize my transgressions and my sin is before me always." He also said, "I have set Hashem before me always; because He is at my right hand, I shall not falter" (Tehillim 16:8).

Only a man who carefully aims his every action towards Hashem can feel true disappointment when he strays from his target. Rabbi Mordechai Gifter observed that the word חֵטְא, *sin*, literally means "to miss the mark." Only the person who strives to achieve that perfect alignment of "I have set Hashem before me always" can fully sense the deep heart-break in, "My sin is before me always." He must be aware at the same time, however, that exaggerated remorse for sin can be counterproductive.

Aharon *HaKohen* (the Priest), says *Ramban*, was the embodiment of the words, "My sin is before me always." The Torah relates that Aharon was guilty of misjudgment in dealing with the Jews' desire to create a Golden Calf (see *Shemos* Ch. 32). This error had a profound impact on Aharon. As he attempted to go about his service of Hashem, he envisioned before him the apparition of a calf, standing in the way of his service being accepted by Hashem. *Ramban* quotes an opinion that in this, Aharon was a victim of מַעֲשֵׂה שָׂטָן, *the guiles of Satan*, who misled him into an obsession of guilt so strong that he felt unworthy and incapable of representing his people in the Sanctuary of Hashem. These fears were finally put to rest by Moshe's words of encouragement on the day when Aharon assumed the role of *Kohen Gadol* (High Priest; see *Ramban* to *Vayikra* 9:7).

The proper way for an individual to resolve this dilemma is to compartmentalize the mind. Surely one must continue to regret his sins even *after* repentance, but that remorse should be isolated to one area of consciousness. The rest of the mind should exult in the opportunity to serve Hashem with renewed enthusiasm and in the awareness of the good which we *have* accomplished which makes us worthy of G-d's grace (Rabbi Avrohom Chaim Feuer in *Tehillim Treasury*).

Exaggerated remorse for sin can be counter-productive.

DAY 54

כ"ד חשון
24 CHESHVAN / CYCLE 1
November 10, 2001
October 30, 2002
November 19, 2003
November 8, 2004
November 26, 2005

כ"ד אדר*
*24 ADAR / CYCLE 2
March 8, 2002
February 26, 2003
March 17, 2004
March 5, 2005
March 24, 2006

כ"ד תמוז
24 TAMMUZ / CYCLE 3
July 4, 2002
July 24, 2003
July 13, 2004
July 31, 2005
July 20, 2006

*During Hebrew leap years a thirteenth month called Adar Sheni (the second Adar) is added to the calendar. For those years, two sets of corresponding dates are given, the first for Adar, and the second for Adar Sheni.

ᵔᷞ The Power of Teshuvah

SEFER SHEM OLAM — Chapter Three:
Approaching Mitzvos with Alacrity (cont.)

There is another method which the yetzer hara uses to wreak spiritual harm. When a person has transgressed many serious sins which cannot possibly be considered insignificant, he may decide that the time has come to repent. At that point, the yetzer hara takes an opposite approach, magnifying the sins to such a degree that teshuvah (repentance) seems impossible. "Your situation is hopeless," the evil inclination tells the sinner. "You can never attain forgiveness for what you've done."

What is the result of this? It is like a doctor who tells his patient, "The situation is hopeless." The patient reasons, "Well, in that case, I might as well enjoy life while it lasts." With the sinner, the result is the same; by despairing of any chance for repentance, he sinks deeper and deeper into the quicksand of sin.

This form of yetzer hara and its fallacy was addressed by the prophet Yechezkel:

> Now, you, Ben Adam, say to the family of Israel: "Thus have you said, saying, 'For our misdeeds and sins are upon us, and through them, we pine away — so how can we live?' "

Say to them: "As I live, the words of my L-rd, Hashem Elokim, I do not desire the death of the wicked one, but the wicked one's return from his way so that he will live. Repent, repent from your evil ways; why should you die, O family of Israel?" (Yechezkel 33:10-11).

When a person returns to Hashem through teshuvah, Hashem responds by drawing him close as if he had never sinned. To the words "Hashem, Hashem," which are the first of the Thirteen Attributes of Mercy, our Sages expound, "I am He [the G-d of mercy] before a person sins, and I am He after a person sins and repents" (Rosh HaShanah 17b). This means that Hashem's ways are very different from the ways of man. When a man sins against his friend and later seeks to correct his mistake and begs forgiveness, even if the friendship will be restored it is doubtful that it will be as it once was. However, Hashem is not this way. Through teshuvah, a person can restore the original closeness with Hashem that he once enjoyed.

In the Book of Yirmiyahu, Hashem declares: "If you repent, O Israel — the word of Hashem — you will return to Me" (Yirmiyahu 4:1), meaning "You will return to your original honor and greatness" (Rashi ad loc.).

Through teshuvah, a person can restore the original closeness with Hashem that he once enjoyed.

(cont. on page 255)

24 Cheshvan — Edith Ozdoba ע"ה לע"נ יהודית חי' בת נחום ע"ה
Dedicated in memory of our dear Edie, by the Izsak family.

24 Adar — לע"נ בן ציון גבריאל בן ר' אליעזר ז"ל
Dedicated by Rabbi & Mrs. Eliezer Hamburger

24 Tammuz — לע"נ חנה בת הניא ע"ה
Dedicated by her children, grandchildren and great-grandchildren

כ"ה חשון
25 CHESHVAN / CYCLE 1

November 11, 2001
October 31, 2002
November 20, 2003
November 9, 2004
November 27, 2005

כ"ה אדר*
*25 ADAR / CYCLE 2

March 9, 2002
February 27, 2003
March 18, 2004
March 6, 2005
March 25, 2006

כ"ה תמוז
25 TAMMUZ / CYCLE 3

July 5, 2002
July 25, 2003
July 14, 2004
August 1, 2005
July 21, 2006

*During Hebrew leap years a thirteenth month called Adar Sheni (the second Adar) is added to the calendar. For those years, two sets of corresponding dates are given, the first for Adar, and the second for Adar Sheni.

❧ Clarity Through Torah

SEFER SHEM OLAM — Chapter Three:
Approaching Mitzvos with Alacrity (cont.)

Know, my friend, that what we have written above, concerning the various ways through which the yetzer hara overcomes a person, only applies to someone who has detached himself from Torah. Such a person is like one who has lost his eyesight; for as King David declared, "The command of Hashem is clear, enlightening the eyes" (Tehillim 19:9). This teaches that without Torah, a person is like someone whose eyes do not function and who therefore can be fooled by unscrupulous people, who might lead him into traps, pits and the like. Someone whose eyes can see cannot be tricked in this way. Without Torah, a person's spiritual vision becomes murky and he has difficulty discerning right from wrong.

Therefore, it is of paramount importance that a person be steadfast in establishing for himself fixed learning periods each day, so that through the Torah's powerful, clear light he will realize what lies before him and will not be easily misled. In this way, he will enjoy a fulfilling life, in this world and in the next.

The following is a letter which the Steipler *Gaon* wrote to a yeshivah student who was experiencing deep pangs of remorse over sins which he had committed:

I have received your letter and I share in your pain. I am hopeful that in the course of time, Hashem will help to rescue you from "the sins of youth," רחמנא ליצלן.

With regard to the past, do not give any thought to it at the present time. Of paramount importance is that you toil in the study of Torah, the Torah of the living G-d, our Rock and Creator, Blessed is His Name. Toil in the study of Torah with intense effort, [with the goal of] understanding all the fine details of a given topic. Toil in the study of Torah even when you find this exceedingly difficult, and without wasting any time...

Do not say: "My soul is sullied; the Torah cannot attach itself to one so earthly as myself." Heaven forfend to think this way! Every word, every bit of logic of Torah is *kodesh kodashim* (holiest of holies), the knowledge and will of Hashem, Blessed is His Name. When it becomes ingrained in one's mind, he becomes sanctified beyond measure with the sanctity of Torah; his body and mind become like a sacred Torah scroll. Ultimately, the sanctity of Torah will, with Hashem's help, rescue you from sin and from sinful thoughts.

...The study of Torah *lishmah* (for its own sake) is the primary way to undo the damage caused by sins. This is especially true of study that is intense and energetic, for it atones like a Temple sacrifice.

(*Karyana D'Igarta* Vol. I, § 11)

Without Torah, a person's spiritual vision becomes murky.

DAY 56

כ"ו חשון
26 CHESHVAN / CYCLE 1

November 12, 2001
November 1, 2002
November 21, 2003
November 10, 2004
November 28, 2005

כ"ו אדר*
*26 ADAR / CYCLE 2

March 10, 2002
February 28, 2003
March 19, 2004
March 7, 2005
March 26, 2006

כ"ו תמוז
26 TAMMUZ / CYCLE 3

July 6, 2002
July 26, 2003
July 15, 2004
August 2, 2005
July 22, 2006

*During Hebrew leap years a thirteenth month called Adar Sheni (the second Adar) is added to the calendar. For those years, two sets of corresponding dates are given, the first for Adar, and the second for Adar Sheni.

❧ The Palace of Our Dreams

SEFER SHEM OLAM — Chapter Four:
The Reward of the World to Come

"*How abundant is Your goodness which You have treasured for those who revere You*" (Tehillim 31:20). This refers to the infinite reward of the World to Come. As the Mishnah teaches:

> R' Yaakov said: "This world is like a lobby before the World to Come; prepare yourself in the lobby so that you may enter the palace'" (Avos 4:21).

When one has an appointment with an important person, he might spend a few hours preparing for the meeting; when scheduled to meet with a king, however, he spends weeks in preparation.

A person's lifespan on this world is seventy or eighty years, yet R' Yaakov teaches us that all those years are alloted to us as preparation time for the Next World. Why should so much preparation be necessary? The answer is that the Heavenly Palace is comprised of many huge rooms and entry to all of them requires the effort of an entire lifetime. Every mitzvah has its own "world" from which man receives his eternal reward. "How abundant is Your goodness which You have treasured for those who revere You."

If we will ponder this concept a bit, we will realize that, to our misfortune, our approach to it is wrong. We can explain this with a parable:

A man purchased a large tract of land upon which he planned to build a palace for himself. He hired an architect and told him: "I have heard that you are among the best in the business. I want to build a massive palace, a work of stunning architecture that will be a sight to behold. I want it to have a beautiful, expansive anteroom, with a large assortment of sofas, coffee tables and armchairs in which my guests can relax before entering the palace chambers. Please draw up plans which will meet these specifications."

The architect studied the land well before telling his client his conclusion. "I have examined the matter well and have determined that you cannot have both. The property which you have purchased is simply not large enough to include both huge palace quarters and the kind of anteroom that you described. Building such an anteroom will mean limiting the size of the structure in a way that will deprive it of any distinctive form. Instead of receiving compliments, you will be laughed at and, I assure you, you will derive no pleasure from all the money which

Man is granted life to prepare for the Next World.

(cont. on page 255)

---

1. While the word טְרַקְלִין is commonly translated as *banquet hall*, the Chofetz Chaim seems to understand it as a *palace*.

כ"ז חשון
27 CHESHVAN / CYCLE 1

November 13, 2001
November 2, 2002
November 22, 2003
November 11, 2004
November 29, 2005

כ"ז אדר*
*27 ADAR / CYCLE 2

March 11, 2002
March 1, 2003
March 20, 2004
March 8, 2005
March 27, 2006

כ"ז תמוז
27 TAMMUZ / CYCLE 3

July 7, 2002
July 27, 2003
July 16, 2004
August 3, 2005
July 23, 2006

*During Hebrew leap years a thirteenth month called Adar Sheni (the second Adar) is added to the calendar. For those years, two sets of corresponding dates are given, the first for Adar, and the second for Adar Sheni.

❧ Know Your Priorities

SEFER SHEM OLAM — Chapter Four:
The Reward of the World to Come (cont.)

In the time allotted to us on this world, we build our palaces in the World to Come. As the Sages comment on the verse, "And all your sons will be disciples of Hashem" (Yeshayahu 54:13): "Do not read it "your sons" (banayich), but "your builders" (bonayich) (Berachos 64a).[1]

King Shlomo said, "The wise among women, each builds her house" (Mishlei 14:1). Metaphorically, a person's soul is called "his wife," and his "house" refers to the palace which he builds for himself in the World to Come. With what does the soul build this house? Midrash Mishlei comments: " '...builds her house' — this refers to Torah." This teaches us that whoever acquires Torah acquires for himself a dwelling in the World to Come, but whoever does not acquire Torah will not acquire a dwelling in the World to Come.

If we contemplate our deeds well, we will find that most of our time is spent building our "anteroom" on this world, acquiring a nice home, food and clothing. We are not satisfied to make do with the minimum; rather, we seek to expand and upgrade every detail of our physical existence. Thus, we leave our-

selves but a small bit of time for the building of our palace in Heaven, and even this bit is not on a steady basis. Sometimes, a person can go weeks without studying Torah, while his tefillah is mere lip service. What a tragedy! Does one truly expect to live in this anteroom forever? Ultimately, we all must uproot ourselves from this world, and if our Heavenly palace will not have been prepared, we will be forced to take up residence out of the province of the Shechinah (Divine Presence), among the shells (of impurity) and external forces.

A wise person will exercise restraint in his personal lifestyle.

While the Chofetz Chaim wrote, "If we contemplate our deeds..." implying that he, too, was guilty of a warped sense of priorities, his simple lifestyle proved otherwise. His son-in-law, Rabbi Mendel Zaks, wrote:

He once confided in me, "Until 5655 (1895), I wore a sheepskin coat (the type worn by beggars in those days), but once I achieved prominence, I was afraid of the possibility of *chillul Hashem*, so I had a *peltz* made — a cloth coat with fur lining." Then he told me, with deep admiration and a touch of envy, how Reb Nachum'ke Horodna[2] owned a sheepskin

(cont. on page 256)

---

1. The Talmud interprets the term "sons" as referring to Torah scholars, the true "builders" of the world. It is striking, notes *Aruch LaNer* (*Yevamos* 122b), that four tractates end with this teaching: בְּרָכוֹת, נָזִיר, יְבָמוֹת, כְּרִיתוֹת. Their initial letters form the word בָּנָיִךְ (builders).

2. A great *tzaddik* who lived his life as a *shamash* (attendant) in a *shul*. As a youth, the Chofetz Chaim traveled to Horodna (Grodno) to observe R' Nachum'ke's ways.

כ"ח חשון
28 CHESHVAN/CYCLE 1

November 14, 2001
November 3, 2002
November 23, 2003
November 12, 2004
November 30, 2005

כ"ח אדר*
*28 ADAR / CYCLE 2

March 12, 2002
March 2, 2003
March 21, 2004
March 9, 2005
March 28, 2006

כ"ח תמוז
28 TAMMUZ / CYCLE 3

July 8, 2002
July 28, 2003
July 17, 2004
August 4, 2005
July 24, 2006

*During Hebrew leap years a thirteenth month called Adar Sheni (the second Adar) is added to the calendar. For those years, two sets of corresponding dates are given, the first for Adar, and the second for Adar Sheni.

❧ No Guests Allowed

SEFER SHEM OLAM — Chapter Four:
The Reward of the World to Come (cont.)

On this world, even a poor Jew who has no place at all to call his home, existing by going from door to door to beg, will not have to sleep in the street. All Jews are obligated to find him a place where he can at least spend his nights. In the World to Come, however, there is no such thing as "inviting a guest" into one's own dwelling. Anyone who lacks personal merit to enter Gan Eden will be denied entry. Even a father cannot gain entry for his own son, as Midrash states: "Avraham will not save Yishmael, Yitzchak will not save Eisav." Thus, whoever will not prepare "food for the road" while he is on this world, will find himself "outside the camp" in the Next World, where he will be vulnerable to harmful spiritual forces.

Of course, it is well known that ultimately, every Jew is cleansed of his sins and attains a portion in the World to Come according to what he accomplished on this world. Nevertheless, the purifying period which precedes this attainment can be extremely painful. And when this purifying process is over, and he is granted entry to Gan Eden, he will receive exactly what he has built for himself through his Torah and good deeds — nothing more. If he did not build properly, meaning that the Torah knowledge and good deeds which he accumulated are far less than what he could have attained given his abilities, then he will be judged accordingly. His Heavenly abode will lack the glory and luster of others, and this will cause him great, eternal shame.

We can liken this to a rich man whose fortunes have fallen, reducing him to poverty. Unable to cover his expenses, he has no choice but to sell his palatial home and move into a small, cramped apartment. When people see this and realize what has happened, the rich man feels terribly embarrassed. In the Next World, there is no concept of jealousy. Nevertheless, one who will receive only minimal reward will experience distress over his situation, telling himself: "I was just as qualified as So-and-so. Why didn't I use my abilities to accomplish more with my life?"

Each person's reward is in exact proportion to his Torah and good deeds.

This is implied in the teaching that in the World to Come, each person will "be burnt by his neighbor's canopy" (Bava Basra 75a). He will be terribly distressed over his inability to gaze at the brilliant, spiritual light emanating from his neighbor's Heavenly place — a light which could have been his own had he only made the necessary effort while on this world.

A wise person will plan for the future and not direct too much of his energies toward the anteroom that is this world. Instead, he will make do with the minimum on this world and focus his thoughts and energies, day in and day out, on acquiring Torah and mitzvos so that the glory of Hashem will shine upon him in his Heavenly abode, forever.

---

28 Cheshvan —

28 Adar — In honor of Rebbetzin Rochel Pernikof, שתחי׳

28 Tammuz — Solomon Nussen לע״נ שלמה בן יוסף דוד ז״ל
Dedicated by Mrs. Ema Nussen and family, Briarwood, NY

כ"ט חשון*
*29 CHESHVAN/CYCLE1

November 15, 2001*
November 4, 2002
November 24, 2003
November 13, 2004*
December 1, 2005*

כ"ט אדר**
**29 ADAR / CYCLE 2

March 13, 2002
March 3, 2003
March 22, 2004
March 10, 2005
March 29, 2006

כ"ט תמוז
29 TAMMUZ / CYCLE 3

July 9, 2002
July 29, 2003
July 18, 2004
August 5, 2005
July 25, 2006

*When this month has only 29 days, the lesson for 30 Cheshvan should also be studied today.

**During Hebrew leap years a thirteenth month called Adar Sheni (the second Adar) is added to the calendar. For those years, two sets of corresponding dates are given, the first for Adar, and the second for Adar Sheni.

כ"ט אדר ב
29 ADAR SHENI

April 2, 2003
April 9, 2005

❧ *Purpose of Redemption*

SEFER SHEM OLAM — Chapter Five:
Approaching Torah Study with Alacrity

*A*ttainment of Torah knowledge is the greatest of all accomplishments, and therefore one should direct constant effort and energy toward this goal. It is well known that Torah study is paramount among all mitzvos.

Many mitzvos — among them Shabbos, Pesach and tefillin — are intertwined with the Exodus from Egypt. The Torah stresses the Exodus so much because through its great miracles, fundamental matters of Jewish faith became clear for all time, as it is written, "Israel saw the great hand that Hashem inflicted upon Egypt... and they had faith in Hashem and in Moshe, His servant" (Shemos 14:31). The Exodus also demonstrated the concept of hashgachah, Hashem's awareness of and involvement in all that transpires on this earth, as the Torah states, "... so that you will know that I am Hashem in the midst of the Land" (ibid. 8:18). For these lessons alone, the Exodus would have been worthwhile.

However, the Torah makes clear that the Exodus served yet another crucial purpose, one which surpassed even those which we have mentioned. The primary goal of the Exodus was that it should serve as a prelude to the Giving of the Torah at Sinai. "[Hashem said to Moshe]: When you take the people out *of Egypt, you will serve G-d on this mountain"* (ibid. 3:12). *And as the Torah states regarding the mitzvah of tefillin, "… it shall be as a sign on your arm and a reminder between your eyes — so that Hashem's Torah may be in your mouth — for [this is why] with a strong hand Hashem took you out of Egypt"* (ibid. 13:9).

The Talmud teaches: "Through what [deeds] do women merit eternal life? Through bringing their children to the synagogue to learn Scripture, through sending their husbands to the study hall [to learn], and for waiting for their husbands until they come home from the study hall" (*Berachos* 17a). The obvious question is: Why not credit women with the many *mitzvos* which they do that are unrelated to Torah study?

As the Chofetz Chaim makes clear in the following segment, there is a degree of spiritual reward that can be attained only through the merit of Torah study. Additionally, notes Rabbi Chaim Pinchus Scheinberg, our Sages teach that to merit *techias hameisim* (the revival of the dead), Torah study is a must. As the Talmud states, the merit to come alive again will come from the "dew" of Torah (*Kesubos* 111b). Only Torah study has this life-giving quality.

Rabbi Scheinberg adds that an unmarried woman can gain merit through support of Torah study. The Torah tells us that the tribes of Yissachar and Zevulun engaged in a partnership whereby Yissachar devoted his life to the study of Torah and was supported by Zevulun (See Day 65). Zevulun's spiritual reward for this "partnership" was equal to that of Yissachar. Anyone, man or woman, can acquire the merit of Torah study through its support (from *Heart to Heart Talks*).

The primary goal of the Exodus was the Giving of the Torah at Sinai.

29 Cheshvan — In gratitude to Hashem for the mercy shown to our grandchildren.

29 Adar — In honor of our children - May they grow to be true עבדי ה'. Dedicated by Jay & Michele Levine

29 Tammuz — Paul Ernst לע"נ שלמה בן ליפא ז"ל Dedicated by Maurice & Phil Ernst

ל חשון*
*30CHESHVAN/CYCLE1

November 5, 2002
November 25, 2003

א ניסן
1 NISSAN / CYCLE 2

March 14, 2002
April 3, 2003
March 23, 2004
April 10, 2005
March 30, 2006

א אב
1 AV / CYCLE 3

July 10, 2002
July 30, 2003
July 19, 2004
August 6, 2005
July 26, 2006

*When this month has only 29 days, the lesson for 30 Cheshvan should be learnt together with 29 Cheshvan.

✑ Source of Life and Light

SEFER SHEM OLAM — Chapter Five:
Approaching Torah Study with Alacrity (cont.)

ashem seeks to grant the Jewish people merit so that they can enjoy eternal life in the World to Come. It is impossible to attain this without Torah, which is the source of spiritual life, as it is written, "...for it is your life and the length of your days..." (Devarim 30:20). Torah is also the source of spiritual light, as it is written, "For a mitzvah is a lamp and the Torah is light" (Mishlei 6:23). When a person attaches himself to Torah, its light casts its glow upon his soul and it is through this light that he lives an eternal life in the World to Come. This is what is meant by "...and eternal life He implanted in us..." which is recited each morning in Shacharis and as part of the closing blessing of the public Torah reading. Specifically, these words refer to תּוֹרָה שֶׁבְּעַל פֶּה, *the Oral Law.*

Conversely, a Jew who separates himself from Torah, separates himself from life itself — literally. We can now understand why Hashem is so exacting when the Jewish people forsake the Torah, as the Talmud teaches: "The Holy One, Blessed is He, was yielding regarding the sins of idol worship, immorality and murder, but He was unyielding regarding the disruption of Torah study [bitul Torah]" (Yerushalmi Chagigah 1:7).

The Jewish people are as precious to Hashem as a child is to a father or mother. Can we imagine the distress of a father who watches as his child swallows a potion that will shorten his lifespan? Hashem's distress, as it were, is many times greater when a Jew forsakes the mitzvah of Torah study, for he is thereby cutting himself off from the source of eternal life.

When a person attaches himself to Torah, its light casts its glow upon his soul.

The Chofetz Chaim refers to the teaching that the Heavenly decree of exile and destruction of the First *Beis HaMikdash* was sealed on account of the Jews' disruption of Torah study. Elsewhere, our Sages teach that the generation was guilty of "not reciting the [required] blessing on the Torah prior to learning" (*Nedarim* 81a). Rabbi Aharon Kotler explained:

> They believed in Torah and *mitzvos* and ful-filled their religious obligations, including involvement and toil in Torah study, but they failed to appreciate the inestimable value of Torah, that without it there is no purpose whatsoever to Creation and that the whole eternal purpose of life can be fulfilled only through Torah. Therefore, they failed to recognize the great importance of offering praise [to G-d] for the Torah [by reciting the Blessing of the Torah]. Because of this, they lacked the benefit of the full spiritual light that radiates from Torah.

(cont. on page 256)

30 Cheshvan — Harriet Segelnick ע"ה לע"נ העננטשע בת מאניס ע"ה
Sponsored by Marc & Michele Segelnick and family

1 Nissan — Abraham Spector ז"ל לע"נ אברהם בן נתן נטע ז"ל
Dedicated by his wife, children and grandchildren

לע"נ דוב בן מרדכי ז"ל — **1 Av**
Dedicated by his family

א כסלו
1 KISLEV / CYCLE 1

November 16, 2001
November 6, 2002
November 26, 2003
November 14, 2004
December 2, 2005

ב ניסן
2 NISSAN / CYCLE 2

March 15, 2002
April 4, 2003
March 24, 2004
April 11, 2005
March 31, 2006

ב אב
2 AV / CYCLE 3

July 11, 2002
July 31, 2003
July 20, 2004
August 7, 2005
July 27, 2006

❧ *A Living Torah Scroll*

SEFER SHEM OLAM — Chapter Five:
Approaching Torah Study with Alacrity (cont.)

"*Only your forefathers did Hashem cherish to love them, and He chose their offspring after them — you — from all the nations, as this day*" *(Devarim 10:15).* In our forefather's merit, Hashem desires to express His love of us by bringing His Shechinah (Divine Presence) to rest upon our souls. As the Torah states: *"Make for Me a Sanctuary so that I shall dwell among them"* (Shemos 25:8), to which our Sages comment: *"[... so that I shall dwell] in each and every one of them"* (Seder Olam Rabbah 6).

How is it possible for the soul to unite itself with the Shechinah? Is the soul not like something physical in comparison to the awesome sanctity of Hashem's Presence?

This is the function of Torah, the intermediary between G-d and His people. Hashem commanded that we attach ourselves to Torah, in which the light of His awesome Presence resides. Through Torah, the light of the Shechinah comes to rest upon one's soul.

Thus, the Torah states (Bamidbar 35:34): *"...for I am Hashem Who rests within the Children of Israel"* — literally. And thus does Zohar teach: *"Israel, the Torah and the Holy One, Blessed is He, are one."*

Through Torah study, the Jewish soul can acquire the sanctity of a sefer Torah (Torah scroll) — literally! It is, therefore, crucial that we approach the mitzvah of Torah study with great zeal and determination.

To the Torah luminaries in every generation, Torah was and is their very lifeblood. They study Torah with incredible diligence and with a joy that can be derived only from learning that which is G-d-given.

One night, as he sat poring over the sacred texts before him, R' Sholom Schwadron grasped the full intent of an explanation recorded by his grandfather, the *Maharsham*. With great excitement, R' Sholom realized how this explanation shed light on the meaning of the Talmudic passage which he sat studying.

R' Sholom could not remain at home and keep this new insight to himself — even until morning. He had to share it with someone else, *now!* And who better to share it with than his illustrious brother-in-law, whom he loved so dearly, R' Shlomo Zalman Auerbach?

R' Sholom stepped out into the dark, empty Jerusalem streets and made his way to his brother-in-law's apartment. His knock was answered by a nephew, who said, "*Abba* (Father) just went into his room to lie down. He's not sleeping yet, but he's finished learning for the night and he's gone to bed."

R' Sholom said, "If he is not sleeping yet, allow me to make him happy."

Soon, R' Shlomo Zalman was sitting transfixed, listening to R' Sholom's explanation. "*Nu,*" said R' Sholom when he had finished, "Isn't it incredible? Let's dance!"

(cont. on page 256)

Through Torah study, the light of the Shechinah comes to rest upon one's soul.

---

1 Kislev — Nathan Samuel Sax ז"ל לע"נ שמואל נאטע בן מרדכי שלמה ז"ל
Sponsored by David and Ann Alden

2 Nissan — Sylvia Feld ע"ה לע"נ זיסל עלקא בת חיים ע"ה
Dedicated by her family

2 Av — Kathryn Kossis ע"ה לע"נ גיטל בת אברהם ע"ה
Dedicated in loving memory by her children

ב כסלו
2 KISLEV / CYCLE 1

November 17, 2001
November 7, 2002
November 27, 2003
November 15, 2004
December 3, 2005

ג ניסן
3 NISSAN / CYCLE 2

March 16, 2002
April 5, 2003
March 25, 2004
April 12, 2005
April 1, 2006

ג אב
3 AV / CYCLE 3

July 12, 2002
August 1, 2003
July 21, 2004
August 8, 2005
July 28, 2006

✺ With All Our Resources

SEFER SHEM OLAM — Chapter Five:
Approaching Torah Study with Alacrity (cont.)

*T*he Torah teaches: אֶת ה' אֱלֹקֶיךָ תִּירָא, *You shall fear Hashem, your G-d (Devarim 10:20). R' Akiva taught (Pesachim 22b) that the extra word אֶת comes to include reverence for talmidei chachamim (Torah scholars). Talmud Yerushalmi (Berachos Ch. 9) quotes R' Akiva as teaching that the word אֶת in this verse comes to include reverence for the Torah itself. These interpretations are really one and the same, for as we have explained, the Torah scholar is sanctified with the light of Torah which rests upon his soul. This is why we are commanded to revere him.*

With this, we can well understand the well-known Talmudic statement:

> *How foolish are those people who stand up in respect for a Torah scroll but they do not stand up in respect for a great person [i.e. a Torah sage], for in the Torah scroll it is written [that for certain sins the transgressor receives] forty lashes, yet the Sages came and subtracted one [i.e. through their Torah wisdom they showed that the verse was not to be understood literally] (Makkos 22b).*

This passage demonstrates the depth of Torah sanctity which the Sages possessed. In interpreting the Written Torah, the Sages were guided by the Thirteen Principles of Torah Interpretation [י"ג מדות שהתורה נדרשת בהן] which were transmitted at Sinai. Through this, they were able to deduce the true intent of every verse, sometimes in a way which is far different from its apparent meaning. Thus, the Sages were sanctified to an incredible degree, through their profound connection to both the Written and Oral Torah.

Midrash records the following incident:

> R' Chiya bar Abba and R' Yochanan were walking down a road when they passed a certain field. R' Yochanan said: "This field used to be mine, but I sold it so that I could devote myself to toiling in Torah, and so too, with another field."
>
> R' Chiya began to weep, exclaiming, "What have you left yourself for your old age?"
>
> R' Yochanan responded, "Why does this bother you? I sold something that was created in six days, as it is written, "...for in six days Hashem made the heaven and the earth..." (Shemos 31:17) and I have acquired something that was taught in forty days, as it is written, "And he [Moshe] was there with Hashem forty days..." (ibid. 34:28).

(cont. on page 256)

We should be prepared to make every sacrifice to acquire Torah knowledge.

2 Kislev — Mrs. Rachel Marder ע"ה לע"נ רחל בת נפתלי ע"ה
Dedicated by Mrs. Ema Nussen, Briarwood, NY

3 Nissan — Jeanne Rush London ע"ה לע"נ ג'ין שרה בת יוסף ע"ה
Dedicated in loving memory by her daughter, Atara London Grenadir

3 Av — Adele Gerstner ע"ה לע"נ אידל הי"ד בת ר' יוסף הלוי הוריוויץ ע"ה
Dedicated by her grandchildren

ג כסלו
3 KISLEV / CYCLE 1

November 18, 2001
November 8, 2002
November 28, 2003
November 16, 2004
December 4, 2005

ד ניסן
4 NISSAN / CYCLE 2

March 17, 2002
April 6, 2003
March 26, 2004
April 13, 2005
April 2, 2006

ד אב
4 AV / CYCLE 3

July 13, 2002
August 2, 2003
July 22, 2004
August 9, 2005
July 29, 2006

✄ *Sacrificing Eternity*

SEFER SHEM OLAM — Chapter Six:
Approaching Torah Study with Alacrity — II

*T*here are many people of good character and superior intelligence who have the potential to accomplish so much with their lives, if only they would not fall prey to the yetzer hara's ploy of keeping them overwhelmed with earthly concerns. These are people who could be acquiring vast knowledge of Torah, developing sincere love and reverence of Hashem, and performing acts of kindness and compassion on a grand scale. Instead, they undertake various business ventures which keep them preoccupied day and night, to the point that they do not set aside time to study Torah, or even to pray with a minyan. They convince themselves that their situation demands such financial efforts. They give no attention at all to their true purpose on this earth, and instead, direct all their energy and ingenuity to improving their material status — both through honest and dishonest means.

The prophet Yeshayahu foretold such tragedies:

> I will now sing on behalf of my Beloved [Hashem], my Beloved's song concerning His vineyard [the Jewish people]:

My Beloved had a vineyard in a fertile corner. He fenced it around and cleared it of stones [i.e. He implanted within His people the qualities of kindness and compassion]; He planted it with choice shoots and built a tower inside it; He even hewed a wine vat in it [i.e. He endowed His people with superior intelligence to delve into the Torah and perceive its wisdom which is likened to wine].[1] He had hoped to produce [fine] grapes, but it produced only inferior grapes [i.e. the people used their intelligence for the wrong goals].

...Now, the vineyard of Hashem, Master of Legions, is the house of Israel (Yeshayahu 5:1-2,7).

Some could be accomplishing so much — if only they would be less preoccupied with earthly concerns.

The Chofetz Chaim offered a classic parable to explain the teaching, "Torah can endure only in one who kills himself over it" (*Berachos* 63b):

A merchant achieved great business success; customers would stream to his store from far and wide. The store occupied his every waking hour, to the extent that he did not even set aside time to pray with a *minyan*.

Years passed; his beard began turning white and his body weakened considerably. He sensed his end drawing near; the time was approaching when he would have to stand judgment for what he had and had not accomplished with his life. He decided to prepare "food for the road" regardless of the consequences.

(cont. on page 257)

---

1. See *Mishlei* 9:5.

ד כסלו
4 KISLEV / CYCLE 1

November 19, 2001
November 9, 2002
November 29, 2003
November 17, 2004
December 5, 2005

ה ניסן
5 NISSAN / CYCLE 2

March 18, 2002
April 7, 2003
March 27, 2004
April 14, 2005
April 3, 2006

ה אב
5 AV / CYCLE 3

July 14, 2002
August 3, 2003
July 23, 2004
August 10, 2005
July 30, 2006

✍ *Attain Your Potential*

SEFER SHEM OLAM — Chapter Six:
Approaching Torah Study with Alacrity — II (cont.)

There are some who delude themselves with the notion that they can fulfill their obligation to study Torah by learning once a week, on the day of Shabbos. This is surely incorrect, for a Jew is obligated to study Torah every day. As the Talmud relates, when a person leaves this world and comes before the Heavenly Tribunal, one of the first questions he is asked is, "Did you set aside fixed times for Torah study?" (Shabbos 31a).

All Jewish souls of all generations were present when the Torah was given at Sinai, and at that time each soul was allotted its portion of Torah knowledge. A person who is born with superior intelligence can assume that he was granted the potential to acquire superior knowledge of Torah. If he will utilize his G-d-given mental gifts primarily for earthly pursuits, while making only a token effort to acquire Torah knowledge, he will be greatly humiliated on the Day of Judgment when he will be told, "Stand up and prepare to recite the Written and Oral Torah which you learned during your lifetime!" For of what value will his Torah have, when compared to the Torah which he could have acquired, had he made proper use of his time and made spiritual accomplishment the primary focus of his life?

In *The Maggid Speaks*, Rabbi Paysach Krohn relates the following story:

Rabbi Naftali Zvi Yehudah Berlin, better known as the *Netziv*,[1] was a foremost luminary of his time. He headed the Yeshivah of Volozhin and authored many works, including *Ha'amek Davar* on the Torah, *Meromei Sadeh* on the Talmud and *Ha'amek Sh'eilah* on *She'iltos D'Rav Achai Gaon*. Upon completion of *Ha'amek Sh'eilah*, the *Netziv* hosted a *seudas mitzvah* (festive meal in honor of a *mitzvah*) and related the following:

> Once, when I was young, I overheard my father crying. I listened from another room and realized that my father and mother were discussing *me*! With pain in his voice, my father said: "I am at a loss as to what to do. I've tried every possible way to inspire our son to learn well — I've offered him all sorts of prizes, but nothing seems to work. It seems that our fervent hope, that he should become a *talmid chacham*, is not to be realized. I guess we'll have to train him to be some sort of laborer."
>
> I was shaken by my father's pain and tears. I rushed into the room and promised my parents that from then on, I would devote myself to the study of Torah. I translated my words into action and became exceedingly diligent in my learning. With Hashem's help,

At Sinai, each soul was alotted its portion of Torah knowledge.

(cont. on page 258)

---

1. ‏נצי"ב‎, *Netziv*, is an acronym for ‏נפתלי צבי יהודה ברלין‎.

ה כסלו
5 KISLEV / CYCLE 1

November 20, 2001
November 10, 2002
November 30, 2003
November 18, 2004
December 6, 2005

ו ניסן
6 NISSAN / CYCLE 2

March 19, 2002
April 8, 2003
March 28, 2004
April 15, 2005
April 4, 2006

ו אב
6 AV / CYCLE 3

July 15, 2002
August 4, 2003
July 24, 2004
August 11, 2005
July 31, 2006

⋙ *The Yissachar-Zevulun Partnership*

SEFER SHEM OLAM — Chapter Six:
Approaching Torah Study with Alacrity — II (cont.)

I know that there are many people who are totally immersed in their business dealings and will find it exceedingly difficult to minimize them [though anyone who understands that this will affect his eternal existence in the Next World should not be deterred from making the necessary changes in his life]. Therefore, I will put forth a way by which they too can attain their eternal reward.

We know that the Tribe of Zevulun were businessmen, as it is written, "Zevulun shall settle by seashores; he shall be at the ship's harbor..." (Bereishis 49:13). Undoubtedly, their involvement in business prevented them from attaining their full potential in Torah study; nevertheless, they found for themselves a correct way by which they would not lack the portion of Torah which they needed to attain. They entered into an agreement with the Tribe of Yissachar; Yissachar would separate himself entirely from earthly pursuits and dedicate his life entirely to the study of Torah, while Zevulun would provide him with his every material need. In this way, the Torah was actually the product of them both, for Yissachar was able to attain unparalleled heights in Torah precisely because he was free from material responsibilities. From the Tribe of Yissachar came the members of Sanhedrin (High Court) and other Torah leaders, as it is written, "And from the sons of Yissachar were those who have understanding of the times [to determine when to declare a leap year]..." (I Divrei HaYamim 12:32). This came about through Zevulun who supported them; therefore, Zevulun shared equally in their Torah achievements. The Torah endorsed Zevulun's practice, as it is written, "Rejoice, Zevulun, in your departures, and Yissachar in your tent" (Devarim 33:18); meaning: "Zevulun, when you go out to do business, do not worry that you will forfeit your portion in Torah, for Yissachar is in your tent."

Zevulun, through his support of Yissachar, shared equally in his achievements.

The same is true today. A person who is heavily involved in business and therefore cannot acquire his alotted portion in Torah through personal study, should strive with all his strength and resources to acquire a "Yissachar partner" so that through this partner, he will merit his own portion in Torah. This can be accomplished in two ways:

He should enter into a partnership with an outstanding talmid chacham, and provide him with his every need, so that he can direct his heart solely toward the study of Torah and service of Hashem. Surely he will thereby

(cont. on page 258)

5 Kislev — In loving memory of Leo Birnbaum לע"נ אליעזר שרגא בן ר' אפרים הכהן ז"ל
Dedicated by his grandchildren and great-grandchildren, Doug & Fran Behrman and family

6 Nissan — In memory of our beloved father Joseph Rosenberg לע"נ יוסף בן אברהם יואל ז"ל

6 Av — Irene Siegel לע"נ שרה בת ר' יחזקאל יהודה ע"ה
Dedicated by her family, Los Angeles, CA

❧ Support of Torah Institutions

SEFER SHEM OLAM — Chapter Six:
Approaching Torah Study with Alacrity — II (cont.)

*T*he second way by which a businessman can acquire his share in Torah is by using his money to support a yeshivah. Support of Torah is a mitzvah which is incumbent upon everyone — even upon those who devote their lives to the study and teaching of Torah. The level of one's obligation is dependent upon his financial status; a wealthy man is required to support Torah generously. This is especially true for someone who seeks to acquire his portion in Torah through support of Torah study. He would have to provide a yeshivah with generous support — approximately what it would cost to support a talmid chacham in full as we discussed above. Each person must give according to his own financial status, in accordance with the blessing which Hashem has bestowed upon him.

Of such a person we can say: fortunate is his lot. Surely he will acquire his portion in Torah in full. This is alluded to in the words "Rejoice, Zevulun, in your departures, and Yissachar in your tent" (Devarim 33:18). When Zevulun will depart this world, he will have nothing to fear; to the contrary, he will be able to rejoice, for surely his portion will be awaiting him in the

Heavenly Academy, where he will attain a great knowledge of Torah through the Torah of Yissachar — who remained immersed in Torah study because of his partner's support.

I have already discussed the mitzvah to support Torah study in Sefer Ahavas Chesed and in Part One of this work. Its reward is exceedingly great, and all the Torah studied by the scholar or by the students of the yeshivah that is being supported, is reckoned to the account of the benefactor [in addition to the accounts of the students themselves]. In a generation which has seen a weakening in the area of Torah study, the reward for support of Torah is many times what it would normally be. As our Sages state (Yerushalmi Berachos 9:5): "If you see a generation whose hands have 'loosened their grip' on the Torah, then stand up and grasp it firmly — and you will receive reward equal to them all."

While a person can acquire his share in Torah through its support, this applies only to acquiring knowledge of Shas and the codes, which requires great toil and much time. In no way, however, can a person absolve himself of the obligation to study those halachos which one needs to know in practice. For this, no amount of support of Torah will suffice; the only option is to study.[1]

Support of Torah is a mitzvah which is incumbent upon everyone.

(cont. on page 259)

---

1. In Chapter Seven, the Chofetz Chaim discusses the obligation upon every Jew to be knowledgeable in practical *halachah*. Our adaptation continues with Chapter Eight.

6 Kislev — May today's learning be a זכות for the Halpern family, Lakewood, NJ.

7 Nissan — Tim Zulberg — לע"נ יוסף מיכאל בן נתן ז"ל

7 Av — In memory of a very special נשמה, Ruth Weissler ע"ה לע"נ רחל בת מרדכי שמואל ע"ה
May she be a מליצת יושר for our entire משפחה. Dedicated by her husband, David Weissler

ז כסלו
7 KISLEV / CYCLE 1

November 22, 2001
November 12, 2002
December 2, 2003
November 20, 2004
December 8, 2005

ח ניסן
8 NISSAN / CYCLE 2

March 21, 2002
April 10, 2003
March 30, 2004
April 17, 2005
April 6, 2006

ח אב
8 AV / CYCLE 3

July 17, 2002
August 6, 2003
July 26, 2004
August 13, 2005
August 2, 2006

≈ *Serious Offenses*

SEFER SHEM OLAM — Chapter Eight:
Intentional Sins

*T*he Mishnah states: *"Do not be a wicked person before yourself"* (Avos 2:18). One interpretation is that a Jew should have fear of Hashem and not sin in private where no human eyes but his own are witness to his behavior. But there is a deeper meaning to this as well.

It is not easy to fulfill all that Hashem expects of us in every situation. In cases involving damages, the Talmud often rules, "He is absolved [of any payment] according to the laws of man, but he is liable according to the laws of Heaven." To achieve a mitzvah b'shleimus, to complete perfection, can require a lot. If a person feels that such accomplishments are far beyond him, then let him at least begin by ensuring that he is not wicked in his own eyes! This means that if he clearly recognizes a given act as a sin, he must carefully avoid it, for if not, then he risks arousing Hashem's wrath, as we shall explain.

If a person recognizes clearly that a given act is wrong, and without any real passion driving him, he convinces himself to sin, then he has committed a very serious offense and retribution may be swift in coming. This applies to any mitzvah; it is imperative that no mitzvah be approached with a carefree atitude, as if it were a matter of choice. Let us offer a few examples:

When a Jew engages in business, he needs to be extremely careful to avoid any hint of gezel (theft). There is no comparison, however-er, between someone who cheats someone through a careless mistake and one who does so intentionally! It is concerning the latter that the Mishnah quoted above is teaching us: When a person knows that something is wrong and does it anyway, he is in effect declaring that he does not truly believe that "an Eye sees, an Ear listens and all your deeds are recorded in a book" (Avos 2:1).

The same applies to matters of speech such as lashon hara, rechilus, or causing someone embarrassment. When a person commits these sins brazenly, acting as if the commandments which prohibit them are not really required of us, he becomes a living illustration of the teaching, "Do not be a wicked person before yourself."

The same applies to the mitzvah to recite Shema every morning and evening. Should a person oversleep and transgress the require-ment to recite the Shema by a certain time, certainly he must repent for allowing this to happen. Nevertheless, the fact that his sin was entirely inadvertent places it in a less severe category. This would not be the case if

It is imperative that no mitzvah be approach-ed with a carefree attitude.

(cont. on page 259)

ח כסלו
8 KISLEV / CYCLE 1

November 23, 2001
November 13, 2002
December 3, 2003
November 21, 2004
December 9, 2005

ט ניסן
9 NISSAN / CYCLE 2

March 22, 2002
April 11, 2003
March 31, 2004
April 18, 2005
April 7, 2006

ט סיון
9 AV / CYCLE 3

July 18, 2002
August 7, 2003
July 27, 2004
August 14, 2005
August 3, 2006

✥ *The Day of Judgment*

SEFER SHEM OLAM — Chapter Eight:
Intentional Sins (cont.)

*O*ne should always bear in mind: No one remains in this world forever. The day will come when the soul will leave its body and ascend Above. Upon death, the soul will seek to return to its source — the Olam HaBeriah (World of Creation), where the souls of all Jewish people dwell. To arrive at that spiritual world, the soul must pass through worlds inhabited by fiery angels, who will ask, "What is a human being doing among us?" To whom will the soul turn for mercy and protection — especially from the angels of wrath created by his sins — if not Hashem? How the soul will cry out and plead to Hashem that it be saved from these spiritual forces! [This, in fact, is what Chapter 116 of Tehillim alludes to: "The pains of death encircled me, the confines of the grave have found me... Then I would invoke the Name of Hashem: 'Please, Hashem, save my soul!' (v. 3-4)].

How shamed the soul will feel at that time when it will recall the lowly sins it committed, that it distanced itself from Hashem and did not give serious thought toward enhancing His honor on this world. It will cry out for

Hashem's help! — but who can be sure that Hashem will not respond, "Why do you come to Me now when you are in distress? Where were you until now?"

One should take this to heart now, when he has the opportunity to mend his ways. Then he will reap the appropriate rewards in the Next World.

Each mitzvah that we perform creates an advocate on our behalf.

The Chofetz Chaim offered the following parable:

A merchant borrowed money from a number of contacts. Then his business collapsed and he was unable to pay back anything. His creditors came to seize his possessions; some were owed thousands of dollars, while others were owed much less. One creditor came to seize property for a ten-dollar loan. "What do you think you're doing?" one of the others demanded. "The man owes you almost nothing! We're here to collect big loans!" "So what?" the man replied. "The money which I lent is owed to me just as yours is owed to you. I have as much right to collect as you do."

Our Sages teach that an accusing angel is created as a result of any sin (*Avos* 4:13). These angels have no power to harm as long a person is alive, but when he dies they stand ready to accuse — regardless of whether the sin is severe or minor.

Conversely, each *mitzvah* that we perform creates an advocate on our behalf. Furthermore, if in the course of our Torah study, we merit to resolve a difficulty in a passage of *Rashi*, *Rambam* or other luminary, the soul of that sage will come to greet us when we ascend to the World of Truth. As the Talmudic

(cont. on page 260)

8 Kislev — May today's learning be a זכות for our family.

9 Nissan — Louis Sherman לע"נ אליעזר בן אליהו ז"ל
Dedicated to a student of the Chofetz Chaim, by his grandson Ronald Greenberg and family

9 Av — Kermit Hirsch לע"נ ר' קלונימוס בן ר' אליעזר ז"ל
Dedicated by Harvey & Yehudis Hirsch and family

DAY 69

ט כסלו
9 KISLEV / CYCLE 1

November 24, 2001
November 14, 2002
December 4, 2003
November 22, 2004
December 10, 2005

י ניסן
10 NISSAN / CYCLE 2

March 23, 2002
April 12, 2003
April 1, 2004
April 19, 2005
April 8, 2006

י אב
10 AV / CYCLE 3

July 19, 2002
August 8, 2003
July 28, 2004
August 15, 2005
August 4, 2006

ஃ *"Today"*

SEFER SHEM OLAM — Chapter Nine:
Reward and Retribution

"*ee, I present before you today a blessing and a curse" (Devarim 11:26). The seemingly superfluous word* היום*, today, can be explained by the words of King Shlomo:*

"*And I returned and contemplated all oppressed ones that are beneath the sun: Behold! Tears of the oppressed with none to comfort them..." (Koheles 4:1). The meaning of this is as follows:*

When a person sins, a ruach hatumah (spirit of impurity) is born which encircles him as he sins and which remains to exact punishment from him when he leaves this world. While he lives on this world in his earthly body, the sinner cannot perceive this accusing spirit which his sin creates, and he goes about with a carefree attitude, happily indulging in forbidden pleasures. When does he begin to sense his troubles? When he dies and is summoned for judgment and the spirits created by his sins surround him from all sides to exact punishment.

One may think that it is then, when he stands in judgment, that he becomes broken and oppressed by the Heavenly beings — but in fact, this is not so. He was broken and oppressed already in his lifetime, as his sins mounted, only he did not perceive this until he died.

This is what Shlomo meant. "And I returned and contemplated all the oppressed ones," and I asked myself, "When did these souls actually become oppressed?" The answer is, "...beneath the sun," as soon as they sinned on this world, for it was then that they were stripped of their inherent kedushah (sanctity) and were clothed instead in a spirit of tumah (impurity).

This is the meaning of, "Do not contaminate yourselves through them [i.e. forbidden pleasures] lest you become contaminated through them" (Vayikra 11:43): If a person allows himself to be drawn after physical pleasures in a way which contradicts the will of Hashem, then the tumah immediately attaches itself to him, though he cannot perceive this.

We can now understand the verse "See, I present before you today a blessing and a curse" (Devarim 11:26). The blessing brought about by mitzvos and the curse which results from sin are immediate, though this is not apparent to the human eye.

The impurity of sin can be eradicated only by the sanctity of mitzvos.

One should constantly bear in mind that the spiritual stains of sin can be cleansed through sincere teshuvah (repentance). *Rabbeinu Yonah* writes:

> [A primary principle of teshuvah is that] one should improve his deeds in the very areas in

(cont. on page 260)

י כסלו
10 KISLEV / CYCLE 1

November 25, 2001
November 15, 2002
December 5, 2003
November 23, 2004
December 11, 2005

רי"א ניסן
11 NISSAN / CYCLE 2

March 24, 2002
April 13, 2003
April 2, 2004
April 20, 2005
April 9, 2006

רי"א אב
11 AV / CYCLE 3

July 20, 2002
August 9, 2003
July 29, 2004
August 16, 2005
August 5, 2006

✑ *Diamonds, Diamonds Everywhere*

SEFER SHEM OLAM — Chapter Nine:
Reward and Retribution (cont.)

*O*nce, a man traveled to a faraway island hoping to engage in some sort of enterprise so that he could provide for his family. He arrived there and discovered a strange situation: diamonds, emeralds and other precious gems were lying in the streets in abundance! Everywhere he turned he saw precious stones lying about like plain pebbles back home. He also noticed that the inhabitants of the island paid no attention to the stones, which seemed worthless in their eyes.

It did not take him long to discover what the locals did value: meat and fish. Both were scarce and were in great demand. Blessed with a keen business sense, the man opened a meat and fish market and was very successful. After a few years, he was a very rich man and he began looking foward to a long-awaited reunion with his wife and children.

He realized that a trip of so many weeks, traversing oceans and continents, would not allow for much baggage. He decided, therefore, that it would be wise to invest his money in some valuable commodities which he would sell for a handsome profit upon his return home. And what could be more valuable than meat and fish!

He set aside the money he would need for the trip, and with the remainder he purchased a few hundred pounds of choice cuts of meat and the very best fish. Carefully, he packed everything into crates and sealed them shut. Then, he wrote to his family, informing them of his date of arrival and that he would be arriving with many crates of valuables. They would have to meet him at the dock and assist him with unloading and transport.

The joyous day arrived. When the crates were unloaded, customs officials demanded that they be opened so that they could assess what duties needed to be paid. The crates were opened — and everyone nearly fainted from the odor! The meat and fish were thoroughly rotten and infested. "Take your 'precious cargo,' " the officials told the man, "and throw it all into the sea before we all become sick from the fumes!"

With the last coins he had in his pocket, the shamefaced entrepreneur hired some workers who hastily disposed of his merchandise.

And so it is with man on this world. He is sent here from Above to amass a genuine treasure — Torah knowledge and good deeds. How unfortunate when a person loses sight of this and instead spends his lifetime indulging in physical pleasures, filling his

The soul descends from Above to amass a genuine treasure — Torah and good deeds.

(cont. on page 261)

DAY 71

י"א כסלו
11 KISLEV / CYCLE 1

November 26, 2001
November 16, 2002
December 6, 2003
November 24, 2004
December 12, 2005

י"ב ניסן
12 NISSAN / CYCLE 2

March 25, 2002
April 14, 2003
April 3, 2004
April 21, 2005
April 10, 2006

י"ב אב
12 AV / CYCLE 3

July 21, 2002
August 10, 2003
July 30, 2004
August 17, 2005
August 6, 2006

❧ "If Only..."

SEFER SHEM OLAM — Chapter Nine:
Reward and Retribution (cont.)

(In the previous lesson, the Chofetz Chaim offered a parable of a man who traveled to a faraway land, only to return with a huge supply of food which rotted.)

The man's wife was, understandably, quite distraught. She waited until they arrived at home before she unburdened herself. "What have you brought us?" she queried. "No clothing, no money, no food — edible food, that is. You have brought nothing home but rotten meat and fish? We are the laughing stock of the entire community. We will never live down such disgrace!"

Her husband was thoroughly drained from his long journey and its aftermath. He mumbled an apology and fell into bed.

While he slept, his wife searched through his suitcases and clothing, hoping to find something of value. In the pocket of one of his jackets, she found a small box containing a precious diamond which he had found on the street in that faraway island. She showed the gem to an expert diamond dealer who had good news for her: "I've never come across a diamond quite like this. It is absolutely exquisite. I am prepared to pay you twenty thousand dollars for it." This offer was accepted and the woman left the dealer's office with a check in hand.

She went to the bank to deposit the money and then went on a shopping spree. She ordered new draperies, bedspreads, a new bedroom and dining room set and paid extra for immediate delivery. Within a couple of hours, their apartment was transformed from a decrepit hovel to a comfortable, nicely-furnished home. While all this was happening, her husband enjoyed a deep slumber. He awoke in the middle of the night and thought that he was dreaming. His house looked beautiful, the table was laden with delicacies and there sat his wife, appearing relaxed and content.

"What's going on?" he asked dumbfoundedly. When his wife explained that all this was the result of one diamond which she had found in his pocket, the man began to weep. "What a fool I've been!" he exclaimed. "On that island, these gems were lying in the streets for anyone to take. Instead of bringing home rotten meat and fish, I could have brought a few boxes of gems — with the profits, we would have become millionaires and been set for life. Instead, I got nothing but disgrace for all my efforts!"

Even the simplest Jew has some merits to his credit. His daily prayers, his answering of "Yehei Shmei Rabbah..." and other mitzvos will gain him eternal reward. After he departs

(cont. on page 261)

Even the simplest Jew has some merits to his credit.

11 Kislev — Henry Kurant לע"נ אלחנן בן פרץ ז"ל
Dedicated by Miriam and Daniel Herenstein and family

12 Nissan — לע"נ אברהם דוד בן ברוך ז"ל
Dedicated by Eli, Marni, Aharon, Avi and Tzivi Polatoff

12 Av — In honor of our parents and our children
Dedicated by Meir Yoel & Susan Laub

י"ב כסלו
12 KISLEV / CYCLE 1

November 27, 2001
November 17, 2002
December 7, 2003
November 25, 2004
December 13, 2005

י"ג ניסן
13 NISSAN / CYCLE 2

March 26, 2002
April 15, 2003
April 4, 2004
April 22, 2005
April 11, 2006

י"ג אב
13 AV / CYCLE 2

July 22, 2002
August 11, 2003
July 31, 2004
August 18, 2005
August 7, 2006

✒ *Inconsolable*

SEFER SHEM OLAM — Chapter Nine:
Reward and Retribution (cont.)

he above parable explains the end of the verse which we quoted above (see Day 69). "...Tears of the oppressed with none to comfort them, and from the hands of their oppressors the power [has been taken] — with none to comfort them" (Koheles 4:1). The tears of the oppressed are shed when they endure the retribution of Gehinnom, where there is no one to comfort them for the suffering which their sins have brought upon them. But even after the power has been taken from their oppressors, when their suffering is over and they are permitted entry into Gan Eden, they still lack consolation. For when they see how great is their reward for but a small amount of mitzvos, and they realize that had they only lived their lives correctly their reward would have been infinitely greater, they are beyond consolation.

Therefore, a wise person will contemplate the future and will dedicate every day of his life to service of Hashem. Then it will be good for him, in this world and in the Next.

The Mishnah states:

> This is the way of Torah: eat bread with salt, drink water in small measure, sleep on the ground, live a life of deprivation — but toil in

Torah! If you do this, "You are praiseworthy and it is well with you" (*Tehillim* 128:2). "You are praiseworthy" — in this world; "and it is well with you" — in the World to Come.

King David said: "Those who seek G-d will not lack any good" (*Tehillim* 34:11). R' Eliyahu Lopian noted: The verse does not say that they will *have* every good; rather, they will *not lack* any good. He explained:

Imagine someone who visits a friend's home and laments that the medicine chest is empty of medications. The homeowner laughs, "How ludicrous! Of course I have no medications — no one in my household is ill!"

Many dedicated Torah scholars live simply, without many of the luxuries which their neighbors consider necessities. Some may view the scholars' lifestyle with genuine pity — but they are wrong. *Those who seek G-d will not lack any good.* Those who are truly devoted to Hashem and His Torah are genuinely happy with their lot — they lack nothing at all.

R' Lopian added another insight: If someone who had never tasted wine before would ask you to explain its taste to him, you might say, "Did you ever taste something sweet? Did you ever taste something sour? Well, the taste of wine is a combination of something sweet and something sour." This may be true, but it will not convey the taste of wine. There is only way to really know how wine tastes — by tasting it.

Similarly, there is only one way to appreciate the happiness of forgoing luxury and indulgence while dedicating one's life to Torah. *If you do this*, *"You are praiseworthy..."* — it must be experienced.

A wise person will contemplate the future.

י"ג כסלו
13 KISLEV / CYCLE 1

November 28, 2001
November 18, 2002
December 8, 2003
November 26, 2004
December 14, 2005

י"ד ניסן
14 NISSAN / CYCLE 2

March 27, 2002
April 16, 2003
April 5, 2004
April 23, 2005
April 12, 2006

י"ד אב
14 AV / CYCLE 3

July 23, 2002
August 12, 2003
August 1, 2004
August 19, 2005
August 8, 2006

⚜ *Like the Angels Above*

SEFER SHEM OLAM — Chapter Ten:
"I set Hashem before Me"

"*I have set Hashem before me always, because He is at my right hand I shall not falter" (Tehillim 16:8). A person's right hand is the one with which he carries out his work; his weaker hand merely lends support. David declared that his primary purpose on this world — indeed, everyone's primary purpose — is to serve Hashem. David saw his physical and material needs as nothing more than "supports," through which his service of Hashem was made possible. Thus he could say with confidence, "I have set Hashem before me always."*

The prayer of Kedushah begins: "We shall sanctify Your Name in this world, just as they sanctify it in Heaven above..." This requires explanation, for dare we compare ourselves to the holy and pure Heavenly angels? Would a commoner dressed in rags come before a king and claim that he could offer the same service as one of the king's close advisors?

The answer to this is that, as we have already stated, a Jew's primary purpose in this world is to serve Hashem by doing mitzvos and offering praise of His exalted Name. "This people which I fashioned for

Myself that they may declare My praise" (Yeshayahu 43:21). For this purpose, we have been granted a neshamah (soul) that is endowed with an awesome sanctity, a חֵלֶק אֱלֹקַ מִמַּעַל, spark of G-dliness from Above. "A man's soul is the candle of Hashem..." (Mishlei 20:27) and its purpose is to sanctify His name, as the Torah states, "I shall be sanctified among the Children of Israel..." (Vayikra 22:32). The Heavenly beings sanctify His Name in the Heavenly spheres, while the Jewish people were created to do the same on this world. This is why we find that in Scriptures, Hashem is referred to both as אֱלֹקֵי צְבָ-אוֹת, G-d of the [Heavenly] hosts, and אֱלֹקֵי יִשְׂרָאֵל, G-d of Israel.

In the Song at the Sea, the Jewish People declared, "This is my G-d and I will build Him a sanctuary, the G-d of my father and I will exalt Him" (Shemos 15:2). The primary purpose of the Exodus was that we should glorify Hashem's Name by studying His teachings and living by them. It is, therefore, not at all strange that the Jewish people declare twice daily, "We shall sanctify Your name in this world, just as they sanctify it in Heaven above..."

In the opening paragraph of *Shulchan Aruch*, *Rama* (based on *Rambam* in *Moreh Nevuchim* 3:52) states:

> *David saw his material needs as nothing more than "supports" which made his service of Hashem possible.*

(cont. on page 262)

13 Kislev — Alfred Katzenberg לע"נ ישראל אלכסנדר בן יצחק הכהן ז"ל
Dedicated by his devoted wife, Blanche, Bernice Lev,
and David & Irwin Katzenberg

14 Nissan — Anita Rubitsky ע"ה לע"נ חנה בת נחמיה אברהם ע"ה
Dedicated by her sons Yehuda, Boruch and Reuven Dubitsky נלב"ע ט"ו ניסן תשמ"ג ת.נ.צ.ב.ה.

14 Av — May today's learning be a זכות for our families.
Dedicated by Bayit V'Gan Bungalow Colony, Ellenville, NY

י״ד כסלו
14 KISLEV / CYCLE 1

November 29, 2001
November 19, 2002
December 9, 2003
November 27, 2004
December 15, 2005

ט״ו ניסן
15 NISSAN / CYCLE 2

March 28, 2002
April 17, 2003
April 6, 2004
April 24, 2005
April 13, 2006

ט״ו אב
15 AV / CYCLE 3

July 24, 2002
August 13, 2003
August 2, 2004
August 20, 2005
August 9, 2006

✒ *Mission Without End*

SEFER SHEM OLAM — Chapter Ten:
"I set Hashem before Me" *(cont.)*

*A*s we have explained, a Jew is placed on this world for one purpose: to faithfully serve his Creator and thereby bring glory to His Name. This truth should be reflected in our every word and deed.

There is not a moment when a Jew can consider himself free of his life's mission. His service of Hashem is not limited to the moments when he is engaged in Torah study, prayer and good deeds. When a Jew eats, drinks, earns a livelihood or engages in other activities which help care for his physical needs, he is also engaged in his mission. The Torah enjoins us to care for our physical well-being: "But you shall greatly protect your souls" (Devarim 4:15) and "Only beware for yourself and greatly protect your souls" (ibid. v. 9). The Torah cautions us to protect our נֶפֶשׁ, soul, rather than our גוּף, body, to hint that when a Jew goes about caring for his physical needs, he must be on guard not to do anything that will cause harm to his neshamah (soul). As one prepares to eat, he should ask himself, "Am I certain that everything on my plate is, in fact, kosher?" When he engages in a business deal, he should ponder, "Is this transaction in full accordance with the laws of Choshen Mishpat?"

After one has determined that what he is about to do is free of all wrong, he should have in mind that our primary purpose in caring for our physical needs is so that we can attain the necessary peace of mind and good health to properly serve Hashem.

Even when a Jew eats, drinks, or earns a livelihood, he is engaged in his life's mission.

The Chofetz Chaim states that before partaking of our food, we must make certain that it is, in fact, kosher. We can take this concept a step further. Even after determining that our food is kosher, we should strive to fulfill the requirement, "You shall be holy," (*Vayikra* 19:2), which *Ramban* understands to mean, "Sanctify yourself in that which is permissible to you." As *Ramban* points out, a person can be in full technical compliance with Torah law and yet be vulgar and indulgent.

In the words of Rabbi Abraham J. Twerski:

Perhaps never before in Jewish history was *Ramban's* teaching as relevant as in modern times. Until fairly recently, people who observed *kashrus* had, as a rule, a rather austere diet. I recall as a child that there were two types of wine available: sweet wine and wine without sugar, primarily used by people who had to restrict their sugar intake. Kosher wines were not for the connoisseur. How different things are today, with a variety of strictly kosher wines available that can satisfy even the most discriminating palate. The same is true of almost all foods, so that virtually every non-kosher product has a kosher counterpart,

(cont. on page 262)

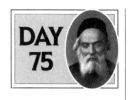
ט"ו כסלו

15 KISLEV / CYCLE 1

November 30, 2001
November 20, 2002
December 10, 2003
November 28, 2004
December 16, 2005

ט"ז ניסן

16 NISSAN / CYCLE 2

March 29, 2002
April 18, 2003
April 7, 2004
April 25, 2005
April 14, 2006

ט"ז אב

16 AV / CYCLE 3

July 25, 2002
August 14, 2003
August 3, 2004
August 21, 2005
August 10, 2006

◈ *The Way of Avraham*

SEFER SHEM OLAM — Chapter Ten:
"I set Hashem before Me" (cont.)

*I*n summation: A G-d-fearing Jew should never forget that Hashem's glory fills the earth and that he constantly stands before Him to carry out His will. When David said, "I have set Hashem before me always," his intention was, "I am forever mindful that I stand before Hashem to carry out His will."

This thought was the foundation of our forefathers' service of Hashem. Hashem told our forefather Avraham, "Walk before Me and be perfect" (Bereishis 17:1), meaning that Avraham should always be cognizant that he is in the presence of Hashem. Avraham fulfilled this directive as testified by his grandson Yaakov: "O G-d before Whom my forefathers Avraham and Yitzchak walked..." (Bereishis 48:15).

Our forefather Avraham's overriding attribute was *chesed* (kindness). Rabbi Yehudah Zev Segal explained that Avraham's benevolence was driven by his sense of mission as a servant of Hashem:

> People do kindness for a variety of reasons. Some are compassionate by nature, others may enjoy the feeling that results from helping someone else, while others may involve themselves in *chesed* simply because they

were brought up that way; helping others is to them a way of life.

Lot (Avraham's nephew) belonged to the latter group. He had spent years in the house of Avraham, where *chesed* was a way of life. Even after joining the community of Sodom, Lot did not lose the inclination toward *chesed* that had developed within him. So ingrained had this quality become that he was willing to take great personal risk for the sake of guests who were strangers.[1]

[By contrast], Avraham may have had an innate tendency toward *chesed*, but this was not the driving force behind his benevolence. Avraham strove to help his fellow man because he had come to recognize his Creator's existence and he perceived that G-d's purpose in creating this world was "to give of His goodness unto others" (*Derech Hashem* Ch. 2). Avraham realized that it is Hashem's will that man emulate His goodness. Hashem knows the needs and suffering of His every creation and provides for each according to his or her particular situation. As a parallel to this, Avraham perfected within himself the quality of נוֹשֵׂא בְּעוֹל עִם חֲבֵירוֹ, *sharing his friend's burden*. When Avraham would see a wayfarer coming down the road, he imagined himself as that hungry, weary, lonely individual. The way in which the wayfarer was welcomed reflected Avraham's unrelenting, incomparable pursuit of *chesed*.

> **Avraham was forever cognizant that he was in the presence of Hashem.**

(cont. on page 262)

---

1. See *Bereishis* Ch. 19.

ט"ז כסלו
16 KISLEV / CYCLE 1

December 1, 2001
November 21, 2002
December 11, 2003
November 29, 2004
December 17, 2005

י"ז ניסן
17 NISSAN / CYCLE 2

March 30, 2002
April 19, 2003
April 8, 2004
April 26, 2005
April 15, 2006

י"ז אב
17 AV / CYCLE 3

July 26, 2002
August 15, 2003
August 4, 2004
August 22, 2005
August 11, 2006

✍ *Hollow Words*

SEFER SHEM OLAM — Chapter Eleven:
Avoiding Contradictions in One's Life

*I*f we ponder our conduct and deeds, and measure them on the barometer of avodas Hashem (service of Hashem), we will find that many of them contradict our very own words.

Picture a man who stands in shul during Shacharis, reciting aloud with the congregation, "We shall sanctify Your Name in this world, just as they sanctify it in Heaven above..." As he exits the shul at the prayers' conclusion, someone thoughtlessly says something insulting. The man is enraged and his tongue becomes like a fiery flame. He becomes oblivious to the fact that we are constantly in Hashem's Presence, and his mouth, which only minutes earlier was engaged in heartfelt prayer, is now spewing forth words of lashon hara, rechilus, strife, and mockery.

On other occasions after leaving shul, he becomes involved in business practices which touch on robbery and deceit. Then, after a few hours of activity, he returns to the synagogue to once again wrap himself in angel's garb and declare, "We shall sanctify Your Name in this world, just as they sanctify it in Heaven above..." In other words, he spends his day changing roles again and again, from a man whose prayers suggest a comparison between himself and the Heavenly angels, to a lowly person whose behavior is nothing short of disgraceful.

Is it conceivable that his prayers will gain acceptance before Hashem? He is like a king's minister who, each day after leaving the palace, earns money shoveling away heaps of garbage. Upon hearing of this, the king becomes incensed. "If you can lower yourself to do such work after having left my palace, then obviously you do not appreciate what a privilege it is to serve me. Remove your royal garb and I will award your position to someone more worthy!"

The same person who compares himself to an angel, can minutes later engage in shameful behavior.

The Chofetz Chaim would note a similar contradiction regarding Torah study. Each morning we implore Hashem, "Our Father, merciful Father, Who acts mercifully, have mercy upon us, instill understanding in our hearts to understand and elucidate, to listen, learn, teach, safeguard, perform and fulfill all the words of Your Torah's teachings with love.." Yet after completing their morning prayers, many do not even enter a *beis midrash* to attempt to study Torah and realize the fulfillment of their prayer. Instead, they waste their time preoccupied with all sorts of non-essentials.

The Chofetz Chaim likens this to a poor man who begs a rich man for a loan. The rich man says, "I have

(cont. on page 263)

16 Kislev — Sara Verschleisser ע"ה לע"נ שרה רוזא בת משה לייב ע"ה
In loving memory of a wife, mother, grandmother and great-grandmother

17 Nisssan — May today's learning be a זכות for all my children.
Dedicated by a loving parent

17 Av — Ernest Grossberger לע"נ שמואל אליהו בן חנניה יום טוב ליפא ז"ל
Dedicated by Pinchus & Judy Friedman and family

DAY 77

🔊 Service of the Heart?

י"ז כסלו

17 KISLEV / CYCLE 1

December 2, 2001
November 22, 2002
December 12, 2003
November 30, 2004
December 18, 2005

י"ח ניסן

18 NISSAN / CYCLE 2

March 31, 2002
April 20, 2003
April 9, 2004
April 27, 2005
April 16, 2006

י"ח אב

18 AV / CYCLE 3

July 27, 2002
August 16, 2003
August 5, 2004
August 23, 2005
August 12, 2006

SEFER SHEM OLAM — Chapter Eleven:
Avoiding Contradictions in One's Life (cont.)

*I*t is unfortunate that we do not fully appreciate the great privilege of being a part of the Chosen Nation, of serving the awesome and all-powerful King, Whose glory and sanctity are beyond our comprehension. This lack of recognition is the underlying cause of our warped sense of priorities, for our tendency to engage in frivolous pursuits even after having devoted time to Torah study, tefillah and other spiritual accomplishments. If we would have proper recognition of who we are and Who we serve, we would not hurl ourselves "from a high roof to a deep pit,'" as we fluctuate between spiritual striving and earthly materialism.

What is the cause of this lack of recognition? How is it that thrice daily we declare in our tefillos that our service of Hashem on earth parallels that of the angels Above, and yet we give little or no thought to what we ourselves say? Undoubtedly, this is because we are too preoccupied with our mundane affairs, to the point that our prayers are mere lip service and we forget completely about our true purpose in life. We pray out of habit, in the same way that we have done since our youth, with little or no thought as to what we are saying and to Whom we are saying it.

But this is wrong. The proper way is as stated in Shulchan Aruch (Orach Chaim

93:1), to pause for at least a bit before begin-ning to pray, in order to rid our minds of mundane thoughts and focus on what we are about to do — to stand before our Creator and plead for ourselves and for our people.

Chovos HaLevavos (*Shaar Cheshbon HaNefesh* 3:9) gives detailed instructions on how to prepare for prayer:

One must disengage himself from this world and free his mind of any thought which will distract his attention from prayer. One should take to heart seriously that he stands before his Maker, and carefully choose both the words and the themes he intends to contemplate.

Understand full well that the words of prayer enunciated by the mouth are merely the shell. The heart's meditation upon these words is the inner kernel. Words of prayer are like a body, while עִיּוּן הַלֵב, *meditation of the heart,* is its soul. One who prays only with his tongue while his mind wanders, resembles an empty body, a husk devoid of a kernel. Such a person is compared to the servant whose master had just returned home from a journey. The servant sent his children to greet the master, while he himself ignored the master's pres-ence. The master was infuriated by this wan-ton disrespect. Similarly, if the heart sends the body and the mouth to greet the Almighty in prayer, but the heart turns its attention else-where, G-d will surely be displeased.

> **Words of prayer are like a body, while meditation of the heart is its soul.**

---
1. An expression borrowed from *Chagigah* 5a.

י"ח כסלו
18 KISLEV / CYCLE 1

December 3, 2001
November 23, 2002
December 13, 2003
December 1, 2004
December 19, 2005

י"ט ניסן
19 NISSAN / CYCLE 2

April 1, 2002
April 21, 2003
April 10, 2004
April 28, 2005
April 17, 2006

י"ט אב
19 AV / CYCLE 3

July 28, 2002
August 17, 2003
August 6, 2004
August 24, 2005
August 13, 2006

❧ An Audience with the King

SEFER SHEM OLAM — Chapter Eleven:
Avoiding Contradictions in One's Life (cont.)

*W*e have become so preoccupied with our earthly existence that we have lost touch with our spiritual emotions.

Imagine the excitement of a person who has been granted an audience with a mighty king. The king is impressed by the man's wise insight and summons his scribe to record his visitor's every word. The man goes home in a state of euphoria. All his problems are forgotten. Wherever he goes he tells people, "Did you hear? I was granted an audience with the king — and he cherished my every word! He had his personal scribe record everything I said." Twenty years later, when meeting old friends at get-togethers, the man proudly tells of that memorable meeting with the king.

What does one gain from having found favor in the king's eyes? The king cannot extend his visitor's life by even a second. At most, he may offer him a prestigious position. In all probability, his reward will be nothing more than the honor derived from having his words recorded by the king's scribe.

Tell me, my brother, does this thought enter your mind once a week, or once a month, or at least once a year?

Now, consider: When a Jew performs a mitzvah and prefaces it with a blessing in which he speaks directly to Hashem ["Blessed are You, Hashem..."] in the way that one addresses his friend; or when he speaks words of Torah learning, surely Hashem's Presence is manifest there, as it is written, "...wherever I permit My Name to be mentioned, I will come to you and bless you" (Shemos 20:21). And surely such efforts find favor in Hashem's eyes and are recorded above, as it is written, "...and a book of remembrance was written before Him for those who fear Hashem and give thought to His Name" (Malachi 3:16). His efforts are announced before myriads of Heavenly angels, for as Zohar states, the angel Gavriel announces man's deeds each night. His efforts in serving the King of kings will earn him eternal praise and splendor, and may extend his life on this world or save him from suffering.

One should be filled with boundless joy when performing a mitzvah and after completing it successfully. That a mere mortal can communicate with G-d like one of the Heavenly beings is suffcient reason to shed tears of joy and to humble oneself before Him in accepting to uphold His Torah with all one's soul and resources.

That a mere mortal can communicate with G-d is sufficient reason to shed tears of joy.

(cont. on page 263)

DAY 79

י"ט כסלו
19 KISLEV / CYCLE 1
December 4, 2001
November 24, 2002
December 14, 2003
December 2, 2004
December 20, 2005

כ ניסן
20 NISSAN / CYCLE 2
April 2, 2002
April 22, 2003
April 11, 2004
April 29, 2005
April 18, 2006

כ אב
20 AV / CYCLE 3
July 29, 2002
August 18, 2003
August 7, 2004
August 25, 2005
August 14, 2006

❧ Serve Hashem with Joy

SEFER SHEM OLAM — Chapter Eleven:
Avoiding Contradictions in One's Life (cont.)

*I*n the Torah's second Tochachah (Admonition) passage, we are told a primary reason for the catastrophies which are detailed there: *"...because you did not serve Hashem, your G-d, amid gladness and goodness of heart, when everything was abundant" (Devarim 21:47)*. As the commentators explain, the opportunity to serve Hashem should fill one's heart with joy more than any earthly pleasure.

There is a tradition that the Arizal merited Ruach HaKodesh (Divine Inspiration) because of his joy when performing a mitzvah, which was greater than that which the soul experiences in Gan Eden (the Garden of Eden). While at first glance this may seem incomprehensible, we can understand it quite easily.

In this world, the more scarce an item is, the greater its value. Iron, which is found in abundance, is cheaper than copper, which is somewhat scarce. Gold is more precious than silver, but less precious than diamonds.

Our Sages teach that one hour of spiritual bliss in the World to Come is greater than an entire life on this world (Avos 4:22). Nevertheless, as far as the soul is concerned, such pleasure is not rare at all. Before descending to this world, the soul resides in the Treasury of Souls before the Heavenly

Throne, where it basks in the glory of the Shechinah (Divine Presence). When a person's life on this world ends, the soul returns Heavenward to delight in Hashem's Presence for eternity. By contrast, the time which we are allotted to perform Hashem's mitzvos is short, for it is only during one's lifetime on this world that such opportunities exist.

When a soul leaves this world and ascends Above, it sees the glory of Hashem surrounded by countless angels, who praise and sanctify His Name with great joy. The soul also sees that when Hashem utters a command to His angels, they hearken to fulfill His will in an instant, joyfully and without any delay. The soul, too, yearns to once again serve as Hashem's emissary, as it did on this world for so many years — but its wish is not granted. In Heaven, only the angels have this privilege. Even if the soul would be willing to forfeit its entire portion in the World to Come for such an opportunity, its wish would be denied.

It is, therefore, not difficult at all to understand the Arizal's joy when performing a mitzvah. Studying Torah or fulfilling any other mitzvah on this world truly is more precious than all earthly pleasures combined. And it is something which can be accomplished only on this world. Thus do our Sages teach: "Better one hour of repentance and good deeds in this world than the entire life of the World to Come" (Avos 4:22).

In Heaven, the soul yearns to serve as Hashem's emissary, as it did on this world.

כ כסלו
20 KISLEV / CYCLE 1

December 5, 2001
November 25, 2002
December 15, 2003
December 3, 2004
December 21, 2005

כ"א ניסן
21 NISSAN / CYCLE 2

April 3, 2002
April 23, 2003
April 12, 2004
April 30, 2005
April 19, 2006

כ"א אב
21 AV / CYCLE 3

July 30, 2002
August 19, 2003
August 8, 2004
August 26, 2005
August 15, 2006

✍ *A Proper Perception*

SEFER SHEM OLAM — Chapter Eleven:
Avoiding Contradictions in One's Life (cont.)

The reason why we lack proper perception of the value of doing mitzvos on this world is that we lack proper perception of the greatness and sanctity of Hashem. Even Moshe Rabbeinu, the greatest of all prophets who attained the forty-ninth level of wisdom, declared, "You have begun to show Your servant Your greatness..." (Devarim 3:24). Were we to perceive this properly, we would naturally realize how precious is our lot, that we merit to serve the King of Glory. This is the meaning of the mishnah, "Know before Whom you toil" (Avos 2:19).

At the tenth anniversary dinner of *Shuvu*, which provides thousands of Russian immigrant children in Israel with a Torah education, the Guest of Honor was Rabbi Abraham Pam, the organization's revered founder and leader. He delivered an emotional address at what would be his last *Shuvu* dinner; he passed away on 28 Menachem Av, 5761. Rabbi Pam began with the following thought:

"On *Shalosh Regalim* (the Three Festivals), we recite a special *tefillah* (prayer) upon opening the *Aron Kodesh* (Holy Ark) to take out the *Sefer Torah*, a *tefillah* which contains a number of requests. One of them is: שֶׁתְּזַכֵּנוּ לַעֲשׂוֹת מַעֲשִׂים טוֹבִים בְּעֵינֶיךָ, meaning, that Hashem should grant us the privilege to do good deeds.

"*Ribono shel Olam*," cried Rabbi Pam, "how can I thank You for giving me the *daas* (wisdom) to initiate and to launch *Shuvu*? *With what shall I approach Hashem [in appreciation], humble myself before G-d on high?*[1] How can I express even a fraction of my gratitude to *HaKadosh Baruch Hu* for granting me such a *zechus* (privilege) and for granting the entire *Shuvu* family such a *zechus*!"

Were we to perceive Hashem's greatness properly, we would realize how precious is our lot.

✌︎⟡✌︎

Someone once accompanied Rabbi Pam on his walk home from yeshivah. As they approached the street on which Rabbi Pam lived, he turned to cross the street in the opposite direction. "I have to mail a letter," he explained, motioning toward the mail box across the street. "I'm going that way anyway," his companion said. "I would be happy to mail the letter for the *Rosh Yeshivah*."

"Thank you," Rabbi Pam replied, "but it's a *tzedakah* envelope. I would rather do the *mitzvah* myself."

In the *Avinu Malkeinu* prayer which we recite during the High Holy days, we beseech Hashem:

אָבִינוּ מַלְכֵּנוּ, כָּתְבֵנוּ בְּסֵפֶר זְכִיּוֹת
Our Father, our King, inscribe us in the book of merits.

The meaning of this prayer[2] is: "Hashem, please grant me the opportunity to accrue *zechuyos* (merits) through the performance of *mitzvos*."

---

1. From *Michah* 6:6.
2. As explained by Rabbi Matisyahu Salomon and Rabbi Moshe Wolfson.

כ"א כסלו
21 KISLEV / CYCLE 1

December 6, 2001
November 26, 2002
December 16, 2003
December 4, 2004
December 22, 2005

כ"ב ניסן
22 NISSAN / CYCLE 2

April 4, 2002
April 24, 2003
April 13, 2004
May 1, 2005
April 20, 2006

כ"ב אב
22 AV / CYCLE 3

July 31, 2002
August 20, 2003
August 9, 2004
August 27, 2005
August 16, 2006

❧ *A Time to Hope*

SEFER SHEM OLAM — Chapter Twelve:
The Birthpangs of Mashiach

We are living in times when the sufferings of our people are great. One may wonder: Why has Hashem brought all this upon us and where is it all leading?

In fact, the increase in suffering is in itself a source for at least partial consolation. It is well known that the Gra (Gaon R' Eliyahu, the Vilna Gaon) wrote that this exile is likened to a pregnancy and the period preceding Mashiach's arrival is like the pangs of childbirth. This is why the Talmud refers to the sufferings of this last period as "the birthpangs of Mashiach" (Shabbos 118a).

Now, when a woman is on the verge of giving birth and the pains become so strong that they seem unbearable, the nurse will comfort her by saying, "If the pain is so intense, then it will not last much longer — you will soon give birth." This is exactly our situation in exile. As long as the travails of exile were relatively "bearable," we had reason to be concerned that it had not yet reached its final stages. However, now that the sufferings have multiplied to a point where they have become unbearable, we can be hopeful that soon, Hashem will bring salvation through the coming of Mashiach.

As our Sages teach (Sanhedrin 98a): "If you see a generation upon which numerous troubles come like a river, expect him [the Mashiach], as it is written, 'For distress shall come like a river...' (Yeshayahu 59:19) and next to that verse it is written, 'A redeemer shall come to Zion.' "

Often there is a break in the pangs of childbirth, which allows the mother to regain some strength before the next pains set in. This exactly describes the period before Mashiach, when the Jewish people sometimes experience somewhat of an easing of their suffering before new travails occur.

When the sufferings seem unbearable, we can be hopeful that Redemption is near.

In his memoirs, the Chofetz Chaim's son, R' Aryeh Leib *HaKohen* Kagan, wrote:

Many of the stories which abound concerning the way in which my father awaited the arrival of *Mashiach* are exaggerated. In truth, however, none of these exaggerations capture the essence of his unshakable faith in *Mashiach's* ultimate arrival. For his faith was not based on mere allusions or even on Aggadic teachings which often are obscure and lend themselves to various interpretations. Rather, it was based on the clearly expressed words of the Prophets, and even more so, the words of the *Chumash*.

Virtually all his life, my father kept a one-volume *Tanach* in his *tallis* bag. Never did he

(cont. on page 264)

כ"ב כסלו
22 KISLEV / CYCLE 1

December 7, 2001
November 27, 2002
December 17, 2003
December 5, 2004
December 23, 2005

כ"ג ניסן
23 NISSAN / CYCLE 2

April 5, 2002
April 25, 2003
April 14, 2004
May 2, 2005
April 21, 2006

כ"ג אב
23 AV / CYCLE 3

August 1, 2002
August 21, 2003
August 10, 2004
August 28, 2005
August 17, 2006

❧ *The Footsteps of Mashiach*

SEFER SHEM OLAM — Chapter Twelve:
The Birthpangs of Mashiach (cont.)

That which the Talmud predicts (Sanhedrin Ch. 11) will take place prior to Mashiach's arrival has, in fact, occurred in our times. The same is true of the predictions in the final mishnah of Masechta Sotah.

The eleventh chapter of *Masechta Sanhedrin* is replete with statements concerning the period preceding *Mashiach's* arrival. One passage there (*Sanhedrin* 97a) is similar to the concluding *Mishnah* of *Masechta Sotah* to which the Chofetz Chaim referred:

> With the footsteps of *Mashiach* insolence will increase, and inflation will soar, the vine will give its fruit but wine will be dear, and the government will turn to heresy, and there will be no rebuke, the places of meeting will be used for immorality, and the Galilee will be destroyed and the Gavlan desolated, and the border dwellers will wander about from city to city, but will not be pitied, the knowledge of scholars will be lost, those who fear sin will be despised, and the truth will be hidden; youths will shame old men and old men will stand up for youngsters; [it will be a time when] "a son shames his father, a daughter rebels against her mother, a daughter-in-law

against her mother-in-law, [and] a man's enemies are the members of his household" (*Michah* 7:6); the face of the generation will be like the face of the dog [i.e. without shame — *Rashi*]; [and] the son is not ashamed before his father. On whom can we rely? [Only] on our Father in Heaven (*Mishnah Sotah* 9:15).

On whom can we rely? [Only] on our Father in Heaven. This means that before *Mashiach's* arrival, the Jewish people will find themselves in a position so precarious that *everyone* will come to the realization that only Hashem can rescue us from our plight (heard from *Rabbi Moshe Wolfson*).

As the Jews headed toward the Sea of Reeds at the time of the Exodus, they found themselves trapped on all sides (see *Shemos* Ch. 14) and they cried out in prayer to Hashem. *Rashi* (citing *Mechilta* and *Tanchuma*) writes: "They adopted the craft of their forefathers," meaning that they prayed the way Avraham, Yitzchak and Yaakov would pray — with a feeling and awareness that without Hashem's intervention they were totally lost. This is what Hashem had been waiting for and He immediately commanded Moshe: "Speak to the Children of Israel and let them journey!" (ibid. v. 15). It is this sort of recognition which the Jewish people will need to demonstrate as a prelude to the Final Redemption (based on the thoughts of *Rabbi Yeruchom Levovitz*).

On whom can we rely? On our Father in Heaven.

כ"ג כסלו
23 KISLEV / CYCLE 1

December 8, 2001
November 28, 2002
December 18, 2003
December 6, 2004
December 24, 2005

כ"ד ניסן
24 NISSAN / CYCLE 2

April 6, 2002
April 26, 2003
April 15, 2004
May 3, 2005
April 22, 2006

כ"ד אב
24 AV / CYCLE 3

August 2, 2002
August 22, 2003
August 11, 2004
August 29, 2005
August 18, 2006

✑ *Hastening the Redemption*

SEFER SHEM OLAM — Chapter Twelve:
Birthpangs of Mashiach (cont.)

*W*e cannot know exactly when the Final Redemption will occur. The duration of the exile following the destruction of the First Beis HaMikdash was explicitly stated by the prophet, "When seventy years are completed for Babylon, I shall remember you" (Yirmiyahu 29:10). Nevertheless, as recorded in the Talmud,[1] many calculated the seventy years and erred. Even the righteous Daniel erred as to when the seventy years began. Certainly no one can know the end of the current exile, for its conclusion has been concealed from us. However, the sufferings of our time indicate that it is drawing to a close.

This is how it was in Egypt; the depth of suffering hastened the redemption. Our forefather Avraham had been told that his descendants would be strangers in a land not their own for four hundred years (Bereishis 15:13), but Hashem calculated the exile as beginning with the birth of Yitzchak. The depths of the Jews' suffering awakened Divine mercy so that the redemption was hastened and their stay in Egypt (from the time Yaakov descended there with *his family) lasted two hundred ten years. Included in those years was the period of Yosef's rule over Egypt when the Jews enjoyed a peaceful existence.*

Over the past eight hundred years, the Jewish people have suffered greatly. Surely this is cause for hope that the exile will not last much longer. It is quite possible that we have already entered the period of "the birthpangs of Mashiach." In Egypt, even after the Jews were informed that the time of redemption had arrived, the situation got worse before it improved. This can explain the situation in which we find ourselves today.

This is how it was in Egypt; the depth of suffering hastened the redemption.

The Chofetz Chaim possessed not only perfect *emunah* (faith), but also a degree of *Ruach HaKodesh* (Divine Inspiration), as can be seen from the following episode, related by Rabbi Shimon Schwab,[2] who spent a memorable Shabbos in Radin in the company of the Chofetz Chaim in 1930:

> An incident took place that Shabbos which gave me a glimpse into the measure of the man. Had I not witnessed it myself, I would not have believed it...
>
> The Chofetz Chaim had eaten a frugal *Shalosh Seudos*... He said, "It's time to *bentch* (recite *Bircas HaMazon*)," and he started to *bentch*, like a simple Jew, saying one word at

(cont. on page 264)

---

1. See *Megillah* 11b.
2. From an address by Rabbi Schwab published in *The Jewish Observer* (January 1984).

23 Kislev — Today's learning is dedicated as a זכות for כלל ישראל.

24 Nissan — Chesna Coren לע"נ ג'עסנא בת יעקב וליקא ע"ה
Dedicated by the Dear family

24 Av — William Schubin לע"נ זאב בן מרדכי יצחק ז"ל
May today's learning be a זכות for his נשמה.

כ״ד כסלו
24 KISLEV / CYCLE 1

December 9, 2001
November 29, 2002
December 19, 2003
December 7, 2004
December 25, 2005

כ״ה ניסן
25 NISSAN / CYCLE 2

April 7, 2002
April 27, 2003
April 16, 2004
May 4, 2005
April 23, 2006

כ״ה אב
25 AV / CYCLE 3

August 3, 2002
August 23, 2003
August 12, 2004
August 30, 2005
August 19, 2006

✑ *Suffering Atones*

SEFER SHEM OLAM — Chapter Twelve:
The Birthpangs of Mashiach (cont.)

You may be wondering: Why must the Jewish people endure so much suffering in order to merit redemption? Is it not possible to redeem us without so much pain and distress? There are many answers to this question. Let us begin with the following:

The prophet states (Yoel 4:2) that at the time of the Redemption, Hashem will gather the other nations at the Valley of Yehoshaphat and judge them for their mistreatment of His beloved people during the two millenium of exile. The gentiles will surely respond that the Jewish people should also be brought to judgment for all their sins. Hashem, therefore, is purifying us now through various tests and sufferings, so that when the time of Redemption comes, we will be truly deserving of it, for we will have atoned for all our sins through our suffering. As the prophet states: "You alone did I know from among all the families of the earth; therefore I will visit upon you all of your sins" (Amos 3:2). Our Sages explain this with a parable:

> *A person lends money to two people, one whom he loves and one whom he*

despises. From his friend he exacts payment little by little so that it should not have too great an effect on him financially. From his enemy he demands the entire payment at one time; and when payment time arrives, he collects it mercilessly.

So, too, Hashem grants the other nations the freedom to do as they choose until they reach "the limits of His endurance" and He exacts punishment without mercy. From the Jewish people, however, He exacts punishment on an ongoing basis so that the scope of their punishment should be limited (Based on Avodah Zara 4a).

The suffering of the Jewish people will make them truly deserving of redemption.

Thus, whereas other nations have achieved great prosperity and prestige and then passed from the stage of history, the Jewish people have undergone sufferings of epic proportions but still exist and will exist forever.

In the words of Rabbi Simchah Wasserman:

In the Torah portion of *Haazinu* (*Devarim* Ch. 32), Hashem tells Moshe *Rabbeinu* that the people will go through many kinds of experiences, many of them very unpleasant, and they will wonder why these things are happening. Hashem commands Moshe to tell the people the song of *Haazinu*: "Tell them that this song will explain everything.

(cont. on page 264)

לע"נ שלמה יעקב בן יונתן ז"ל — **24 Kislev**
לע"נ שטאתה רחל בת אברהם הכהן ע"ה
25 Nissan — Freida Magid ע"ה לע"נ פריידא בת יצחק ע"ה
Dedicated by her children, Zalman & Hillel Magid and families
25 Av —

כ"ה כסלו
25 KISLEV / CYCLE 1
December 10, 2001
November 30, 2002
December 20, 2003
December 8, 2004
December 26, 2005

כ"ו ניסן
26 NISSAN / CYCLE 2
April 8, 2002
April 28, 2003
April 17, 2004
May 5, 2005
April 24, 2006

כ"ו אב
26 AV / CYCLE 3
August 4, 2002
August 24, 2003
August 13, 2004
August 31, 2005
August 20, 2006

⮦ *Bread of Humiliation*

SEFER SHEM OLAM — Chapter Twelve:
The Birthpangs of Mashiach (cont.)

There is another quite obvious reason for the trials and travails which the Jewish people have endured during this long and difficult exile.

A fundamental principle of Jewish belief is that a person is placed on this world to accrue merit through fulfillment of Torah and mitzvos in order to earn the eternal reward of the World to Come. Hashem, Whose goodness is beyond our comprehension, could have granted the neshamah this spiritual pleasure without sending it down to this lowly world. However, as recorded in earlier works, this would have been נַהֲמָא דְכִסוּפָא, bread of humiliation. The soul would feel shamed to receive a magnanimous gift which it did not earn.

Therefore, Hashem sends the soul down to this world, clothes it in a physical form and tests it by implanting within it tendencies such as passion, anger and jealousy, which attempt to distract it from its lofty mission. The soul's sanctity can light the way of truth so that it can overcome these destructive forces and persevere. This battle is a difficult one and it lasts one's entire lifetime. Therefore, when after its life on this earth, the soul emerges victorious with its mission accomplished, it can ascend to receive its reward without any sense of shame.

This discussion continues in the next segment. The concept which the Chofetz Chaim discusses here is the focus of the opening chapter of *Mesilas Yesharim*, the ethical classic by R' Moshe Chaim Luzzato:

> ...Only union with G-d constitutes true perfection, as King David said, "But as for me, the nearness of G-d is my good" (*Tehillim* 73:28) and "One thing I asked of Hashem, that I shall seek: to dwell in the house of Hashem all the days of my life" (ibid. 27:4). This alone is the true good and anything aside from this which people may consider good is nothing but deceptive worthlessness. For a person to obtain the true good it is appropriate that he first labor and persevere in his efforts to acquire it by means of those actions which will achieve this end. These actions are the performance of *mitzvos*.
>
> G-d put man in a place where there are many factors which can distract him [from his mission]. These are the physical desires, which, if a person indulges in them, cause him to progressively distance himself from the true good. Thus, man is actually placed in the midst of a raging battle, because everything that he will encounter in the world, whether good or bad, is a test for a person.

(cont. on page 265)

The soul would feel shamed to receive a magnanimous gift which it did not earn.

לזכות שרה ברכה בת דינה רבקה שתחי׳ — **25 Kislev**

26 Nissan — Boruch Gerstenblit לע״נ ברוך בן יהושע ז״ל
Dedicated by his children and grandchildren

26 Av —

כ"ו כסלו
26 KISLEV / CYCLE 1

December 11, 2001
December 1, 2002
December 21, 2003
December 9, 2004
December 27, 2005

כ"ז ניסן
27 NISSAN / CYCLE 2

April 9, 2002
April 29, 2003
April 18, 2004
May 6, 2005
April 25, 2006

כ"ז אב
27 AV / CYCLE 3

August 5, 2002
August 25, 2003
August 14, 2004
September 1, 2005
August 21, 2006

✎ *A Nation of Prophets*

SEFER SHEM OLAM — Chapter Twelve:
The Birthpangs of Mashiach (cont.)

*H*ashem has promised the Jewish people that after the coming of Mashiach, everyone will merit to learn Torah directly from Him, just as we merited to hear the first two of the Ten Commandments directly from Him at Sinai. At that glorious time, all Jews will ascend to the level of prophets, as it is written, "And it will be after this, I will pour out My spirit upon all flesh, and your sons and daughters shall prophesy; your elders shall dream, your young men shall see visions" (Yoel 3:1).

This, however, presents a problem which we can explain by way of a parable. If a worker was expecting a ruble for a day's work and instead was given two rubles by his employer, he would probably be quite pleased with himself. He would assume that the employer was very pleased with his work and decided to reward him by doubling his wages. However, such would not be the case if the employer were to give him a thousand rubles instead of one. In this case, the worker would view the money as a gift and would quite likely be uncomfortable accepting it. This is the נַהֲמָא דְכִסוּפָא, *bread of humiliation*, of which we spoke above.

We can apply this to our own situation. We know that we are light years away from the spiritual greatness of Rishonim (Early Commentators) such as Rif, Rambam and others of that period. We are far, far more removed from the levels of the Tanaaim (Sages of the Mishnah) and even more so from that of the Anshei Knesses HaGedolah (Men of the Great Assembly) led by Ezra the Scribe. Were we to live a thousand years and never once veer from the path of Hashem and His Torah, we could not attain the level of prophecy through our own merit. How, then, will we be able to comfortably attain this level in the End of Days without feeling that it is bread of humiliation?

This is the secret of this long exile, in which Hashem has concealed His Presence from us. Our enemies rise up against us and from all sides we are surrounded by suffering and pain. Despite all this, we cling faithfully to the mitzvos and our love of Torah does not wane. Many of our brethren have endured enormous hardship for the sake of Shabbos observance, happily forgoing financial opportunities for the sake of this cornerstone of Jewish belief. Others have been denied monetary improvement because of their refusal to socialize with gentile counterparts and join them at parties or the like. Throughout the exile, we have borne shame, scorne and insults because of our beliefs.

Despite our suffering, we cling faithfully to the mitzvos and our love of Torah does not wane.

(cont. on page 265)

26 Kislev — רפואה שלמה לחי לאה מלכה בת שרה בתושחי"י
Dedicated by Leah & Jay Starkman and family

27 Nissan — Ella Zalmanson ע"ה לע"נ אלה בת שלמה ורחל
Dedicated by Dalit & James Burgess

27 Av — Philip Blum לע"נ שרגא פייוול בן דוב בער ז"ל
Dedicated by his great nephew, Mayer Blum

כ"ז כסלו
27 KISLEV / CYCLE 1

December 12, 2001
December 2, 2002
December 22, 2003
December 10, 2004
December 28, 2005

כ"ח ניסן
28 NISSAN / CYCLE 2

April 10, 2002
April 30, 2003
April 19, 2004
May 7, 2005
April 26, 2006

כ"ח אב
28 AV / CYCLE 3

August 6, 2002
August 26, 2003
August 15, 2004
September 2, 2005
August 22, 2006

✑ *The Time is Now*

SEFER SHEM OLAM — Chapter Twelve:
The Birthpangs of Mashiach (cont.)

*T*o the verse (Koheles 12:1), "So remember your Creator in the days of your youth before... those years arrive of which you will say, 'I have no pleasure in them,' " our Sages comment: "These are the days of Mashiach when there will be no opportunity to acquire merit or liability" (Shabbos 151b). Therefore, it is crucial that we strengthen ourselves now in fulfillment of Torah and mitzvos, before Mashiach arrives. For at that time, when the people of Hashem will be an object of glory before the world and all the nations will call out in Hashem's Name — what sort of test will it be to serve Hashem? Each person's spiritual level and reward hinges primarily on his accomplishments prior to Mashiach's arrival.

Tana D'Vei Eliyahu states: "In the future, the Holy One, Blessed is He, will sit in His great study hall in Jerusalem, and all the tzaddikim of the world will sit before Him, and to each He will grant a radiant countenance in proportion to the Torah which he has attained."

The Chofetz Chaim once explained the proliferation of immorality and corruption before *Mashiach's* arrival as consistent with a natural phenomenon: When a force is on the threshhold of destruction, it gathers strength for several moments before it dies out forever. For example, before a candle burns out, its flame shoots up one final time... And so it is regarding the world situation at the End of Days. Zechariah prophesied that when *Mashiach* arrives, "...[G-d] will remove the spirit of impurity from the land" (*Zechariah* 13:2). Therefore, the forces of impurity attack with renewed strength prior to *Mashiach's* arrival.

Rabbi Avraham Pam noted: the unprecedented power these forces have shown in recent years — infinitely more so than in the time of the Chofetz Chaim — indicates that they are mustering their final strength before their obliteration. This further explains why *now* is the time to strengthen oneself in Torah and *mitzvos*. The arrival of *Mashiach* will signal the destruction of the Evil Inclination and as explained above (Day 85), man's purpose in this world is to persevere in his struggle to overcome this inclination.

The twelfth of the Thirteen Principles of Faith as formulated by *Rambam* is:

> I believe with perfect faith in the coming of *Mashiach*, and even though he may delay, nevertheless I anticipate every day that he will come.

In other words, anticipating *Mashiach's* arrival is a basic obligation incumbent upon every Jew. In his code, Rambam states unequivocally: "Whoever does not believe in *Mashiach* or does not await his arrival, not only negates the validity of the prophets, but also denies the authenticity of the Torah and Moshe *Rabbeinu*."

Internalizing this truth should inspire us to strengthen our service of Hashem so that we will be spiritually prepared to greet *Mashiach*, possibly tomorrow and hopefully in the very near future.

Each person's spiritual reward hinges primarily on his accomplishments prior to Mashiach's arrival.

27 Kislev — Alex Missry לע״נ אליהו בן בוליסה ז״ל
Dedicated by Mr. & Mrs. David M. Gindi, Mr. & Mrs. Morris D. Gindi, and families

28 Nissan — Today's learning has been dedicated as a z'chus for Victor Salem and family.

28 Av — Jackie Wiesner זכות חנה בת עטא שתחי׳
Dedicated by Dov, Debby, and grandchildren

כ״ח כסלו
28 KISLEV / CYCLE 1
December 13, 2001
December 3, 2002
December 23, 2003
December 11, 2004
December 29, 2005

כ״ט ניסן
29 NISSAN / CYCLE 2
April 11, 2002
May 1, 2003
April 20, 2004
May 8, 2005
April 27, 2006

כ״ט אב
29 AV / CYCLE 3
August 7, 2002
August 27, 2003
August 16, 2004
September 3, 2005
August 23, 2006

❧ Two Forms of Redemption

SEFER SHEM OLAM — Chapter Thirteen:
The Birthpangs of Mashiach — II

*T*he Prophet states: אֲנִי ה׳ בְּעִתָּהּ אֲחִישֶׁנָּה, *I, Hashem, in its time I will hasten it (Yeshayahu 60:22), to which the Talmud comments:*

> *R' Yehoshua ben Levi noted a contradiction: On the one hand it is written* בְּעִתָּהּ, *in its time, which implies that the Redemption will occur at its preordained time. But on the other hand it is written* אֲחִישֶׁנָּה, *I will hasten it, which implies that Hashem will bring the Redemption before its preordained time.*
>
> *The answer to this is: If the Jews are deserving, Hashem will hasten it; if they are not deserving, the Redemption will come in its time (Sanhedrin 98a).*

Thus, Mashiach can appear at any time, so we should never despair of his imminent arrival. Do not wonder: How is it possible that earlier generations which were far superior to us did not merit the Redemption, yet we in our lowly state will merit it? We can answer this by citing a law in the Torah.

In a passage dealing with Jewish slaves (Vayikra, Chapter 25), the Torah states that if an impoverished Jew sold himself to a non-Jewish resident of Eretz Yisrael, there is a responsibility upon his relatives to redeem him. In doing so, the relatives may not deprive the gentile owner of his legitimate property rights. They must calculate how much the gentile paid for the slave, how much of that money has already been earned by the slave through his labor, and they must pay the difference. Obviously, the longer the slave has been working for his master, the less the relatives will have to pay.

Our redemption from exile is dependent on "spiritual currency."

For example: If the Jew sold himself to the gentile for six years for a sum of six hundred silver pieces, he would earn one hundred pieces for each year of work. If his relatives wished to redeem him after a year, they would have to pay the gentile five hundred pieces; if they would do so after five years, however, the cost would be only one hundred pieces.

Our redemption from this bitter exile is dependent, of course, on "spiritual currency." As Eliyahu the Prophet told R' Yehoshua ben Levi (Sanhedrin 98a), the hastening of the Redemption is directly related to our level of repentance and mitzvah performance: "Today, [Mashiach can arrive] if you heed His [Hashem's] voice!" (Tehillim 95:7). As each day, with its trials and tribulations, goes by, the merits of the Jewish people increase and we become ever more deserving of the dawn of redemption.

כ"ט כסלו*
*29 KISLEV / CYCLE 1

December 14, 2001
December 4, 2002
December 24, 2003
December 12, 2004*
December 30, 2005

ל ניסן
30 NISSAN / CYCLE 2

April 12, 2002
May 2, 2003
April 21, 2004
May 9, 2005
April 28, 2006

ל אב
30 AV / CYCLE 3

August 8, 2002
August 28, 2003
August 17, 2004
September 4, 2005
August 24, 2006

*When this month has
only 29 days, the lesson
for 30 Kislev should also
be studied today.

~ *Don't Despair*

SEFER SHEM OLAM — Chapter Thirteen:
The Birthpangs of Mashiach — II (cont.)

"*B*ecause of our sins we were exiled from our Land." These words, from the Mussaf Shemoneh Esrei of yom tov, indicate that the purpose of exile is to atone for our sins so that we may merit redemption. In advance of each exile in Jewish history, Hashem calculated exactly how long it needed to last before the people could be cleansed of their sins sufficiently. Hashem informed our forefather Avraham that the Egyptian exile would have to last four hundred years [beginning with the birth of Yitzchak]. The Babylonian exile was destined to last exactly seventy years: "Seventy years have been decreed upon your people and your holy city..." (Daniel 9:24). The current exile, too, has a fixed time [בְּעִתָּה] by which it must end. Though this date has not been revealed, the prophet did say that it would be long in coming:*

> *For many days the Children of Israel shall sit, with no king nor officer and no sacrifice nor pillar and no ephod and teraphim. Afterward the Children of Israel shall return and they shall seek Hashem their G-d and David their king, and they shall tremble for Hashem and*

for His goodness in the end of days (Hoshea 3:4-5).

Though earlier generations were superior to our own, they would have required an enormous degree of merit to have brought the Redemption in the way of אֲחִישֶׁנָה, I will hasten, that is, before the final, hidden date by which Mashiach must appear regardless of our collective merit. As with our analogy of the Jewish slave who sold himself to the gentile, the earlier the generation, the more merit they would have required. Thus, though we are not on the spiritual level of earlier generations, it is easier for us to merit Mashiach's arrival before the final date. The sufferings of our people in recent times may have left us with comparatively little work to do to be deserving of that glorious moment for which we all yearn.

The Torah mentions a case where a Jew actually sells himself into slavery to chop wood or draw water for a house of idolatry (Vayikra 25:47). Though the Jew was wrong for doing so (as it could well lead to his assimilation), Hashem took pity on him and decreed that if his relatives do not redeem him, then he must go free in any case when Yovel (the fiftieth year of the agricultural cycle) arrives. Surely, then, Hashem takes pity upon His beloved people, who sacrificed themselves for His sake during this exile, and He will ultimately redeem them.

Earlier genera-tions, though superior to our own, would have required enormous merit to have achieved the Redemp-tion.

29 Kislev — May today's learning be a ז"כות לרפואה שלמה רפאל יצחק בן דבורה עטל נ"י
30 Nissan — רפואה שלמה לנעמי בת חיה שתחי', בתושח"י
Dedicated by her family
30 Av — In memory of our father Myron Greenfield לע"נ מאיר בן ברוך ז"ל
Dedicated by his daughter and son-in-law, Sari & Ari Bacon and family

DAY 90

ל כסלו*
'30 KISLEV / CYCLE 1

December 15, 2001
December 5, 2002
December 25, 2003
December 31, 2005

א אייר
1 IYAR / CYCLE 2

April 13, 2002
May 3, 2003
April 22, 2004
May 10, 2005
April 29, 2006

א אלול
1 ELUL / CYCLE 3

August 9, 2002
August 29, 2003
August 18, 2004
September 5, 2005
August 25, 2006

When this month has only 29 days, the lesson for 30 Kislev should be learnt together with 29 Kislev.

❧ A Nation of Merit

SEFER SHEM OLAM — Chapter Thirteen:
The Birthpangs of Mashiach — II (cont.)

*O*ne may be thinking: Perhaps our nation lacks merit and we will have no choice but to wait until the Redemption of בְּעִתָּה, in its time, the final, hidden date by which Mashiach must arrive regardless of our collective merit?

This should not be cause for concern. Firstly, it is possible that the date of בְּעִתָּה, in its time, will be reached in our day. As already mentioned, the travails of our day point towards this. "If you see a generation upon which numerous troubles come like a river, expect him [the Mashiach], as it is written, 'For distress shall come like a river...' (Yeshayahu 59:19) and next to that verse it is written, 'A redeemer shall come to Zion.' " (Sanhedrin 98a).

Furthermore, to suggest that the Jewish nation is completely without merit is wrong and incomprehensible. Our people lived by the Torah in all situations under the most adverse conditions. Today, thank G-d, we live under the rule of a gracious government, but there were times, such as that of the Cossak uprisings of 1648-1649, when hundreds of thousands of our people died for the sanctification of His Name. We have suffered scorn and degradation, deprivation and hunger for remaining steadfast in our beliefs. Anyone with some knowledge of history knows that the death, persecution and suffering which our people has endured for clinging to its faith is indescribable. How can anyone dare suggest that the Jewish nation is without merit and that we will therefore have no choice but to wait until the final date of בְּעִתָּה, in its time, for this exile to end? Surely we have reason to hope each day for our imminent salvation. As our Sages teach, when a person departs this world and stands before the Heavenly Court in judgment, one of the first questions he is asked is, "Did you await the salvation [through the coming of Mashiach]?" (Shabbos 31a).

We know from past history that even when Hashem establishes a specific length for an exile, He employs various means to hasten its end. Hashem informed Avraham, "...for your offspring shall be strangers in a land that is not their own... for four hundred years..." (Bereishis 15:13), yet He calculated this period as beginning with the birth of Yitzchak [who himself was born into a land not his own]. Others are of the opinion that Hashem calculated the 210 years of the Jews' sojourn in Egypt as being equivalent to 400 years because their suffering was so intense. We, too, should hope that Hashem will find a way to hasten the date of בְּעִתָּה, due to the intensity of suffering which our people have endured or because of some other factor. Perhaps this is alluded to in the words אֲנִי ה' בְּעִתָּה אֲחִשֶׁנָּה, I, Hashem, in its time I will hasten it (Yeshayahu 60:22), which can be interpreted: Hsahem, in His mercy, will hasten [אֲחִשֶׁנָּה] the final date of בְּעִתָּה.

> To suggest that the Jewish nation is completely without merit is wrong and incomprehensible.

(cont. on page ???)

30 Kislev — In honor of our daughter Victoria Zarotsky's marriage to Alexander Gorbatov
Dedicated by her parents
1 Iyar — Dr. Bernard Farber לע"נ בערל ז"ל בן בנימין הלל יבלח"ט
Dedicated by friends of Tanya, Ahuvie, Estie, Rivky and Toby
לע"נ ר' יוסף ארי' בן ר' יעקב יששכר הכהן ז"ל — **1 Elul**
Dedicated by his son, Shlomo Moskowitz

‎א טבת
1 TEVES / CYCLE 1

December 16, 2001
December 6, 2002
December 26, 2003
December 13, 2004
January 1, 2006

‎ב אייר
2 IYAR / CYCLE 2

April 14, 2002
May 4, 2003
April 23, 2004
May 11, 2005
April 30, 2006

‎ב אלול
2 ELUL / CYCLE 3

August 10, 2002
August 30, 2003
August 19, 2004
September 6, 2005
August 26, 2006

❧ *Above Nature*

SEFER SHEM OLAM — Chapter Fourteen:
Anticipating the Redemption

"*Look to the rock from which you were hewn, and at the hollow of the pit from which you were dug; look to Avraham your forefather and Sarah who bore you, for when he was yet alone did I summon him and bless him and make him many*" (Yeshayahu 51:1-2).

With these words, the prophet comforts the Jewish people, who have been scattered and downtrodden in this long, difficult exile. According to the natural order of the world, there seems to be no possible way for the Jews, so shamed and despised, to extricate themselves from their situation and rise to become a light unto the nations. Therefore, the prophet says: "This should not worry you at all. The destiny of the Jewish people is unlike that of any other nation. Other nations rise and fall little by little, in a natural ascent or descent. The Jews, however, are beyond the plane of nature.

"And if you require proof of this, look to the '*rock from which you were hewn,*' that is, your roots. When were your ancestors, Avraham and Sarah, finally blessed with a child? The birth of Yitzchak was an open miracle, for at that time Avraham was one hundred years old and Sarah was ninety."

The Torah relates that when Hashem informed Avraham of Yitzchak's birth, "He took him [Avraham] outside, and said, "Gaze, now, toward the Heavens, and count the stars if you are able to count them... so shall your offspring be!" (Bereishis 15:5). As Midrash explains, Avraham had seen in the constellations that according to the natural order of the world, he was not destined to have a child. Hashem "took him outside," meaning that Avraham was shown that he was "outside" natural limitations; because he alone was Hashem's faithful servant in a world sunk in idolatry, Hashem had placed his destiny — and that of his offspring — beyond the plane of nature.

The destiny of the Jewish people is unlike that of any other nation.

Though we live in a time of *hester panim* (Divine concealment) when the guiding hand of Providence is not revealed in an obvious way, one *can* recognize Hashem's involvement in this world merely by taking note of the miraculous survival of the Jewish people, physically and spiritually.

R' Eliyahu Meir Bloch was one of the Torah luminaries whom Providence saved from the flames of the Holocaust to build Torah in America. R' Bloch overcame great personal loss to revive the glory of Telshe, Lithunania as he founded the great Telshe Yeshivah on these shores.

During the dark days of the Second World War, R' Bloch entered one of the few Judaica stores in

(cont. on page 266)

1 Teves — Dedicated in loving memory לע"נ חי' לאה בת שעפסיל ע"ה
May it serve as a זכות for her נשמה.

2 Iyar — Perla Spinzi   לע"נ פרלה בת סמריה ע"ה
Dedicated by her children

2 Elul — Sarah Penn לע"נ חי' שרה בת יהודה ליב ע"ה
Dedicated in loving memory by her sons, Ronnie and Baruch Penn and families

ב טבת
2 TEVES / CYCLE 1

December 17, 2001
December 7, 2002
December 27, 2003
December 14, 2004
January 2, 2006

ג אייר
3 IYAR / CYCLE 2

April 15, 2002
May 5, 2003
April 24, 2004
May 12, 2005
May 1, 2006

ג אלול
3 ELUL / CYCLE 3

August 11, 2002
August 31, 2003
August 20, 2004
September 7, 2005
August 27, 2006

❧ Remember the Exodus

SEFER SHEM OLAM — Chapter Fourteen:
Anticipating the Redemption (cont.)

*C*onsider the situation of the Jewish people during the worst moments of the
Egyptian bondage. Backbreaking work involving the mixing of mortar and the laying of
bricks, quotas that needed to be filled at the
threat of merciless beatings, decree upon
harsh decree... Who could have imagined at
that time that the Jews, a nation of more than
a million souls, would depart Egypt "with an
upraised arm" (Shemos 14:8) before the very
eyes of their oppressors? Moreover, the Torah
relates that after the slaying of the firstborn,
Pharaoh arose from his bed in the middle of
the night and with his servants and subjects
trailing behind, actually begged the Jews to
leave (ibid. 12:31)! At the splitting of the Sea
of Reeds, the entire nation rose to a level of
prophecy which surpassed the esoteric visions
of the prophet Yechezkel and less than two
months later, when they received the Torah at
Sinai, they rose to yet a higher level, as it is
written, "Face to face did Hashem speak to
you on the mountain..." (Devarim 5:4).

Our Sages teach that certain specific merits gained
the Jews redemption from Egypt: they did not adopt the
Egyptian way of dress or the Egyptian manner of

speech and they used Jewish, not Egyptian, names. The miracle of the splitting of the sea was attained specifically through the merit of Yosef. Yosef had fled from the house of his master Potiphar, when the latter's wife attempted to convince him to sin.[1] In this merit, the Sea of Reeds "fled" [i.e. parted] when the Jewish people arrived at its shores bearing Yosef's coffin.[2]

Yosef was a slave in a home of immorality and idolatry and was subjected to the daily enticements of Potiphar's wife. He was all alone in an environment permeated with moral decadence. Because of the spiritual strength which he demonstrated under such trying conditions, Yosef earned the appelation *HaTzaddik* (the Righteous One). And it was in his merit that the sea parted.

The lesson of Yosef is especially crucial in our times, when the world has sunk to an astonishing level of spiritual decay.

> Even in the most difficult situations and generations, Hashem provides us with ways and remedies through which we can be saved. In today's world, which (morally) is like the world was at the time of the Flood, when the spiritual filth is powerful and widespread... one must constantly be immersed in an atmosphere of Torah, for only by surrounding oneself with Torah, sanctity and G-dliness can he be saved from the world's filth. Total immersion in the ocean of Torah is the antidote to the depravity that has permeated the world's atmosphere.
>
> *(Nesivos Shalom)*

Who could have imagined that an entire nation would depart Egypt before the very eyes of their oppressors?

---

1. See *Bereishis* Ch. 39.
2. See *Shemos* 13:19.

2 Teves — George Lambert לע"נ גד אשר בן יהושע מרדכי ז"ל
Sponsored by his children
3 Iyar — Ida Tuchman לע"נ איצלע איידא בת מרדכי ע"ה
Dedicated in memory of our beloved mother and Bubby, by the Atlas family
3 Elul — Rabbi David Singer לע"נ ר' דוד בן אליהו ז"ל
Dedicated by his children, Eli & Renee Singer

ג טבת
3 TEVES / CYCLE 1

December 18, 2001
December 8, 2002
December 28, 2003
December 15, 2004
January 3, 2006

ד אייר
4 IYAR / CYCLE 2

April 16, 2002
May 6, 2003
April 25, 2004
May 13, 2005
May 2, 2006

ד אלול
4 ELUL / CYCLE 3

August 12, 2002
September 1, 2003
August 21, 2004
September 8, 2005
August 28, 2006

✌ *The Purim Miracle*

SEFER SHEM OLAM — Chapter Fourteen:
Anticipating the Redemption (cont.)

*Consider the situation of the Jewish peo-
ple in the days of Haman, when a royal
decree was signed and sealed to annihilate
the Jews from young to old, men, women and
children on a single day, the thirteenth of
Adar. At the time the decree was issued, who
would have thought that on that very day, the
thirteenth of Adar, the situation would completely reverse itself and the Jews would overpower their enemies and do with them as
they pleased? Whereas initially the Jews were
filled with fear and foreboding, in the end
"many of the people of the land claimed to be
Jews, for the fear of the Jews had fallen upon
them" (Esther 8:17). Haman, as the king's
viceroy, went to have Mordechai hung on the
gallows which he had prepared, but instead,
Haman was hung on the very same gallows
and Mordechai became the king's viceroy!*

*The matter was summed up well by
Haman's evil wife and advisors:[1] "If Mordechai,
before whom you have begun to fall, is of
Jewish descent, you will not prevail against
him, but will undoubtedly fall before him"
(ibid. 6:13). Our Sages explain their words:
They knew that the Jews are compared to both
the dust of the earth and the stars in heaven.
When they begin to fall, they fall all the way*

*down to the dust; but when they begin to rise
they can reach the stars (Megillah 16a).*

Where is there an allusion to Esther in the
Torah? וְאָנֹכִי הַסְתֵּר אַסְתִּיר פָּנַי, *And I will utterly
conceal My countenance (Devarim 31:18).*

(*Chullin* 139b)

The above verse speaks of a time when the Jewish
people will sin grievously and as a result will be subject to Divine wrath. The double form הַסְתֵּר אַסְתִּיר represents utter concealment, when only those of pure
faith can perceive the hand of Hashem at work.

The miracle of Purim happened during the period
between the First *Beis HaMikdash* and the Second,
when the Jews were in exile. It serves as an eternal
reminder that G-d never abandons His people. Even in
the darkness of exile, when the sword of our oppressors
is on our necks and when Hashem's Presence is hidden,
there is never room for despair (based on *Kol Eliyahu*).

Furthermore, the Purim deliverance involved no
open miracles; rather, the entire story, from the feast
of King Achashveirosh to the hanging of Haman and
his sons, was a tapestry of hidden miracles in which
the guiding hand of Providence is plainly apparent. It
was a declaration of Hashem to His beloved people,
"When you were exiled, My *Shechinah* (Divine
Presence) accompanied you, and it has never departed from your midst. I am here guiding and protecting
you, and I will always be with you, even when My
Presence is not readily discernible."

*Who
would
have
thought
that the
Jews
would
overpower
their
enemies
and do
with them
as they
pleased?*

---

1. Haman had informed his cohorts of the king's command that Haman
lead Mordechai through the streets of Shushan as he rode the king's
horse and wore the king's royal attire. They understood that this development was not coincidental; it meant the beginning of the Jews' rise and
of Haman's downfall.

ד טבת
4 TEVES / CYCLE 1
December 19, 2001
December 9, 2002
December 29, 2003
December 16, 2004
January 4, 2006

ה אייר
5 IYAR / CYCLE 2
April 17, 2002
May 7, 2003
April 26, 2004
May 14, 2005
May 3, 2006

ה אלול
5 ELUL / CYCLE 3
August 13, 2002
September 2, 2003
August 22, 2004
September 9, 2005
August 29, 2006

❧ A Difficult Form of Return

SEFER SHEM OLAM — Chapter Fourteen:
Anticipating the Redemption (cont.)

*I*n these turbulent times, when our brethren are being threatened and attacked, we should not become dispirited; to the contrary, this is an indication that Hashem may soon redeem us and from the depths of degradation He will uplift us. Instead of the shame and derision to which we have been subjected, we will be the object of praise and reverence among the nations. We will merit the fulfillment of the verses of Hallel: "I thank You for You have answered me and become my salvation. The stone the builders despised has become the cornerstone" (Tehillim 118:21-22). And in the words of the prophets:

> Instead of your being forsaken and despised, without wayfarers, I will make you into an eternal pride, a joy for generation after generation (Yeshayahu 60:15).

> In the place where it was said to them, "You are not my nation," it shall be said to them, "the children of the living G-d" (Hoshea 2:1).

Our people were in a similar situation in the days of King Chizkiyahu, when the *mighty armies of Sancheriv, King of Assyria, laid seige to Jerusalem. Sancheriv directed brazen words toward Hashem and His people. He also boasted that the dust of Jerusalem would not suffice for the feet of his myriad soldiers and that his armies and their animals had used up the water sources of the nations which they had ravaged.*

How did that episode end? That very night, as the Assyrian army was positioned to attack, Hashem dispatched an angel to slay Sancheriv's one hundred eighty-five thousand men as they slept.

In our times, we have witnessed situations where our enemies rose up against us and it seemed as if all was lost. Then suddenly, Hashem showed His might as He took pity on us and rescued us from our oppressors. Anyone with a discerning heart can perceive clearly the guiding Hand of Providence in our people's fortunes.

All of the above should serve as a lesson to us that Hashem has not given us over to the forces of nature. Rather, we are guided by His hand alone, and should it be His will, He can redeem us at any moment.

> **Anyone with a discerning heart can perceive the hand of Providence in our people's fortunes.**

Our generation, too, has been privileged to witness salvation through Divine intervention in an obvious way. A decade ago, the dictator of Iraq, Saddam

(cont. on page 266)

✎ *Three Reasons for Hope*

SEFER SHEM OLAM — Chapter Fourteen:
Anticipating the Redemption (cont.)

"*Let Israel hope for Hashem, for with Hashem is kindness, and with Him is abundant redemption. And He shall redeem Israel from all its sins" (Tehillim 130:7-8). The meaning of this is as follows:*

Even a person who is genuinely kind and generous may not always be prepared to grant someone's request for help. This could be for one of three reasons:

1) The benefactor has just been enraged by someone else and has not had time to calm down. Until he calms down, he finds himself unable to listen to new requests.

2) He simple lacks the resources to fulfill the request.

3) He feels that his petitioner is unworthy of having his request granted. (For example, the man has requested a loan but he has a poor history of repayment.)

The above verses teach us that these reasons are irrelevant when we put our requests before Hashem, and therefore we can hope that our salvation will come at any moment.

The first reason mentioned above does not apply, because Hashem is the Source of kind-

ness and goodness and these attributes are inseparable from Him, as it is written, "Hashem's kindness surely has not ended, nor are His mercies exhausted" (Eichah 3:22). This is the meaning of, "Let Israel hope for Hashem, for with Hashem is kindness."

The second reason mentioned above is also not applicable, because nothing is beyond Hashem's power. This is the meaning of, "and with Him is abundant redemption."

Therefore, one should not wonder how we can be anticipating and praying for a speedy redemption when we are caught in the thick of calamity. Nothing is beyond Hashem's power and He has many forms of redemption at His disposal. There is a process of redemption which lasts months or years, as was the redemption from Egypt. And there is a redemption which lasts but a single night from start to finish. This was the redemption mentioned above which occurred in the days of King Chizkiyahu. The mighty armies of Sancheriv beseiged Jerusalem as Sancheriv blasphemed toward Hashem and His people. Then, in a single night, an angel slew his entire army and Sancheriv returned to his homeland in disgrace.

These variant forms of redemption are alluded to in a passage in which Hashem warns Pharaoh about a forthcoming Plague.

Nothing is beyond Hashem's power and He has many means of redemption at His disposal.

(cont. on page 267)

לכבוד הילד היקר נדב אריא-ל חביבי — **5 Teves**
שיפתח ד' את לבו לתלמיד תורתו אמן.

לע"נ זאב בן יצחק יעקב ז"ל — **6 Iyar**
May today's learning be a זכות for his נשמה. Dedicated by the Farberas family

לזכות חיים צבי מנחם מענדיל גאלדענבערג נ"י ומשפחתו — **6 Elul**

DAY 96

ו טבת
6 TEVES / CYCLE 1

December 21, 2001
December 11, 2002
December 31, 2003
December 18, 2004
January 6, 2006

ז אייר
7 IYAR / CYCLE 2

April 19, 2002
May 9, 2003
April 28, 2004
May 16, 2005
May 5, 2006

ז אלול
7 ELUL / CYCLE 3

August 15, 2002
September 4, 2003
August 24, 2004
September 11, 2005
August 31, 2006

✍ Guaranteed Redemption

SEFER SHEM OLAM — Chapter Fourteen:
Anticipating the Redemption (cont.)

bove, we said that an earthly benefactor will not grant his petitioner's request if he feels that the person is not deserving of it. However, Hashem's way is different. When He determines that the exile must end, He redeems the Jewish people regardless of their spiritual level. This is what is meant by, "And He shall redeem Israel from all its sins" (Tehillim 130:8).

The Midrash relates:

> *"The voice of my Beloved! Behold it came suddenly to redeem me, as if leaping over mountains, skipping over hills" (Shir HaShirim 2:8).*
>
> *R' Nechemia said: "The voice" was that of Moshe. When Moshe informed the Jews, "In this month you will be redeemed," they responded, "Moshe, our teacher — how can we be redeemed? We do not possess good deeds!" Moshe replied, "Because He desires to redeem you, He is not taking note of your evil deeds.[1] And of whom does He take note? — the righteous among you and their good deeds, such*

as Amram (Moshe's father) and his court" (Shir HaShirim Rabbah).

Therefore, no one should despair of Hashem's mercy; rather, he should anticipate redemption at any time.

Rabbi Avraham Pam explained the above as follows: Certainly the *Midrash* does not mean to imply that Hashem ignored grievous sins and did not require any sort of soul-cleansing, just as we know that He did not "disregard" His decree of a four hundred-year exile. As our Sages teach, Hashem, in His infinite kindness, calculated the exile as beginning with the birth of Yitzchak, which occurred exactly four hundred years prior to the redemption. In a similar sense, Hashem, in His infinte mercy, "reckoned" the Jews' meriting redemption despite their spiritual failings at that time.

The essence of Moshe's response to the people, "Because He desires to redeem you, He is not taking note of your evil deeds..." was taught to him by Hashem, when the exile actually worsened after Moshe's first appearance in Pharoah's palace as prophet and leader of his people. As *Maggid Meisharim*[2] puts it, Hashem's response was: "My ways are not your ways, for I accomplish judgment and compassion simultaneously." The redemption process had, in fact, begun, but that did not preclude what appeared to be Divine judgment directed toward the Jewish people. Incomprehensible? Possibly, to the limited grasp of human intellect. *"My ways are not your ways."*

> **Ultimately, the Jewish people must be redeemed, regardless of its spiritual level.**

---

1. This is the meaning of leaping over mountains, skipping over hills.
2. A collection of teachings which an angel revealed to Rabbi Yosef Karo, author of *Shulchan Aruch* and the *Beis Yosef* commentary to *Tur*.

לע"נ שמעון בן ר' יעקב ז"ל — **6 Teves** — Samuel Klaus
ואשתו באשא בת ר' מרדכי נתן — Bessie Klaus

לע"נ חנה בת שמואל זאנוויל ע"ה — **7 Iyar** — Anna Rubin
Dedicated in loving memory by her grandchildren, Steve & Shari Goranson and family

לזכות אברהם קלונימוס בן גיטל נ"י — **7 Elul**
לזכות שמואל מנחם אהרן בן יוטא לאה נ"י

Book III:

Selected
Letters

Letters of the
Chofetz Chaim
to his generation

published in
Kol Kisvei Chofetz Chaim,
Volume III

ז טבת
7 TEVES / CYCLE 1

December 22, 2001
December 12, 2002
January 1, 2004
December 19, 2004
January 7, 2006

ח אייר
8 IYAR / CYCLE 2

April 20, 2002
May 10, 2003
April 29, 2004
May 17, 2005
May 6, 2006

ח אלול
8 ELUL / CYCLE 3

August 16, 2002
September 5, 2003
August 25, 2004
September 12, 2005
September 1, 2006

❧ *Why Do You Slumber?*

LETTER ONE

Some weeks ago, I publicized a call to teshuvah (repentance) following the great storm which struck our Holy Land. I wrote how that storm was a warning from Above to the entire world to repent of its evil ways, for we know that all is from Hashem and none of the frightening occurrences of the past year were mere happenstance.

Now we have received yet another frightening report — of the catastrophic flood in our country and the great storm in Russia in which thousands of men, women, children and livestock were killed. In many instances, the people's homes became their graves.[1]

Surely any thinking person should be gripped by fear and trembling when hearing such news. What is this that G-d has done to us?[2] Hashem is the "King Who is good and Who does good for all,"[3] and "His mercies are upon all His works."[4] Hashem does not want even a wicked person to die, as it is written, "As I live — the words of Hashem — I do not desire the death of the wicked one, but only the wicked one's return from his way that he may live" (Yechezkel 33:11).

The wise person will understand that Hashem is warning us to repent. He is demonstrating to everyone that He can do whatever He pleases and that He is not beholden to any power above or below. I am certain that if there were prophets alive today, surely they would stand watch to exhort their fellow Jews to return to their Father in Heaven. Because, to our misfortune, there is no prophecy today, He warns us through other "emissaries" — as it is written, "He makes the winds His messengers, the flaming fire His attendants" (Tehillim 104:4).

The Talmud states (*Yevamos* 63a):

> Rabbi Elazar ben Avina said: Misfortune comes to the world only on account of Israel, as it says, "I have eliminated nations, their towers have become desolate; I have destroyed their streets" (*Tzephaniah* 3:6) and it is written (ibid. v. 7), "I said [in wreaking this destruction], 'Just fear me, [O Israel,] extract a lesson.' "

Maharal explains that basic to Jewish belief is that all that Hashem does is for the good. But what good can come from natural disasters if the nations of the world view them as the "onslaught of Mother Nature"? It must be that these catastrophies are for the benefit of the Jewish people, who know that "everything is a miracle, there is nothing natural at all" (*Ramban* to *Shemos* 13:16). The Jews will see these happenings as a message from Heaven and will take the necessary measures towards repentance and self-improvement.

> **If there were prophets alive today, surely they would exhort their fellow Jews to return to their Father in Heaven.**

---

1. This letter is dated *Erev Yom Kippur* 5685 (1925).
2. *Bereishis* 42:28.
3. From *Bircas HaMazon.*
4. *Tehillim* 145:9.

ח טבת
8 TEVES / CYCLE 1

December 23, 2001
December 13, 2002
January 2, 2004
December 20, 2004
January 8, 2006

ט אייר
9 IYAR / CYCLE 2

April 21, 2002
May 11, 2003
April 30, 2004
May 18, 2005
May 7, 2006

ט אייר
9 ELUL / CYCLE 3

August 17, 2002
September 6, 2003
August 26, 2004
September 13, 2005
September 2, 2006

❧ *Preparing for the Wedding*

LETTER TWO

ome have asked me: Virtually all the signs which our Sages have said would be apparent in the period preceding Mashiach's arrival have already appeared. Furthermore, the dreadful desecration of Hashem's Name which this exile has brought about should be further reason to expect that redemption is imminent. This is indicated in the opening blessing of the Shemoneh Esrei in which we say:"...and Who brings redemption to their children's children for the sake of His Name..."

Yet we continue to suffer the wrath of our oppressors while salvation seems distant and the footsteps of Mashiach have yet to be heard. What is this that G-d has done to us?[1] Surely Hashem's judgment is without flaw! This is what people have asked me.

And this is what I answered them: Surely nothing is beyond Hashem's power and His salvation can come in the blink of an eye. And surely He is concerned for the desecration of His Name. I am certain, however, that Hashem is delaying our Redemption a bit more so that we can prepare ourselves for Mashiach's arrival, so that we will not go for-

ward to greet him while sorely deficient in Torah and mitzvos.

This can be likened to a wealthy man who invited his poor friends and neighbors to the wedding of his son. The man had invited some wealthy business acquaintances to the wedding and did not want to be embarrassed by the tattered rags which his relatives and neighbors were liable to wear. So he requested of them: "Please make sure to come dressed presentably."

Hashem is likened to a groom and we are His bride, as it is written: "As a bridegroom rejoicing over his bride, so will your G-d rejoice over you" (Yeshayahu 62:5). As the time of redemption approaches, we must prepare ourselves with our spiritual garments — Torah and good deeds — so that we will be properly "attired" to greet our Groom on that glorious day. Surely each one of us will want to greet Him and bask in the radiance of His Presence. However, if we will not be spiritually ready, and will be lacking in Torah and mitzvos, we will be forced to hide our faces in shame.

Hashem is likened to a groom and we are His bride.

The Chofetz Chaim owned a ledger in which he recorded his daily spiritual accounting, which he would examine so that he could repent for what, to

(cont. on page 267)

---

1. *Bereishis* 42:28.

8 Teves — Benjamin M. Garfunkel לע"נ החבר ברוך מרדכי בן כלב ז"ל
Dedicated in loving memory by Nosson & Lisa Garfunkel and family
9 Iyar — לזכות דוד ישעי' בן רבקה נ"י
Dedicated by the Rivlin family
9 Elul — May today's learning be a z'chus for my loving wife, Brina and family.
Dedicated by Dovid Davis

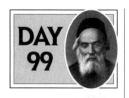

DAY 99

ט טבת
9 TEVES / CYCLE 1
December 24, 2001
December 14, 2002
January 3, 2004
December 21, 2004
January 9, 2006

י אייר
10 IYAR / CYCLE 2
April 22, 2002
May 12, 2003
May 1, 2004
May 19, 2005
May 8, 2006

י אלול
10 ELUL / CYCLE 3
August 18, 2002
September 7, 2003
August 27, 2004
September 14, 2005
September 3, 2006

✍ *The Thirteen Principles of Faith*

LETTER TWO (cont.)

I *would also like to awaken my brethren to a matter of great importance: It is well known that the luminaries of earlier generations instituted the reciting of the Thirteen Principles of Faith each morning after Shacharis. This custom is based on the Talmudic teaching that the prophet Chavakuk established one mitzvah as the foundation for observance of the entire Torah: "And a righteous person lives by his faith" (Chavakuk 2:4)*

In our time, it is a great mitzvah upon everyone to strengthen himself in this and to recite these Thirteen Principles as our ancestors did.[1]

A man who lived in Radin and was a contemporary of the Chofetz Chaim is reported to have said: "We believe in *Olam Haba* (the World to Come) and the Chofetz Chaim believes in *Olam Haba*. The difference is that our belief is somewhat abstract, while to the Chofetz Chaim, *Olam Haba* is as real as the room next door." The same can be said of the Chofetz Chaim's belief of all the basic principles of Jewish faith. Each principle was to him like a tangible reality.

In a letter, his son-in-law, Rabbi Mendel Zaks, wrote:

So firm was my father-in-law's *emunah* (faith) that he was impatient when listening to proofs of G-d's existence, for he viewed such proofs as entirely superfluous.

When he spoke of *kedushah* (sanctity), such as when citing the verse, "You shall be holy because I, Hashem, your G-d, am holy" (*Vayikra* 19:2), he would smack his lips and say, "It is sweeter than honey!"

I often overheard him in direct conversations with G-d, talking to Him in *Yiddish*, "You always listen to my prayers; please listen to me again this time."

Whenever he spoke of prophecy, one could see his intense yearning for the spiritual level it represented.

He frequently quoted the passage: "Better one hour of repentance and good deeds in this world than the entire life of the World to Come" (*Avos* 4:22), which was followed by a number of parables. "In one minute well spent on this world,' he would add, "one can become an *eved Hashem* (servant of Hashem). With all the joys which the World to Come brings, one cannot do anything there to elevate his status."

> *To the Chofetz Chaim, the World to Come was as real as the room next door.*

---

1. *Tzaddikim* have taught that reciting the Thirteen Principles is auspicious for enhancing one's level of *emunah*.

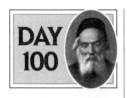

✺ Sarah's Laughter

LETTER THREE

*T*he Torah relates at great length the episode where the angel informed Avraham that in a year's time Sarah would give birth to a son. Sarah, who was listening from her place in the tent, laughed incredulously upon hearing the angel's words:

> *And Sarah laughed to herself, saying: "After I have withered shall I again be young? And my husband is old!" (Bereishis 18:12).*

Hashem expressed displeasure to Avraham over Sarah's apparent lack of faith:

> *Then Hashem said to Avraham: "Why is it that Sarah laughed, saying, 'Shall I in truth bear a child though I have aged?' — Is anything beyond Hashem? At the appointed time I will return to you at this time next year, and Sarah will have a son."*
>
> *Sarah denied it, saying, "I did not laugh," for she was frightened. But He said, "No, you laughed indeed." (vs. 13-15).*

When I studied this passage well, I was struck by great difficulties. We know that there is not one extra letter in the Torah and *that each letter has been invested with an awesome, inestimable sanctity by the Giver of the Torah. Therefore it seems astonishing that the Torah would relate this episode, which is so uncomplimentary to the righteous Sarah, in such great detail.*

I told myself that this passage must allude to something of major significance. Then, Hashem enlightened me and I perceived the message of this episode.

Our Sages teach: "The deeds of our forefathers are a symbol for their descendants." The episode of Sarah's laughter is recorded in the Torah as a sign of what will transpire in Ikvisa D'Meshicha, the period before Mashiach's arrival in which we now find ourselves.

The deeds of our forefathers are a symbol for their descendants.

The oft-quoted phrase: מַעֲשֵׂה אָבוֹת סִימָן לְבָנִים, *the actions of the forefathers are a symbol for their descendants,* is rooted in a *Midrash:* "G-d gave a sign to Avraham that all which would happen to him would be visited upon his children" (*Midrash Tanchuma, Lech Lecha* 9). The Patriarchs and Matriarchs embodied in their words and deeds the entire, still-unfolding course of Jewish history. The Chofetz Chaim proceeds to show us how Sarah's laughter, and subsequent response when her laughter was challenged, parallels the attitude of many G-d-fearing Jews at the End of Days.

10 Teves — Lester Richmond לע"נ אליעזר משה בן יחזקא-ל ז"ל
Dedicated in loving memory by the Siegel, Silverman, and Kramer families

11 Iyar —

לע"נ מאיר בן אברהם ז"ל — **11 Elul**
Dedicated in loving memory by Michael & Shelley Eizelman

י"א טבת
11 TEVES / CYCLE 1

December 26, 2001
December 16, 2002
January 5, 2004
December 23, 2004
January 11, 2006

י"ב אייר
12 IYAR / CYCLE 2

April 24, 2002
May 14, 2003
May 3, 2004
May 21, 2005
May 10, 2006

י"ב אלול
12 ELUL / CYCLE 3

August 20, 2002
September 9, 2003
August 29, 2004
September 16, 2005
September 5, 2006

~ *A Weakness of Faith*

LETTER THREE (cont.)

*T*he episode of Sarah's laughter alludes to the following:

In Ikvesa D'Meshicha (the period leading to Mashiach's arrival), there will be Torah luminaries who will act as the prophets of old in exhorting the people to repent and to strengthen their emunah (faith in G-d). As our Sages state, "All the 'Ends' [i.e. the times which the Sages predicted as suited for the Redemption] have passed and the matter [of Mashiach's arrival] depends only on repentance and good deeds" (Sanhedrin 97a). These leaders will encourage their brethren to prepare themselves with Torah and good deeds so that they will be ready to greet Mashiach when he arrives.

However, the Torah is hinting to us that at that time, there will be people weak in faith, who will not believe the words of those who seek to reprove and encourage them. These people will say, "How it is possible that at a time like this, with the Jewish people steeped in suffering and travail, that redemption should suddenly occur?" With this attitude, they will turn a deaf ear to those who seek to reprove them, as was the case in Egypt: "...and they did not heed Moshe, because of shortness of breath and hard work" (Shemos

6:9). *The Torah alludes to this situation where Hashem tells Avraham, "Is anything beyond Hashem?" Surely it is within His power to redeem us on any day at any time. Those who, in Ikvesa D'Meshicha, will be guilty of a lack of faith will be taken to task for this.*

Sarah attempted to defend herself, saying, "I did not laugh." Similarly, those whose faith will be wanting in Ikvesa D'Meshicha will attempt to defend themselves, saying, "Certainly we believe in Mashiach's ultimate arrival and in Hashem's power to effect the redemption at any time. We are familiar with the story of Purim, where in a single night the situation turned around from despair to salvation. However, we doubt that redemption is imminent; it seems that the matter is still years away."

They will be held accountable for this attitude. The prophet states explicitly, "...suddenly the lord who you seek [i.e. Mashiach] will come to his sanctuary, and the messenger of the covenant [the prophet Eliyahu] for whom you yearn, behold, he comes, says Hashem..." (Malachi 3:1). Accordingly, each and every day we must at least entertain the possibility that today Mashiach will appear. This is why the Talmud rules that if one vows, "I accept upon myself to be a nazarite on the day on which the scion of David [Mashiach] will appear," he is forbidden to drink wine for

Each day, we must entertain the possibility that today Mashiach will appear.

(cont. on page 268)

11 Teves — לע"נ ירחמיא-ל ז"ל בן שמחה יבלח"ט
May today's learning be a זכות for our son.
Dedicated by his parents and brothers, the Renzoni family

12 Iyar — Sruly Miller לע"נ ישראל מרדכי הכהן ז"ל בן ר' אליעזר יבלח"ט
Dedicated by Highland Park Bungalow Colony

12 Elul — לע"נ שיינדל בת ר' דוד ע"ה
Sponsored by Dov & Adena Goldman

י"ב טבת
12 TEVES / CYCLE 1

December 27, 2001
December 17, 2002
January 6, 2004
December 24, 2004
January 12, 2006

י"ג אייר
13 IYAR / CYCLE 2

April 25, 2002
May 15, 2003
May 4, 2004
May 22, 2005
May 11, 2006

י"ג אלול
13 ELUL / CYCLE 3

August 21, 2002
September 10, 2003
August 30, 2004
September 17, 2005
September 6, 2006

✑ *Shemiras HaLashon*

LETTER FOUR

Through the kindness of Hashem, I have attained the age of "strength," the ninth decade of my life, and virtually all my life I have not diverted my attention from pondering matters of speech. Shemiras halashon (guarding one's tongue) involves numerous positive and negative commandments, and has come to be virtually ignored by multitudes who think that it is nothing more than a good habit for those who choose to adopt it.

I wish to awaken thoughtful people who are knowledgeable in Torah, but who fail to equate the sin of lashon hara with that of eating non-kosher food. Consider the following: If someone will cause his fellow Jew to eat non-kosher food, the sinner will be distressed about this for months and he will bear ill will for years towards the one who caused him to sin. By contrast: What would be the same person's reaction if he accepted an evil report about someone and subsequently humiliated the person in public — only to discover later that the report was pure fabrication? In all probability, his anger toward the gossiper would last but a few days, at the most. The reason for this is as we have stated, that the multitudes do not view lashon hara as a sin and they give no thought at all to the rights and wrongs of speech. This affects even those who are knowledgeable in Torah, so that they treat the matter lightly and do not accord it much attention.

To the verse: "Remember what Hashem, your G-d, did to Miriam on the way, when you were leaving Egypt" (Devarim 24:9), Ramban comments:

> We are commanded to inform our children of this episode [where Miriam was punished for speaking negatively of her brother Moshe — see Bamidbar 12:1-16] and to relate it to future generations, though it would have seemed more fitting to conceal it so as not to speak disparagingly of the righteous Miriam. Nevertheless, the Torah commands us to relate it and make it known, so that the prohibition of lashon hara will be well known to all. For lashon hara is a terrible sin which brings about much harm and in which many frequently stumble.

Ramban teaches us that aside from our obligation to carefully avoid the sin of lashon hara, we are also commanded to instruct our children and others regarding the severity of this sin. When a person fulfills the mitzvah of, "Remember what Hashem, your G-d, did to Miriam..." by informing others about shemiras halashon, this will be greatly beneficial

Lashon hara is a terrible sin which brings about much harm.

(cont. on page 268)

12 Teves — Poppi ז"ל לע"נ שמחה בן יעקב
Dedicated by Yaakov, Miriam and Izak

13 Iyar — Frieda Glicker לע"נ פרומא בת יוסף מאיר הלוי ע"ה
Dedicated by the Gottesman family

13 Elul — Priscilla Greenberg לע"נ פערל בת יעקב יצחק ע"ה
By her husband, Bernard, and children, Howard, Ira, Ellen and Roseanne

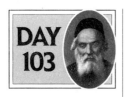
י"ג טבת
13 TEVES / CYCLE 1

December 28, 2001
December 18, 2002
January 7, 2004
December 25, 2004
January 13, 2006

י"ד אייר
14 IYAR / CYCLE 2

April 26, 2002
May 16, 2003
May 5, 2004
May 23, 2005
May 12, 2006

י"ד אלול
14 ELUL / CYCLE 3

August 22, 2002
September 11, 2003
August 31, 2004
September 18, 2005
September 7, 2006

≈ *Sins of Mass Destruction*

LETTER FIVE

*I*t is well known that the Second Beis HaMikdash was destroyed on account of sinas chinam and lashon hara (see Yoma 9b). Satan still "dances" among us, as these sins are still all too prevalent. The Early Commentators observed: if these sins had the power to destroy an existing Beis HaMikdash, then certainly they have the power to prevent the Beis HaMikdash from being rebuilt. The Midrash informs us that lashon hara causes the Shechinah to depart from our midst (Devarim Rabbah 5:10).

If we were to recount in full detail the harm which lashon hara causes to the speaker and to the entire world, and the punishments which the speaker is liable to incur in this world and the next, we would never finish. Below, we will mention a few points:

We know that regarding certain mitzvos, "the fruits [secondary reward] a person enjoys in this world, while the principal [primary reward] remains intact for him for the World to Come." By contrast, certain sins carry with them a primary punishment for the actual sin, and a secondary punishment for the sin's harmful effects. Lashon hara is such a sin. If the speaker's words have caused harm, then he will suffer retribution for that in this world, while the primary punishment will await him in the Next World, as is stated in Tosefta (Masechta Pe'ah), Rambam (Hilchos Dei'os 7:3) and Smag (negative commandment 11).

Our Sages teach: "The Holy One, Blessed is He, said: 'I can rescue you from all sufferings that come upon you, but when the tongue roams — hide yourself!'"[1] (Iyov 5:21). Because the sin of lashon hara is so destructive, Hashem does not expend effort, as it were, to save the sinner from punishment. Furthermore, the Torah records a specific curse for this sin, as it is written, "Accursed is one who strikes his fellow in secret" (Devarim 27:24).

Worst of all, the sin of lashon hara can cause one to forfeit whatever merit he has attained through Torah study, as the Midrash (Shochar Tov to Tehillim Ch. 52) teaches in interpreting the verse, "Let not your mouth bring guilt upon your flesh... Why should G–d be angered by your speech and destroy the work of your hands?" (Koheles 5:5).

Is there any other sin of which the Torah speaks at such length in so many places and which involves transgression of so many positive and negative commandments?

(cont. on page 269)

Lashon hara can cause one to forfeit whatever merit he has attained through Torah study.

---

1. This is based on *Iyov 5:19,21*.

13 Teves — Sarah Feldman ע"ה לע"נ שרה בת משה ע"ה
Dedicated in loving memory by her children, Moishe & Malky Feldman

14 Iyar — May today's learning be a z'chus for Leo Billet.
Dedicated by the Werstein Family Trust

14 Elul — In honor of our parents and grandparents
Sponsored by Sandy & Charles Edward Gros

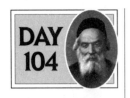

י״ד טבת
14 TEVES / CYCLE 1

December 29, 2001
December 19, 2002
January 8, 2004
December 26, 2004
January 14, 2006

ט״ו אייר
15 IYAR / CYCLE 2

April 27, 2002
May 17, 2003
May 6, 2004
May 24, 2005
May 13, 2006

ט״ו אלול
15 ELUL / CYCLE 3

August 23, 2002
September 12, 2003
September 1, 2004
September 19, 2005
September 8, 2006

❧ *Is this Honor?*

LETTER FIVE (cont.)

In the prayers of Shabbos eve, we declare: "Render to Hashem honor and might, render to Hashem the honor due His Name" (Tehillim 29:1-2). In our daily Shacharis prayers, we even call to the nations: "Render to Hashem, O family of nations, render to Hashem honor and might" (I Divrei HaYamim 16:28). Yet we ourselves detract from His honor by frequently engaging in conversations which the Torah, in numerous places, clearly prohibits!

Let each person make a personal reckoning of how many times each week he is guilty of speaking lashon hara, rechilus (lashon hara which causes ill will), falsehood and deceit and how many times he has transgressed the grievous sins of ona'as devarim (speaking hurtful words) and halbanas panim (humiliating someone). All too often, many of these sins are transgressed by a single person in a single day. In short, the passages in the Torah which discuss these sins are woefully ignored.

Our Sages state that the mitzvos are Hashem's "emissaries": Hashem says: "If you honor My commandments, it is as if you honor Me, and if you disgrace My commandments, it is as if you disgrace Me."

To what can this be compared? To a group of people who shout, "Fire, fire!" and their cries bring out all the townspeople with buckets of water. But no matter how hard the people try, the fire continues to rage. And what is the reason? The very people who shouted for help are adding fuel to the fire!

And so it is in our situation. The very people who cry, "Render to Hashem honor..." utter statements and enagage in conversations which show their utter disregard for His sacred commandments. But what of "rendering honor" to Him? Is this honor?

In Sefer Shemiras HaLashon (Shaar HaTevunah), I have explained the underlying cause of this widespread carelessness. The yetzer hara prevents us from pondering an essential truth: if Hashem has made clear in His holy Torah, through numerous positive and negative commandments, that shemiras halashon is an absolute imperative, then surely He has granted every one of us the ability to control our tongues and save ourselves from these terrible sins.

At the present, however, lashon hara is widespread; the sin which brought about the Destruction has not been corrected and Mashiach, therefore, has yet to appear. Each yom tov we plead, "Our Father, our King: reveal the glory of Your Kingship upon us, speedily," yet we fail to contemplate that as long as we remain mired in the sin of lashon

(cont. on page 269)

If we honor Hashem's commandments, it is as if we honor Him.

לזכות חי' ברכה בת דבורה שתחי' — **14 Teves**
לזכות אורה בת מלכה שתחי'

15 Iyar — May today's learning be a זכות for our משפחה.
Dedicated by Menachem & Erica Kaiman

לזכות אשר מנחם בן פייגא ברכה נ"י — **15 Elul**

ט"ו טבת

15 TEVES / CYCLE 1

December 30, 2001
December 20, 2002
January 9, 2004
December 27, 2004
January 15, 2006

ט"ז אייר

16 IYAR / CYCLE 2

April 28, 2002
May 18, 2003
May 7, 2004
May 25, 2005
May 14, 2006

ט"ז אלול

16 ELUL / CYCLE 3

August 24, 2002
September 13, 2003
September 2, 2004
September 20, 2005
September 9, 2006

✍ Parting Words

LETTER SIX

From his youth, the Chofetz Chaim was possessed by a burning desire to ascend to Eretz Yisrael and serve Hashem amid the rarified atmosphere of our precious Holy Land. In 1925, at age eighty-seven, he attempted to realize this dream. As he and his family packed their belongings and a house was being readied for him in Petach Tikvah, the great Torah leaders of Eastern Europe worried over how Torah life in their lands would be affected by the departure of the *tzaddik hador* (most righteous of the generation). In the end, Heaven intervened and the journey had to be postponed again and again until it was finally cancelled.

In preparation for his journey, the Chofetz Chaim issued the following public letter to the Jews in the Diaspora:

As in His mercy, Hashem has granted me the privilege of attaining the age of "strength," the ninth decade of my life, and I intend with His help to go up to our Holy Land to find favor in her stones and to cherish her dust, I wish to bid farewell with a blessing to my brethren in these lands.

I pour out my heartfelt prayer before Hashem, the Guardian of Israel, that He should take pity on His people who are mired in troubles and captivity, that He should grant them survival and take them out from trouble to relief. May He send them His Mashiach to bring them good tidings and comfort.

My precious brethren! It is difficult for me to part from you at this trying hour, when judgments are poised against us, may the Compassionate One save us from them, and when each day's tragedies seem to surpass those of the previous day. The spiritual destruction is awesome. For this reason, I feel it incumbent upon myself to make mention of our obligations to the One Above.

When the disciples of R' Eliezer the Great asked him, "What shall a person do to escape the 'birthpangs' of Mashiach?" he replied, "He should occupy himself with Torah and acts of kindness." R' Eliezer found no other suggestion for how to escape the bitter sufferings of that period other than Torah and chesed...

...As we say in the Selichos of Ne'ilah at Yom Kippur's conclusion, "We have nothing left to us but this Torah." The four cubits of halachah[1] within the confines of the study halls of our yeshivos have been left to us as a refuge, through Hashem's mercy. Yet on account of economic depression and poverty, the very existence of the yeshivos is in danger.

It is well known that the purpose of our coming into this world is for each one of us to attain his portion in Torah. As R' Yochanan ben Zakkai taught, "If you have learned a great amount of Torah, do not take credit for yourself, for this is the purpose for which you were created" (Avos 2:9).

One can escape the "birth-pangs" of Mashiach through Torah and chesed.

(cont. on page 270)

---

1. An expression borrowed from an Aggadic teaching; see *Berachos* 8a.

ט"ז טבת
16 TEVES / CYCLE 1

December 31, 2001
December 21, 2002
January 10, 2004
December 28, 2004
January 16, 2006

י"ז אייר
17 IYAR / CYCLE 2

April 29, 2002
May 19, 2003
May 8, 2004
May 26, 2005
May 15, 2006

י"ז אלול
17 ELUL / CYCLE 3

August 25, 2002
September 14, 2003
September 3, 2004
September 21, 2005
September 10, 2006

≈ *A Parting Request*

LETTER SIX *(cont.)*

The Chofetz Chaim continues his farewell letter to the Torah community of Eastern Europe, in which he stresses the importance of maintaining the great yeshivos which thrived there before the Second World War.

he world was created for the sake of the Torah, as it is written, "So said Hashem: 'Were it not for My covenant [which is to be studied] day and night, I would have not put forth the orders of heaven and earth'" (Yirmiyahu 33:25). If we grow lax in our attachment to Torah and thereby cause disgrace to the Torah and its students, then all of Creation is virtually without purpose, neither for our souls nor for our physical beings.

...Therefore, my final request, as I take leave of you, concerns the strengthening of the Torah and the yeshivos. I make mention to you of the last prophecy of the last prophet, in which the promise of, "Behold, I send you Eliyahu the prophet before the coming of the great and awesome day of Hashem" (Malachi 3:23), is preceded by, "Remember the Torah of Moshe My servant... for all of Israel" (v. 22). This, the Torah, is the foundation and primary purpose of our lives and the primary source of merit for our redemption.

I beseech my brethren, young and old, to take to heart this last request of mine, to guard the lamp of our holy Torah which illuminates our sacred halls of Torah study. We have been stripped of virtually everything, whatever we had has been taken from us, except for the source of life which Hashem blew into our nostrils — our holy Torah which is still vibrant and enduring.

The holy ark of Hashem has not been captured! — it still "goes with you to fight for you with your enemies, to save you."[1] Guard the Torah properly, guard it like the apple of your eye. Arise, everyone, like one man, to lend help to the ark of Hashem which resides in the study halls of our holy yeshivos. Grant honor to Hashem and His Torah! Contribute to the support of Torah, in accordance with your means and Hashem's blessings upon you.

Virtually everything has been taken from us — except for our holy Torah, which is still vibrant and enduring.

When Rabbi Aharon Kotler spent a few weeks in Florida recuperating from illness, it was decided to make use of the opportunity to raise badly needed funds for his yeshivah in Lakewood.

One day, the student who had accompanied R' Aharon was asked to pick up two wealthy men and drive them to the *Rosh Yeshivah's* residence for a meeting. On the way, one of the men remarked to the other, "I guess this meeting is going to cost us $10,000 — *nu,* what can we do?" At the meeting, R' Aharon gave a fiery talk about the obligation to support Torah study, adducing proofs from both the Written and Oral Torah — but he never made a formal request for

(cont. on page 270)

---

1. From *Devarim* 20:4.

16 Teves — לע"נ חנה גיטל בת ר' אברהם אבאיש ע"ה
Dedicated by the Nussen family, Briarwood, NY and Lakewood, NJ

17 Iyar — Piri Steinharter לע"נ פעסל בת יצחק ארי' ע"ה
Dedicated by Avrohom Steinharter

17 Elul — Hanna Rosenstein לע"נ חנה בת משה ע"ה
Dedicated in loving memory by the Rosenstein and Greenberg families

י"ז טבת
17 TEVES / CYCLE 1
January 1, 2002
December 22, 2002
January 11, 2004
December 29, 2004
January 17, 2006

י"ח אייר
18 IYAR / CYCLE 2
April 30, 2002
May 20, 2003
May 9, 2004
May 27, 2005
May 16, 2006

י"ח אלול
18 ELUL / CYCLE 3
August 26, 2002
September 15, 2003
September 4, 2004
September 22, 2005
September 11, 2006

✑ *The Fundamental Principle*

LETTER SEVEN

In an address commemorating the Chofetz Chaim's fiftieth *yahrtzeit*, Rabbi Avraham Pam referred to the above letter of the Chofetz Chaim. The following is drawn from that address:

Surprisingly, in his farewell letter, not a single word was mentioned about *shemiras halashon*, to which he devoted so much of his life. Instead, he urged his people to support and strengthen the yeshivos and Torah institutions. The Chofetz Chaim's reasoning is obvious:

If Torah as a whole will be strengthened, then each individual *mitzvah* will be observed properly, both *mitzvos* between man and Hashem and between man and his fellow. This, in turn, will lead to love amongst Jews, and acts of kindness will abound — no one will seek to belittle someone else or to besmirch his name. As a result, there will be a significant improvement in matters of *shemiras halashon*.

The Chofetz Chaim told of a scholar who made his rounds amongst the communities, rousing them to improve their ways. When he asked the Vilna *Gaon* which *mitzvos* to stress, he was told, "Speak about strengthening Torah study, for this is the fundamental principle upon which all of Judaism depends."

During the last years of his life, when he was very frail and sickly, the Chofetz Chaim traveled by train from Radin to Grodno to attend an important meeting of the *Vaad HaYeshivos* (Committee for the [Preservation of the] Yeshivos). When he arrived he said, "In my physical condition, taking such a journey is literally putting my life in jeopardy. I would not have undertaken it for a hundred *mitzvos*. For the sake of strengthening Torah and the yeshivos, however, one must be willing even to sacrifice his life."[1]

It is impossible to talk about the Chofetz Chaim without mentioning *shemiras halashon*. The Chofetz Chaim wanted all Jews to feel the same love for each other as he felt for them. A person does not come down to this world to cause pain and unpleasantness to others. To the contrary, his soul was dispatched from the celestial worlds to bring joy, aid and pleasure to his fellow Jews.

Among the many arguments the Chofetz Chaim presented against *lashon hara*, he pointed out that as low as a Jew may stoop, he would never incriminate his fellow Jew by informing against him to the Czarist government. Yet when one slanders a fellow Jew, he in effect becomes an informer; because as long as no one mentions other people's faults, Hashem, in His mercy, tends to delay punishing the guilty. Once a person calls

(cont. on page 270)

The Chofetz Chaim wanted all Jews to feel the same love for each other as he felt for them.

---

1. Rabbi Pam himself demonstrated great self-sacrifice for the cause of Torah in the last years of his life, when he was extremely frail and suffered from various ailments. On July 11, 2001, a little more than a month before his passing, R' Pam was brought by ambulance to address the annual parlor meeting for the benefit of *Shuvu*, the organization which he founded to provide Torah education to Russian immigrant children in Eretz Yisrael.

---

17 Teves — Daniel Saul Douglas לע"נ דוד שלמה בן אל' הלוי ז"ל
Our learning is a זכות for Dad's נשמה, our family and כלל ישראל. Linda & Norman Mintz

18 Iyar — In memory of our Rebbe, Rabbi Moshe Rosenberg לע"נ ר' משה בן ר' ישראל ז"ל
Dedicated by Seniors תש"ס, Bais Kaila, Lakewood, NJ

18 Elul — May Hashem open our hearts and minds
to perform the מצוה of שמירת הלשון properly.

י"ח טבת
18 TEVES / CYCLE 1

January 2, 2002
December 23, 2002
January 12, 2004
December 30, 2004
January 18, 2006

י"ט אייר
19 IYAR / CYCLE 2

May 1, 2002
May 21, 2003
May 10, 2004
May 28, 2005
May 17, 2006

י"ט אלול
19 ELUL / CYCLE 3

August 27, 2002
September 16, 2003
September 5, 2004
September 23, 2005
September 12, 2006

❧ *The Grateful Guest*

LETTER EIGHT

*O*ur Sages teach: "What does a good guest say? 'Whatever effort my host has expended, has been for my sake.' And what does a bad guest say? 'Whatever effort my host has expended, has been for his own benefit'" (Berachos 58a). The meaning of this is obvious. A good guest, who is given room and board by his host and observes all that the host does in providing for his every need, will easily recognize and appreciate that, indeed, his host is working hard for his sake. Only a fool would say that his host's hard work was all for himself.*

All of us are like guests on this world, in which Hashem is, of course, the Host. As King David said, "I am a visitor in the world," (Tehillim 119:19). We believe with perfect faith "that the Creator, Blessed is His Name, creates and guides all creatures, and that He alone made, makes and will make every-thing."[1] All happenings are directed by Hashem and all wondrous occurrences and great wisdoms which become revealed in this world are all from Hashem, Who stands watch over everything, and Who instills wis-dom and understanding into the hearts of inventors who create wondrous inventions. Everything is available in its proper time, and all is for the benefit of man. It is, therefore, incumbent upon every individual to recognize all the good that his Creator showers upon him. We shall demonstrate this point by way of the following:

In years past, when a person needed to embark on a distant journey, he traveled for months via a horse-drawn wagon over rough road in inclement weather. The difficulties which he encountered were awesome. But later, Hashem gave man the wisdom to invent the locomotive and railroad system. Now, a trip which used to take weeks, takes only a day or two. The trip itself is quite comfortable, and does not involve many of the difficulties which are common to wagon travel.

Of course the railroad did not turn every man's journey into a smooth ride from start to finish. There were many small towns and hamlets which had no rail service. It was still necessary to travel by wagon to the nearest train station and this first part of the journey often involved great hardship. But then the automobile was invented. Every town and hamlet has at least one or two autos which can transport passengers from their home to the nearest station, in a short amount of time and in comfort.

A person must ask himself: "For what purpose have these inventions been revealed?"

(cont. on page 270)

> *It is incumbent upon every individual to recognize all the good that his Creator showers upon him.*

---

1. From the Thirteen Principles of Faith as formulated by *Rambam*.

DAY 109

י"ט טבת
19 TEVES / CYCLE 1

January 3, 2002
December 24, 2002
January 13, 2004
December 31, 2004
January 19, 2006

כ אייר
20 IYAR / CYCLE 2

May 2, 2002
May 22, 2003
May 11, 2004
May 29, 2005
May 18, 2006

כ אלול
20 ELUL / CYCLE 3

August 28, 2002
September 17, 2003
September 6, 2004
September 24, 2005
September 13, 2006

✑ The Purpose of Modern Transportation

LETTER EIGHT (cont.)

I have pondered well the question of why Hashem has granted recent generations such inventions as the railroad system and automobile, which make life so much easier. And I have arrived at the following conclusion:

As all of us know, the primary purpose of a Jew in this world is to accrue merit through Torah study, doing mitzvos and good deeds so that he will thereby attain eternal life in the World to Come. As the Torah states: "Hashem commanded us to perform all these decrees, to fear Hashem our G-d, for our good, all the days, to give us life as this very day" (Devarim 6:24). This world, as we know, is but an anteroom to the World to Come, the banquet hall of reward (Avos 4:21).

In earlier generations, people were healthier physically and Jewish communities were stronger spiritually. The sounds of Torah study reverberated in every community and the people clung steadfastly to Hashem and His Torah. An arduous journey in those days was not as traumatic as today and it did not present spiritual pitfalls. Even as they traveled, Jewish men remained engrossed in Torah and exchanged Torah thoughts with one another.

In recent generations, however, there has been a marked decline in man's physical stamina; a long wagon journey would require a recuperation period. Furthermore, there has been a general weakening of Torah knowledge in the world. Were travel to be as difficult and dangerous as in earlier generations, Torah study would suffer and much Torah would be forgotten from among the Jewish people.

Hashem, in His infinite mercy, wishes to make us righteous and to increase Torah among us. Therefore, He instilled wisdom and understanding in the minds of scientists and inventors to develop means of transportation which would make travel easier for the Jewish people. A wise person who has been blessed by Hashem with the mental capacity for learning should appreciate that Hashem has made travel so much easier for him. He should express his thanks to Hashem that due to these discoveries, he is able to devote more time to the study of Torah.

Were travel to be as difficult as in earlier times, Torah study would suffer.

In a footnote, the Chofetz Chaim cites the verse, "For the ways of Hashem are straight, and the righteous shall walk with them and the wayward shall stumble over them" (*Hoshea* 14:10). He applies it to those who abuse the great gifts of modern inventions with which Hashem has blessed recent generations, by using them for sin. We see this vividly in our days

(cont. on page 271)

19 Teves — Chaya Rosenberg ע"ה לע"נ חי' בת ר' יצחק ע"ה
Dedicated by her children

20 Iyar — לע"נ ליפא אורי בן משה הלוי ז"ל
Dedicated by his family

20 Elul — In loving memory ע"ה לע"נ שפריינצא בת שלמה יואל ע"ה
May it serve as a זכות for her נשמה.

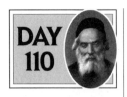
כ טבת
20 TEVES / CYCLE 1

January 4, 2002
December 25, 2002
January 14, 2004
January 1, 2005
January 20, 2006

כ"א אייר
21 IYAR / CYCLE 2

May 3, 2002
May 23, 2003
May 12, 2004
May 30, 2005
May 19, 2006

כ"א אלול
21 ELUL / CYCLE 3

August 29, 2002
September 18, 2003
September 7, 2004
September 25, 2005
September 14, 2006

✍ *Make Every Minute Count*

LETTER EIGHT (cont.)

R' Elazar was asked by his students: "What can a person do to be spared the 'birthpangs' of Mashiach [i.e. the pre-Messianic period]?" [He responded]: "One should occupy himself with Torah and acts of kindness" (Sanhedrin 98b).

*A*s is well known, we are living in Ikvesa D'Meshicha, the period preceding the arrival of Mashiach, for many of the descriptions of that era as stated by our Sages have already materialized. The sufferings increase from day to day and every Jew is in need of great merit so that he can be saved from these travails. The primary source of merit, which has no equal, is that of Torah study; it shields us in time of difficulty or danger.*

Therefore in our day, when with the advent of the railroad and automobile, traveling has become so much easier and less time-consuming, we must take advantage of this and utilize wisely the time which we have been granted. A person who is capable of learning Torah should dedicate additional time for Hashem's sake and set it aside for the study of Torah, rather than waste it on nonsense. Even while one is at home and not traveling, he should feel gratitude toward Hashem that in general his life has been made easier and he has been granted more time for himself through the modern methods of travel — and that this affords him the opportunity to accomplish more in the realm of Torah and mitzvos.

Many have noted a strange and unfortunate fact. Our generation has been granted an incredible array of appliances and other conveniences which should make life easier. As the Chofetz Chaim noted, travel had already been made easier in his time. We know that life within the home has been made easier as we have unlimited access to virtually every sort of staple at any given time. Gone are the days when water was drawn from the well, clothing were washed by hand and man's bodily functions needed to be attended to out in the fields.

One should feel gratitude toward Hashem that modern inventions have made his life easier.

Yet life has not become more relaxed. To the contrary, it seems that our ancestors' lives in pre-war Europe were far more serene than our own, and they devoted themselves to the service of Hashem with far greater peace of mind. To at least some degree, the lack of serenity that we experience is our own fault.

We live in a very small world; information can be transmitted across the globe via phone, fax, media and other means in a matter of seconds. But does this mean that we must enslave ourselves to this "communication explosion"? Certainly we do not need the radio, with its flood of immorality and violence, as our ever-present companion. Other, even more harmful methods of communication, need not be mentioned.

Let us use the blessings of technology for spiritual benefit, such as listening to tapes of Torah lectures and the like. At the same time, let us be careful to avoid the dangerous traps that our modern world presents.

Book IV:

Selected Insights

Insights of the
Chofetz Chaim
as recorded by his son,

R' Aryeh Leib HaKohen Kagan, in
Kol Kisvei Chofetz Chaim,
Volume III

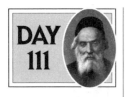
כ"א טבת
21 TEVES / CYCLE 1

January 5, 2002
December 26, 2002
January 15, 2004
January 2, 2005
January 21, 2006

כ"ב אייר
22 IYAR / CYCLE 2

May 4, 2002
May 24, 2003
May 13, 2004
May 31, 2005
May 20, 2006

כ"ב אלול
22 ELUL / CYCLE 3

August 30, 2002
September 19, 2003
September 8, 2004
September 26, 2005
September 15, 2006

❧ *Fine-Tuning*

INSIGHTS OF THE CHOFETZ CHAIM

The amount of merchandise a laborer is expected to produce is in proportion to the material he is given to work with.

A person is expected to accomplish in the spiritual realm in accordance with the inborn abilities with which Hashem has blessed him. When he stands before the Heavenly Tribunal, he will be held accountable if his accomplishments fall short of his potential.

R' Aryeh Leib related that as a youth, he tried his hand at making some pocket money through buying and selling. His father reprimanded him, "Is it for this that Heaven has given you superior intellect? You are taking a utensil intended for collecting precious gems, and are using it to shovel refuse."

On another occasion, the Chofetz Chaim admonished his son not to go in the way of youths who disrupt their Torah learning to engage in idle conversation. Young Aryeh Leib replied, "But it is not proper to ignore a friend or acquaintance who approaches me in the *beis midrash*!'"The Chofetz Chaim replied:

> *"Have you ever noticed how on market day every merchant is totally preoccupied with selling his wares to the throngs who crowd around his stand? Now, what if at that time the merchant would be approached by a relative whom he has not seen for a very long time?*

Do you think that he will engage him in lengthy conversation as the customers stand waiting? Certainly not! He will greet his relative and then beg forgiveness for being unable to converse at that time, and he will ask the relative to return after dark when the market is closed for the day. Then he will greet him warmly and spend more time with him."

Once, when the Chofetz Chaim and his son were studying the laws of the *arba minim* (four species), they came upon the case of *hadasim* (myrtles) which have lost their freshness. If all the leaves of a twig have dried up it is invalid, but if they are merely wilted it may be used. However, if all the leaves below the top level are dry, then according to some opinions the twig is fit for the *mitzvah* only if the top leaves are fresh (and not wilted). At this point, the Chofetz Chaim sighed and commented:

"In a generation when most Jews observe Torah and mitzvos, then even when their service of Hashem is somewhat wanting and they are like a 'wilted twig,' Hashem will accept their service as passable. In our days, however, when to our misfortune, the majority of Jews are 'dried leaves,' devoid of any faith in Hashem and His Torah, and a small minority remain to shield the generation, it is crucial that our Torah and mitzvos be wholesome, and that our deeds bring about kiddush Shem Shamayim (sanctification of Hashem's Name)."

We will be held accountable if our accomplishments fall short of our potential.

כ"ב טבת
22 TEVES / CYCLE 1

January 6, 2002
December 27, 2002
January 16, 2004
January 3, 2005
January 22, 2006

כ"ג אייר
23 IYAR / CYCLE 2

May 5, 2002
May 25, 2003
May 14, 2004
June 1, 2005
May 21, 2006

כ"ג אלול
23 ELUL / CYCLE 3

August 31, 2002
September 20, 2003
September 9, 2004
September 27, 2005
September 16, 2006

❧ Chillul Hashem

INSIGHTS OF THE CHOFETZ CHAIM

The Chofetz Chaim would often caution his son to avoid any action which could lead to disgrace of the Torah and its students. Once, his son asked, "I am not a renowned personality from whom others will learn — why must I be so careful concerning my actions?" The Chofetz Chaim replied:

*D*o not think this way. True, generally speaking, people do not look at you as a renowned personality. However, when you do something improper, the same people will say scornfully, 'Look how So-and-so — a supposedly distinguished individual — is so lax regarding a mitzvah.' At that time, they will portray you as a man of enormous stature, so that your infraction will appear that much worse. Therefore, you must be extremely careful in all your actions."

To his mind, the worst sin of all was *chillul Hashem* (desecration of Hashem's Name). He would often quote the words of *Sefer Yerei'im* (7): כִּי כָתוּב זֶה נוֹקֵב וְיוֹרֵד עַד הַתְּהוֹם, וְעַל לָאו זֶה יְדְוּ כָּל הַדְּוּיִם , *For this verse (regarding chillul Hashem-Vayikra 22:32) pierces and descends to the very depths, and it is for this [negative commandment] that all those who feel pain are pained.*

Towards the end of the Chofetz Chaim's life, when it became exceedingly difficult for him to study from a text, he would ask that a *sefer* (usually a *chumash*) be opened before him. Though such study was difficult for him, he did this to prevent *chillul Hashem* lest someone enter his room and think that he was sitting idle. This is similar to a Talmudic teaching: "What is *chillul Hashem*? ...R' Yochanan said: 'Someone like me, who goes four *amos* without Torah and without *tefillin*' " (*Yoma* 86a).

In a certain community, a number of people had flagrantly violated *halachah* by going to secular court to voice accusations against their fellow Jew. The Chofetz Chaim wasted no time in penning a strong letter to the community's *rav*, decrying such open transgression of the laws of *lashon hara*, as well as the *chillul Hashem* of taking one's grievances against his fellow Jew to a secular court.

> *This matter has become public knowledge in the outlying communities, that for every trivial matter they do this [to seek reparations in secular court], and this is a great disgrace to the Jewish people. Why does his honor not rebuke them concerning the awesome chillul Hashem which results from this, that the name of Israel has become an object of scorn and derision among the nations?*
> *...And how will each person respond? — "So-and-so is the intentional sinner in this case, while I am only an inadvertent*

(cont. on page 271)

The Chofetz Chaim took great pains to avoid any possibility of chillul Hashem.

לע"נ הרבנית רחל ע"ה בת ר' אהרן זצ"ל — **22 Teves**
Dedicated by Yitzchok & Rivka Mashitz

23 Iyar — Tillie Herman ע"ה לע"נ טאבא בת ר' ישראל ע"ה
Dedicated by Ruth & Philip Kipust and family

לע"נ רישקא בת אליעזר ע"ה — **23 Elul**
Dedicated by Avraham Yaakov & Sorah Levin and family

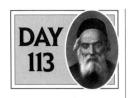

DAY 113

כ"ג טבת
23 TEVES / CYCLE 1

January 7, 2002
December 28, 2002
January 17, 2004
January 4, 2005
January 23, 2006

כ"ד אייר
24 IYAR / CYCLE 2

May 6, 2002
May 26, 2003
May 15, 2004
June 2, 2005
May 22, 2006

כ"ד אלול
24 ELUL / CYCLE 3

September 1, 2002
September 21, 2003
September 10, 2004
September 28, 2005
September 17, 2006

✍ *A Time of Drought*

INSIGHTS OF THE CHOFETZ CHAIM

The Chofetz Chaim's nephew, R' Leib Leibowitz, once bemoaned the fact that the difficulties of earning a living often disturbed his concentration during *tefillah*. The Chofetz Chaim consoled him by way of a parable:

"*Have you ever seen the wholesale grain merchants as they purchase grain from the farmers? They test a sampling of the grain to determine the sand content mixed into the grain, and this is deducted from the price. However, this is so only when there is an abundance of grain and prices are low. If, however, there is a drought and grain is scarce, the merchants will accept the grain as it is and will pay the full price regardless of the sand content.*

"*So it is, my dear nephew, regarding our spiritual efforts. In previous generations when the vast majority of Jews were faithful to Hashem and observed His mitzvos, a Jew's good deeds were scrutinized carefully in Heaven before they gained acceptance. Today, when unfortunately the generation's spiritual level has fallen drastically, due to the difficulties of life and the influence of heretics, it is a time of 'spiritual drought.' Heaven is not*

> *so exacting in judging our deeds and they are readily accepted, as long as we act for the sake of Hashem."*

Above (Day 111), the Chofetz Chaim stated that, "In our days, when the majority of Jews are... devoid of any faith in Hashem and His Torah, and a small minority remain to shield the generation, it is crucial that our Torah and *mitzvos* be wholesome, and that our deeds bring about *kiddush Shem Shamayim*." Here, however, he states that "it is a time of 'spiritual drought.' Heaven is not so exacting in judging our deeds..." To resolve this apparent contradiction, we suggest:

To serve as a "shield" for the generation, one's service of Hashem must be of a superior quality. On an individual level, however, a person's good deeds are more readily acceptable in Heaven during a time of "spiritual drought," when comparatively few hearken to the word of Hashem.

If the Chofetz Chaim considered his time one of "spiritual drought," how much more so is this true in our times, when the world is steeped in materialism and self-gratification. Every *mitzvah*, word of Torah and *tefillah*, or act of kindness that we accomplish is exceedingly precious to Hashem and has enormous impact in the Upper Worlds.

As the Chofetz Chaim noted above (Day 88), with each succeeding generation, the collective merit of the Jewish people increases and it becomes easier to hasten *Mashiach's* arrival. We have every reason to be hopeful that our generation, whose spiritual efforts brings such pleasure to Hashem, will be the one that will merit to greet *Mashiach*.

Every mitzvah that we accomplish is exceedingly precious to Hashem.

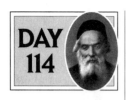

כ"ד טבת
24 TEVES / CYCLE 1

January 8, 2002
December 29, 2002
January 18, 2004
January 5, 2005
January 24, 2006

כ"ה אייר
25 IYAR / CYCLE 2

May 7, 2002
May 27, 2003
May 16, 2004
June 3, 2005
May 23, 2006

כ"ה אלול
25 ELUL / CYCLE 3

September 2, 2002
September 22, 2003
September 11, 2004
September 29, 2005
September 18, 2006

✍ *A Stranger Comes to Town*

INSIGHTS OF THE CHOFETZ CHAIM

The Chofetz Chaim once said:

Hashem conducts this world with exacting precision; nothing is left to chance. We, however, who cannot fathom His ways and often wonder why things are the way they are, are like the guest who arrived in a city and came to the local shul on Shabbos morning. During krias HaTorah (the public Torah reading), he observed how the gabbai summoned one person from one corner of the shul, and a second person from the opposite corner, seemingly without any order or system. Later, the guest approached the gabbai and said, "It seems to me that you were just calling people up haphazardly. Wouldn't it make more sense to call them to the Torah in the order of how they are seated?"

The gabbai replied, "You are a stranger here and have only recently arrived. Were you to be here for a few months' time, you would know by now that there is a system to how I call people to the Torah. Some were called to the Torah last week because of a yahrtzeit or some other reason, and therefore they were not called today. No one is simply ignored or passed over..."

We are like that guest. We come to this world for a relatively short period of time and are wholly unaware of, for example, what transpired in a particular family in centuries gone by. We do not know their good and bad deeds, the sufferings they endured or the good times which they enjoyed. We also do not know what the future holds in store for that family — and yet we question Hashem's ways!

We must always be mindful of the Torah's words: "The Rock! — perfect is His work, for all His paths are justice; a G-d of faith without iniquity, righteous and fair is He" (Devarim 32:4).

Hashem conducts this world with exacting precision; nothing is left to chance.

When Yosef *HaTzaddik* (the Righteous) revealed himself with the words, "I am Yosef," (*Bereishis* 45:3), his brothers "could not answer him for they felt disconcerted before him." Until the moment that Yosef revealed himself, the sons of Yaakov had found the actions of Egypt's viceroy, who was actually their long-lost brother, to be baffling, at the very least. He had accused them of being spies, demanded that they bring their youngest brother before him, imprisoned them, then sent all but Shimon home with their money returned and provisions for the road... When they returned, he invited them to join him for a meal at which they were seated according to age and maternal descent (without their having revealed this information) with Binyamin seated next to his brother Yosef. Then as they headed home, the chief of Yosef's household staff overtook them. Having "discovered" the

(cont. on page 271)

24 Teves — Sarah Riva Cantor לע"נ שרה ריבא בת ר' יעקב ע"ה
Dedicated to a beloved mother, by the Altman and Cantor families

25 Iyar — Etty Perl לע"נ אסתר ראצא בת דוד ע"ה
Dedicated by her daughter and son-in-law, Yaakov & Rayze Abraham

25 Elul —

DAY 115

◥ *All for the Best*

INSIGHTS OF THE CHOFETZ CHAIM

*T*he Chofetz Chaim once overheard some-one ask his friend, "So how are you?" to which the friend replied, "Baruch Hashem, it wouldn't hurt if things were a little better." The Chofetz Chaim interjected, "How do you know it wouldn't hurt? Perhaps it would!"

The Chofetz Chaim was alluding to the teaching: "Whatever Hashem does He does for the good," (*Berachos* 60b). In an address, Rabbi Avraham Pam cited the Chofetz Chaim's comment and elaborated upon it:

> One must be careful not to react when hearing of severe judgments that befall others, by saying: "What did he ever do to deserve such *tzaros* (sufferings)?" or similar remarks that seem to question Divine judgment. Rather than making such comments, we should remain firm in our faith that when *Mashiach* comes and the spirit of prophecy will return, events that puzzle us today will become clear.
>
> There are times when events that seem incomprehensible to some *can* be understandable to us. One's level of faith and trust has much to do with how we interpret events.
>
> My mother, of blessed memory, once related to me an incident that was told to her by her father, the Shedlitzer *Rav*, זצ"ל.

A Jew in Shedlitz had sufficient Torah knowledge to qualify easily as a *rav*. Instead, the man chose to be a merchant and indeed was very successful. Then it happened that the man received a telegram informing him that a ship carrying a huge quantity of his merchandise had sunk in a storm — all of its cargo was lost. The merchant would never be able to recover from the financial setback he had suffered. He had been reduced to poverty overnight.

When the man's wife and children read the telegram, they despaired: what would life be like now? As for the man himself, he stood stock-still, simply holding the telegram in his hands and muttering over and over again, "This (telegram) is a *k'sav rabbanus* (a certificate of rabbinic appointment)..."

Upon hearing this strange remark, the family wondered if the shock of the news had affected the man's mind. Then he explained.

"I became a merchant thinking that it was the right thing to do. This telegram is a message from Heaven informing me that I erred. The *Ribono shel Olam* wants me to be a *rav*."

> **Whatever Hashem does, He does for the good.**

כ"ו טבת
26 TEVES / CYCLE 1

January 10, 2002
December 31, 2002
January 20, 2004
January 7, 2005
January 26, 2006

כ"ז אייר
27 IYAR / CYCLE 2

May 9, 2002
May 29, 2003
May 18, 2004
June 5, 2005
May 25, 2006

כ"ז אלול
27 ELUL / CYCLE 3

September 4, 2002
September 24, 2003
September 13, 2004
October 1, 2005
September 20, 2006

❧ *There is None Besides Him*

INSIGHTS OF THE CHOFETZ CHAIM

The first of the Thirteen Principles of Faith begins: "I believe with complete faith that the Creator, Blessed is His Name, creates and guides all creatures..." Said the Chofetz Chaim:

Every person must ask himself: "Do I truly believe that whatever happens in my life is through hashgachah pratis (exacting Divine Providence)?" One whose faith is truly wholesome does not bear a grudge towards anyone, including someone who has harmed him. We find this with David, who, after being cursed by Shimi ben Geirah, said, "Hashem told him to curse" (II Shmuel 16:10), meaning that Heaven had incited him to do this.

The Talmud (Chullin 7b) teaches that when a Jew's emunah (faith) is perfect, he is not afraid of any form of harm or adversary. Thus, R' Chanina was unafraid when a Roman matron attempted to harm him through sorcery. He explained his serenity by quoting the verse (Devarim 4:35), "אֵין עוֹד מִלְבַדּוֹ, ... there is none besides Him." By this, he meant to say, "I fear no one but Hashem." It is through such faith that he overcame her powers. This is what the Talmud means when it states, "R' Chanina was different, for his merit was abundant."

In a famous explanation of the above Talmudic incident, Rabbi Chaim Volozhiner teaches an important principle:

> Surely the Talmud does not mean that Rabbi Chanina viewed himself as someone whose Torah and good deeds had earned him abundant merit to ensure that he would not fall prey to the power of sorcery. Rather, the meaning is...that in reality, the forces of impurity [from which sorcery derives its power] have no independent power, Heaven forfend. It is Hashem Who has established these powers, superior to the natural forces of the stars and constellations, so that they can produce actions which can even alter the natural order of the world. *Were it not for Hashem's will [that this be], these forces would cease to exist.*
>
> Rabbi Chanina did not rely on the merit of the sanctity of his Torah study and his abundant good deeds. Rather, he knew that established within his own heart was the firm belief that אֵין עוֹד מִלְבַדּוֹ, *there is none besides Him* — there is no power in this world at all other than Hashem. With the sanctity of his thoughts, Rabbi Chanina attached himself to the Master of All Powers, the One and Only Ruler Whose glory fills every world. Therefore, he was certain that the power of sorcery, which derives its strength from the forces of impurity, would have no dominion over him. This is what Rabbi Chanina meant when he said [to the sorceress], "You will not succeed — for it is written, 'there is none besides Him.'"

When a Jew's emunah (faith) is rock-firm, he is not afraid of any harm or adversary.

(cont. on page 272)

26 Teves — Yehuda (Jerry) Sostchin לע"נ יהודה טביה בן דוד ז"ל
Lovingly dedicated by his Ima, grandparents, sister and Aunt Bayla

27 Iyar — In honor of our children Menachem Mendel, Devorah Ruth and Deana Erin Davis
Dedicated by Brina & Dovid Davis

27 Elul — L'zichron Olam, our father לע"נ ר' משה אברהם בן אלטר זצ"ל
Dedicated by his daughter, Hana Lipkovitz and family

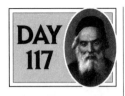

כ"ז טבת
27 TEVES / CYCLE 1

January 11, 2002
January 1, 2003
January 21, 2004
January 8, 2005
January 27, 2006

כ"ח אייר
28 IYAR / CYCLE 2

May 10, 2002
May 30, 2003
May 19, 2004
June 6, 2005
May 26, 2006

כ"ח אלול
28 ELUL / CYCLE 3

September 5, 2002
September 25, 2003
September 14, 2004
October 2, 2005
September 21, 2006

❧ On Spiritual Growth

INSIGHTS OF THE CHOFETZ CHAIM

"And these matters that I command you *today* shall be upon your heart" (*Devarim* 6:6).

When approaching a mitzvah, a person should view it as if it is his only mitzvah, as if he is the only person in the world and as if this is the only day on which he can perform it.

"Remove your shoes from your feet, for the place upon which you stand is holy ground" (*Shemos* 3:5).

A Jew should always strive to ascend to a higher spiritual level. Do not think: "My abilities are pitiful, there is no way that I can attain spiritual heights — now, if I had the intellect and perception of So-and-so, then I would be able to amount to something!" This is a mistake, for "the place upon which you stand," that is, your present spiritual level — whatever it may be — "is holy ground," it can eventually lead to sanctity and upliftment. Therefore, "Remove your shoes from your feet," cast aside sin and strive to grow in your service of Hashem.

The halachah states that when reciting Shemoneh Esrei, one praying outside Eretz Yisrael should face Eretz Yisrael, one praying in Eretz Yisrael should face Jerusalem, and one praying in Jerusalem should face the site of the Beis HaMikdash. It does not say that one praying outside Eretz Yisrael should face the Beis HaMikdash, for in spiritual growth one must ascend slowly a level at a time and not attempt many levels at once.

The Talmud states (Succah 52b): "A man's evil inclination threatens every day to overpower him and seeks to kill him, as it says (Tehillim 37:32), 'the wicked one watches for the righteous person and seeks to slay him.' And if not for the Holy One Who aids him, he would be unable to withstand it, as it says (ibid. v. 33), 'Hashem will not leave him in his hand, nor condemn him in His judgment.' "

This means that even if a person has succeeded in prevailing once or twice, the yetzer hara will not give up and will seek to overpower him once more — we need Hashem's help constantly in order to prevail. It is obvious that a person can hope for such Divine assistance only if he gathers all his spiritual strength [to fight against his inclination]; otherwise, he cannot expect Hashem to help him.

An analogy to this is the mitzvah to help a fellow Jew to load his animal. One is obligated in this only if the animal's owner will share the work; however, if the owner says, "It is your mitzvah, I will sit on the side while you do the work," then there is no obligation (Devarim 22:4 with Rashi).

In a similar sense, Hashem helps those who help themselves.

One must ascend slowly, one spiritual level at a time and not attempt many levels at once.

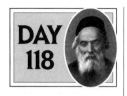

DAY 118

כ"ח טבת
28 TEVES / CYCLE 1

January 12, 2002
January 2, 2003
January 22, 2004
January 9, 2005
January 28, 2006

כ"ט אייר*
29 IYAR* / CYCLE 2

May 11, 2002
May 31, 2003
May 20, 2004
June 7, 2005
May 25, 2006

כ"ט אלול*
29 ELUL* / CYCLE 3

September 6, 2002
September 26, 2003
September 15, 2004
October 3, 2005
September 22, 2006

✌ *What to Ask For*

INSIGHTS OF THE CHOFETZ CHAIM

In the *Ahavah Rabbah* prayer we say: "Enlighten our eyes in Your Torah, attach our hearts to Your commandments... so that we may not feel inner shame nor be humiliated." The Chofetz Chaim explained this by way of a parable:

"When I was in the city of Snovisk, I saw a little girl playing with a doll. I thought to myself: 'If I would put this doll away and offer it to this girl twenty years from now, wouldn't she laugh? That which was precious to her as a child would have no value to her at that age.'

"So it is with a person when he ascends to the World of Truth. He will feel shamed over what he considered valuable during his life on this world. For in the World of Truth, nothing but Torah and good deeds has any value."

When a person wants to ask something of Hashem, He should not ask, "Ribono shel Olam, give me this and that," for a person does not know what is truly in his best interests. Wealth, for example, is not always good for a person, as it says, "...riches hoarded by their owner to his misfortune" (Koheles 5:12)... Rather, the proper way to pray is, "Ribono shel Olam, if this request is good for

* On 29 Iyar and 29 Elul, the lesson for Day 119 should be learnt together with today's lesson.

me, then please grant it to me." This can be better understood by way of a parable:

A man told his neighbor who owned a candy store, "When my little boy comes by your store, give him some candy and I will pay you later." The storekeeper, however, was not a very smart man and he gave the boy far too much candy, causing him to become sick! When the man came to the boy's father to be paid, he was told, "Fool that you are! Why did you feed my child so much candy until he became sick? For this I should pay you? I had meant that you should give him a few candies — not an entire bag!"

The two went to beis din (Rabbinical court) — and who do you think won? The child's father, of course.

This is how it is with man on this world. He thinks to himself, "If only I had this and that, I would be happy" — and he complains inwardly when his prayers for these items are not granted. However, he should know that if his prayers would be answered, then when he would arrive at the World of Truth, he would see clearly that attaining these things was really not to his benefit. Then he would say, "Ribono shel Olam, why did You give me this? You knew that it was not good for me, so why did You grant it to me?"

This is why Hashem does not grant us what He knows is not to our advantage. Such being the case, why should one complain when his requests are not granted?

A person does not know what is truly in his best interests.

DAY 119

כ"ט טבת
29 TEVES / CYCLE 1
January 13, 2002
January 3, 2003
January 23, 2004
January 10, 2005
January 29, 2006

כ"ט אייר
29 IYAR / CYCLE 2
May 11, 2002
May 31, 2003
May 20, 2004
June 7, 2005
May 25, 2006

כ"ט אלול
29 ELUL / CYCLE 3
September 6, 2002
September 26, 2003
September 15, 2004
October 3, 2005
September 22, 2006

✍ *With an Eye Towards Heaven*

INSIGHTS OF THE CHOFETZ CHAIM

Once, a distinguished gentleman of great wealth, with whom the Chofetz Chaim was well acquainted, came to seek his advice. His business enterprises were all doing very well, and he now had the opportunity to embark on a new, lucrative venture. While the venture seemed very promising, undertaking it would mean that even more of his time and energy would be channeled towards business. Should he undertake it?

The Chofetz Chaim initially replied by citing the Mishnah, "Anyone excessively occupied in business cannot become a scholar" (Avos 2:6). He then added:

Our Sages teach that a person's earnings for the year are decreed on Rosh Hashanah. Therefore, overexerting oneself by undertaking excessive involvement in business will not earn anyone an extra cent.

This can be likened to a person who sought to increase the amount of wine in his cellar. He hit upon what to his mind was a brilliant idea: He added a few extra spouts to each barrel of wine, thinking that, this way, more wine would come out. Of course, he actually accomplished nothing for the amount of wine remained the same.

The Chofetz Chaim's son, R' Aryeh Leib, concludes: "It is told that the rich man heeded my father's advice and did not undertake this venture. Those who did, however, lost all their money."

In an address during the *Aseres Yemei Teshuvah* (Ten Days of Repentance), the Chofetz Chaim said:

> *When a person stands in judgment before the King of Glory, he is in need of great mercy. Above all, he is need of mercy that the Accuser [Satan] should not stand and accuse. Like in a court case on this world, if the prosecutor is silent, the defendant is exonerated. Initially we plead, "Our Father, our King, exterminate every adversary and foe from upon us," meaning, that the Accuser should be denied presence at our judgment. However, if we lack sufficient merit for this, then we plead that at least, "Our Father, our King, seal the mouths of our adversaries and accusers," meaning, that the Accuser should not be permitted to voice his accusations against us.*

How does a person merit that the Accuser cannot speak against him? One must know that Hashem judges us מִדָּה כְּנֶגֶד מִדָּה, measure for measure; the way we deal with others is the way that Hashem deals with us. Therefore, if we are careful not to speak against others, then Hashem will not permit the Accuser to speak against us.

(cont. on page 272)

Hashem judges us מִדָּה כְּנֶגֶד מִדָּה, **measure for measure.**

29 Teves — לע"נ שמעון בן אביגדור ליבלינג ז"ל
Dedicated by the Liebling family

29 Iyar — Lewis Buckman לע"נ אליעזר בן יצחק הלוי ז"ל
Dedicated in loving memory by Yaakov & Rana Reisman and family

29 Elul — Freda Adler לע"נ פרעדא בת אברהם ע"ה

Continuations...

CONTINUED FROM DAY 5 — PAGE 11

this people has drawn close, with its mouth and its lips it has honored Me, yet it has distanced its heart from Me" (*Yeshayahu* 29:13), and he would conclude his message with, "מיר זאלען זוכה זיין צו אבערקאלע אמת, *May we merit a bit of truth!"* (*Lev Eliyahu,* Vol. I, p. 22).

CONTINUED FROM DAY 7 — PAGE 15

returned to R' Shraga and informed him that he wished to make his purchase at the price which had been quoted.

To the man's surprise, R' Shraga said, "I will be happy to sell you the goods — but at a cheaper price than I had originally quoted.

"You see, after you left I thought it over and I realized that I really *could* offer you a reduction, since as you maintained, you were making an unusually large purchase. And although you returned to me prepared to accept my original price, I will sell it to you for less, in keeping with the verse, "Hashem, who may reside in Your tent?.... One who speaks truth in his heart" *(B'Derech Eitz Chaim).*

CONTINUED FROM DAY 8 — PAGE 17

R' Weismandel was taken aback. Back home, he was accustomed to seeing a store full of anxious customers, carefully examining *esrog* upon *esrog* for points of beauty or possible blemishes. Acquiring an *esrog* for this precious *mitzvah* by nonchalantly picking one out of a pile seemed to be trivializing the *mitzvah.*

On the following morning, as a congregant stepped up to the pulpit to serve as a *chazzan,* another man exclaimed angrily, "Yesterday, he told an untruth — how dare he serve as *chazzan!"*

R' Weismandel reflected, "True, we seek to acquire an *esrog* which is free of the minutest blemish. Are we as meticulous in our demands for truth, that a person who represents us before our Creator should be without a blemish of falsehood?"[1]

---

1. The man who voiced his outrage over the *chazzan* may have sinned grievously by shaming the *chazzan* in public (unless the untruth which he uttered was public knowledge and he should have had the sense not to ascend the pulpit). Nevertheless, R' Weismandel was moved by the man's utter intolerance of falsehood.

CONTINUED FROM DAY 10 — PAGE 21

It should be noted that "קַדֵּשׁ עַצְמְךָ בַּמּוּתָר לָךְ, *sanctify yourself even with that which is permissible*" (*Yevamos* 20a), states *Ramban* (*Vayikra* 19:2), is required of every Jew. In *Ramban's* famous words, a person who lives a life of physical indulgence while making sure to do so within the confines of *Halachah* is branded as a "נָבָל בִּרְשׁוּת הַתּוֹרָה, *a degenerate person within the framework of Torah.*" This is a primary reason why even one who *does* have the means to enjoy an indulgent lifestyle should exercise restraint when partaking of the pleasures of this world.

CONTINUED FROM DAY 15 — PAGE 31

individuals from purchasing his *sefarim* if he felt that they would not make use of the *sefer*. "I want buyers who are *bnei Torah*, not benefactors who seek roundabout ways to support me. This is not the proper way."

His brother-in-law, the Steipler *Gaon* (R' Yaakov Yisrael Kanievsky) also displayed a powerful trust in Hashem. The Steipler would allow certain individuals of means to contribute funds towards the publication of his many *sefarim*. Once, he was short a certain sum of money which was needed to publish the next volume of *Kehilos Yaakov*. A family member wanted to contribute this sum, but he knew that the Steipler would never accept it from him (for he really could not afford it). The person gave the money to a second party who presented it to the Steipler as "a gift from someone who wishes to remain anonymous." The Steipler refused the money, saying, "I do not accept money unless I know its source." No sooner had he said these words than a regular contributor toward his *sefarim* entered the house and, without being asked, handed the Steipler the exact sum which was needed! The Steipler turned to the person who had attempted to present the anonymous contribution and said, "Do you see? When something is needed, Hashem provides."

CONTINUED FROM DAY 17 — PAGE 35

R' Segal's personal standards in money matters earned him the reverence of all, including gentiles. Once, he found himself unable to concentrate properly on his studies while sitting in the noisy second-class section of a train. He moved to the first-class section with the intention of paying the additional charge when the ticket attendant would make his rounds. By some error, the attendant never appeared, so upon disembarking, R' Segal approached the station attendant, who said to "forget about it." R' Segal, however, went to the station master to pay the fee. The astounded fellow declared that R' Segal was "one in a million."

CONTINUED FROM DAY 18 — PAGE 37

Maharal (Chiddushei Agados) explains that a man needs his earnings to sustain himself and his family; to rob him of even a small amount is to deprive him of that degree of sustenance. This is why robbing one's fellow is akin to taking his life.

In the modern world, we can see how causing someone a small loss can have major ramifications in his life. Someone can receive a small check which he deposits, only to have it returned because of insufficient funds. Because this check bounces, the depositor's own mortgage check bounces. This damages his credit rating and later, when he needs to obtain a loan for his business, the bank is unwilling to extend credit to him. Thus, the loss caused by a bounced check of a few dollars has led to disastrous results.

CONTINUED FROM DAY 19 — PAGE 39

The Torah teaches that when an animal is offered as an olah, it is entirely burned upon the Altar. However, when a bird is offered, its innards are thrown away. This, says the Midrash (cited by Rashi to Vayikra 1:16), is because an animal eats from its owner's feeding trough, while a bird eats that which it "steals" from private property. This wondrous distinction teaches us that anything which contains a trace of robbery will find no favor before Hashem. Rather, it will be rejected and repulsed.

CONTINUED FROM DAY 20 — PAGE 41

---

affair, on which was printed: "Proceeds to *ma'os chittim*" (Passover fund for the needy). They asked R' Elchonon: "What will be the verdict when this money reaches the Heavenly Court — will it be judged a *mitzvah* of *tzedakah* since it was given for *ma'os chittim*, or a sin since it was raised through gambling and mixed dancing?" R' Elchonon replied, "Who knows whether such money will ever reach the Heavenly Court?"

CONTINUED FROM DAY 21 — PAGE 43

When a person lives a life of dishonesty and deceit, his misdeeds will ultimately come back to haunt him. Conversely, one whose actions are upright and sincere will never regret his way of life, regardless of any short-term difficulties.

CONTINUED FROM DAY 22 — PAGE 45

din (rabbinical court) has ruled against him incorrectly. At such times, one should bear in mind that it is impossible to see matters objectively when one's own interests are involved.

The *Ksav Sofer* (Rabbi Shmuel Binyamin Sofer) relates the following story, which he heard from his father the *Chasam Sofer* (Rabbi Moshe Sofer):

> R' Yehoshua Falk Katz, author of *S'ma*, had a monetary dispute with someone, and later had occasion to raise the question during a gathering of Torah luminaries. He presented the case to them and pointed out why he felt his position was right. One of the scholars opened a volume of *Choshen Mishpat* with the commentary of *S'ma* and showed him that, according to his very own words, his position was wrong! R' Yehoshua arose and declared, "Now I understand the comment of our Sages that 'no man is capable of seeing his own faults.' "

Even a great Torah sage cannot rely on his own reasoning when he is a party to a monetary dispute; he, too, must seek the opinion of other *talmidei chachamim*.

CONTINUED FROM DAY 24 — PAGE 49

more you attempt to flee from your responsibilities as a Jew on this world, the more you will be brought to judgment in the Next World. You will have to return to this world again and again, for you will be forced to rectify your misdeeds — so what is the point of fleeing from your responsibilities?"

CONTINUED FROM DAY 25 — PAGE 51

ly wild and dangerous and to approach it was to endanger one's life. If he still wanted the bull, it would cost him eighty rubles. The Jew offered forty rubles which the gentile quickly accepted. The gentile advised the man to hire several men to transport the dangerous animal but the man declined. To the utter amazement of the gentile and his friends, the Jew slipped a rope over the bull's horns and led the now tame animal away.

The bull was brought to Kovno where it was slaughtered by a G-d-fearing *shochet* in the presence of R' Yehoshua Leib. A portion of its meat was given to the *Rav* while the rest was distributed among the city's *talmidei chachamim* (from *Guardian of Jerusalem [Ish al HaChomah]*).

CONTINUED FROM DAY 26 — PAGE 53

---

fellow. "We have been informed that before leaving the island, you were warned to settle any monetary claims. You have only yourself to blame. All that we will grant you is to open the city gates for a few moments so that you and your family can see each other from a distance."

Imagine the pain of the man and his family as the city gates are opened and then shut a short time later — after many years of separation and months of anticipation. Imagine the man's regret that he did not heed his friend's advice to settle his accounts before leaving the island!

This is the sort of regret the soul would feel were it to stand at the entrance to Gan Eden, only to be denied entry because of the sin of gezel.

CONTINUED FROM DAY 27 — PAGE 55

In the Volozhiner Yeshivah, Torah was studied in shifts, around the clock.[1] R' Chaim Volozhiner would often walk the halls of the yeshivah late at night, keeping watch over the students who were learning. On one particular night, R' Chaim was walking alone, when suddenly he found himself face-to-face with the deceased student! Maintaining his composure, R' Chaim spoke to this soul, which had returned from the Upper World, and asked how it had fared before the Heavenly Tribunal. This was the student's reply:

It had been decided that he be granted immediate entrance to *Gan Eden*, for the sufferings of his illness had atoned for any sins he might have committed. However, as he approached the entrance to *Gan Eden*, Satan blocked his way and declared that he had left this world without having repaid his debt to the innkeeper.

The Heavenly Tribunal was in a quandary. The boy had done all he could to repay the debt; he was certainly not to blame for his friend's memory lapse. Still, he had come to the World of Truth owing someone money. How could he be rid of this blemish on his account?

It was decided that since he was blameless, he would be permitted to return to this world to request of his teacher that he rectify the matter. R' Chaim promised to see to it, and immediately the soul of the student disappeared. R' Chaim summoned the other student, who was left trembling by his teacher's words. The next morning, he set out for the inn and the bill was paid.

---

1. The world's continued existence was predicated upon the Jews' acceptance of the Torah at Sinai. In *Nefesh HaChaim* (4:25), R' Chaim Volozhiner taught that as a corollary of this, were even a moment to pass without Torah being studied somewhere on this earth, the world would cease to exist. This is why he arranged for Torah to be studied in his yeshivah twenty-four hours a day.

CONTINUED FROM DAY 29 — PAGE 59

style," which often means compromising acceptable standards of *tznius* (modesty). He continued:

> There is yet another point to consider. Dressing in style is expensive, as is decorating one's home in elaborate style. A woman who places excessive emphasis on dress and interior decorating also places undue pressure on her husband to provide the money for her expensive tastes. This contradicts a woman's duty to ensure that her husband dedicate himself to the study of Torah to the best of his ability. Furthermore, it is precisely these sorts of pressures which can lead a man to engage in dishonest business practices. When a man's budget is beyond his means, a feeling of desperation can set in, and this can drive one to acquire through deception, that which he simply cannot earn honestly (*Inspiration and Insight*, Vol. I).

CONTINUED FROM DAY 33 — PAGE 67

point, the householder still has the option of hiring someone else. If the householder is a talmid chacham, he should certainly follow this practice, for if the worker were to go away dissatisfied, a chillul Hashem (desecration of Hashem's Name) would likely result, for the worker will say that "the rabbi cheated him."

CONTINUED FROM DAY 36 — PAGE 73

Hashem in business dealings between Jews and non-Jews, and between devout Jews and irreligious Jews. Quite a number of such cases are known to me, and I stand up in reverence for those who sanctify Hashem's Name in our times.

CONTINUED FROM DAY 37 — PAGE 75

legal means. Certainly he will not resort to trickery and theft to increase his income, for such practices will surely lead to distress.
Conversely, Hashem will surely provide for those who sincerely walk in His ways.

CONTINUED FROM DAY 40 — PAGE 81

the Chazon Ish's *yahrtzeit*, the Steipler told a visitor, "I am suffering pain and distress. In the course of the *shiur*, I cited an opinion of the *Birkei Yosef* regarding *tefillin*. I had come across the comment of *Birkei Yosef* in R' Akiva Eiger's glosses to *Rambam's* laws of the Yom Kippur service. I forgot to mention this during the *shiur*. I have been guilty of *geneivas da'as* (deceit), for those who attended the *shiur* now think that I am fluent in the writings of *Birkei Yosef*...

"What can I do? I am old and I forgot to mention this..."

CONTINUED FROM DAY 41 — PAGE 83

Sarah laughed incredulously, for how could a couple so old be granted a child? Hashem was displeased with Sarah's laughter and He confronted Avraham, asking, "Why did Sarah laugh, saying, 'Can it be true that I will give birth when I am old?' " (*Bereishis* 18:13). In fact, Sarah had also said, "...and my husband is old." As *Rashi* states, Hashem altered the truth for the sake of peace, for Avraham might have felt hurt that his wife referred to him as "old."[1]

---

1. See *Chofetz Chaim: A Daily Companion,* Days 92 and 114.

CONTINUED FROM DAY 43 — PAGE 87

ported me, and You have stood me erect before You forever" (Ibid. 41:13).

An outgrowth of this sterling quality is the quality of truth, which is one of the Thirteen Qualities (of Mercy) associated with Hashem Himself.

CONTINUED FROM DAY 45 — PAGE 91

As a young man in Russia, he came before the draft board and was accused by an army officer of having appeared the day before under a different name. "I have never told a lie my entire life," R' Yaakov said emphatically. The manner in which he spoke convinced the officer that he was telling the truth.

R' Yaakov went to great lengths to honor his word. He had agreed to attend the dedication of a new *sefer Torah* in Monsey, but later, the *vort* (engagement celebration) of one of his granddaughters was scheduled for the same day in Baltimore. R' Yaakov would not break his word, even for a grandchild's *simchah* (celebration). He traveled to Baltimore for Shabbos to celebrate with his family and returned to Monsey on *Motzaei Shabbos* so that he could attend the *hachnasas sefer Torah* the next day.

CONTINUED FROM DAY 46 — PAGE 93

To R' Yaakov, there was no question. "The Purim *seudah* (festive meal) is a Rabbinic *mitzvah*; "Distance yourself from falsehood" (*Shemos* 23:7) is a verse in the Torah." Reb Yaakov added that the Vilna *Gaon* had always made his Purim *seudah* early in the morning in keeping with the general rule that the zealous perform *mitzvos* at the first opportunity.

CONTINUED FROM DAY 47 — PAGE 97

and love in your heart — a tremendous reverence and respect, beyond any limit. When you take a closer look, you see the face of an angel, a ministering servant of G-d. The Divine Presence rests upon that face and you have to shut your eyes from the radiance streaming from those two grey piercing eyes. When he stands on the dais speaking, two rabbis support him with their arms. The entire assembly stands as it listens to him. His voice is weak, but clear. He summons the Jews to unity, to peace, to goodness, to fear of Heaven, to love of fellow man, to good deeds...

So, I imagine, Hillel the Elder, a sage in the Talmud, must have looked.

CONTINUED FROM DAY 48 — PAGE 99

desires through its worship of false gods whose "doctrines" satisfied their every craving. Body and soul could not have been more distant, more "out of touch" with each other. Then along came Avraham, who taught the world pure faith in Hashem and the way to serve Him. Thus, he "stitched" the "tear" between body and soul, and between mankind and Hashem.

CONTINUED FROM DAY 49 — PAGE 101

How much more true is it today when society at large has sunk to astounding levels of immorality and violence! As the Chofetz Chaim writes, the way to emerge unscathed from this spiritual war is by remaining steadfastly attached to Torah.

Those to whom Torah is their very lifeblood remained immersed in it under the most trying circumstances.

Once, R' Sholom Schwadron, accompanied by a son-in-law, went to ask the Brisker *Rav* a question on a statement of *Rambam* concerning the laws of sacrifices. It was a difficult question. The *Rav* listened attentively, then turned to his son, R' Yosef Dov, and said, "Tell them the answer — and the circumstances under which we arrived at it." Before saying the answer, R' Yosef Dov related the following:

"During the Second World War, when we were running for our lives towards Vilna, enemy aircraft were bombing the area ceaselessly. As we hurried down the road by wagon, the enemy noticed large numbers of refugees. They began to bomb the road itself — literally, right over our heads.

"In the grip of terror, we tried desperately to turn our wagon off the road to take shelter. We searched for concealment beneath the trees. At the very moment that we drove beneath the thick foliage and stopped, my father announced, 'I understand the *Rambam's* meaning!'

"That was the very *Rambam* you asked about now" *(Voice of Truth)*.

CONTINUED FROM DAY 50 — PAGE 103

talmidim, as he supervised the baking of the *matzos* which he would use on the holiday. As the baking process proceeded, he would hurry from worker to worker ensuring that each step in the process was being carried out correctly and with utmost haste. Whatever weariness he might have felt was hidden by his radiance and by the genuine joy which he derived from performing a *mitzvah*.

CONTINUED FROM DAY 51 — PAGE 105

severity of the subject's misdeed, so that the speaker becomes convinced that the subject is a rasha (evil person) and that it is a mitzvah to ridicule him. In reality, a Jew should take the opposite approach; he should judge his neighbor favorably and minimize his apparent misdeeds.

CONTINUED FROM DAY 52 — PAGE 107

because of it, for this [spiritual accomplishment] is his purpose in life. "If you have studied much Torah, do not take credit for yourself, for that is what you were created to do" (*Avos* 2:9).

CONTINUED FROM DAY 54 — PAGE 111

Rambam writes (*Hilchos Teshuvah* 7:6):

Great is *teshuvah* for it brings one close to the Divine Presence, as it is written, "Return, Israel, unto Hashem, your G-d" (*Hoshea* 14:2)... Yesterday, this man was contemptible, distant from G-d — but today, he is loved and desired, close and beloved... Yesterday, he was separated from Hashem, G-d of Israel — but today, he cleaves to the Divine Presence, as it is written, "You who cling to Hashem, your G-d — you are all alive today" (*Devarim* 4:4).

CONTINUED FROM DAY 56 — PAGE 115

you plan to invest. And remember, you plan to live in this edifice. If you limit yourself by according the anteroom such importance, you will regret the day that you purchased the property.

"My advice to you, therefore, is: Let us design the palace according to your desire, leaving but a small area for the anteroom. After we have completed the plans for the structure to your satisfaction, we will design an anteroom which will be the best one possible of such dimensions."

The lesson of this parable is obvious.

peasant's jacket which he wore on winter days, used as a cover on cold nights, rolled up under his head as a pillow, and used as a basket to haul groceries when necessary...

The Chofetz Chaim had no silver in his house — no silver Chanukah *menorah*, spice box or *esrog* box. The candlesticks used for Shabbos were brass. The only exception was an heirloom silver wine goblet, which he used for *Kiddush*.

Benches were used in his home rather than chairs. "So many people can sit on one bench," the Chofetz Chaim explained. "Two legs hold up the plank, and support several people. Why does each person need four legs?" Other times he elaborated, "G-d's throne is not complete until *Amalek* is defeated[3]... How can we sit so royally on grand chairs?"

The Chofetz Chaim once said that while the Jews languish in exile, Hashem contains His glory, as it were; His Presence is concealed within layer upon layer. It is only fitting, then, that we exercise restraint in our personal lifestyles.

---

3. See *Rashi* to *Shemos* 17:16.

Though the First *Beis HaMikdash* was destroyed because of the three cardinal sins which were found among a portion of the people, nevertheless, had their appreciation for Torah been adequate, G-d would have been yielding — because they would have been in a position to repent and better their ways. However, once they lacked a proper appreciation of Torah, it was impossible to ignore their sins.

(*Mishnas Rabbi Aharon*, based on *Rabbeinu Yonah* as cited by *Ran*)

R' Shlomo Zalman, by now no less excited than his brother-in-law, grasped R' Sholom's hands and together they sang and danced, the dance of joyous Torah study (from *Voice of Truth*).

We know that there is nothing which is not alluded to in the Torah. Where do we find an allusion that it is correct for a per-

son to sell all his possessions [leaving for himself just the bare minimum] so that he can acquire proper knowledge of Torah? The answer is, as we have said above, that the word אֶת *in the verse* אֶת ה' אֱלֹקֶיךָ תִּירָא *comes to include reverence for Torah. It follows, then, that the word* אֶת *in the verse* וְאָהַבְתָּ אֵת ה' אֱלֹקֶיךָ, *And you shall love Hashem, your G-d (Devarim 6:5) also includes love of Torah. That verse states that we should love Hashem with all our heart, with all our soul and with all our resources. Therefore, we must love the Torah in the same way, and like R' Yochanan, we should be prepared to make every sacrifice to acquire its sacred knowledge.*

CONTINUED FROM DAY 63 — PAGE 129

He began to pray with a *minyan* each morning and remain in the *beis midrash* afterwards for two hours to study Torah, despite the fact that customers and fellow merchants were waiting for him.

When, on the first day of his new schedule, he arrived at the store three hours later than usual, his distraught wife demanded, "Where were you? The store is packed with customers who are anxious to be on their way!" The man replied simply, "My delay was unavoidable."

When, on the second morning, the man again was late, his wife went to find him. How astounded she was to find him learning in the *beis midrash*! She began to shout at him: "What has gotten into you? Have you gone mad? The store is full of customers and you are sitting and learning! It is not so much the present loss that bothers me, but the fact that we will lose all those customers to our competitors!"

"My dear wife," her husband replied, "let me ask you a question. What would you do if the Angel of Death would come to me and say, 'Come, let us go, the time has come for you to depart this world.' Would you interject, 'No, not now — not when the store is full of customers!'

"Well, for these three hours each morning, consider me dead. The fact that I shall subsequently arise from the dead to tend to my store is irrelevant!"

Torah can endure only in one who considers himself dead during the time that he has designated for Torah study. With this approach, one will never free himself from learning with the excuse that he has no time — and in this merit, he will be granted eternal life (*Chofetz Chaim al HaTorah, Parashas Chukas*).

I acquired sufficient knowledge to even author some *sefarim*, including the *Ha'amek Sh'eilah* which I have now merited to complete.

Imagine for a moment where I might be today had I not heard my father's anguished words. I would have grown up to be a tailor, a shoemaker, or a carpenter. Coming from such a family, I would have been honest in business and each night after a day's work, I would have sat down to learn some *Mishnayos*, *Chumash* or *Ein Yaakov* [the Aggadic passages of the Tamlud]. I would have lived with the feeling that I had followed the proper path all my life and that I had a reward to anticipate in the World to Come.

But after my time on this world would have ended, I would have come before the Heavenly Court and they would have asked me, "But where is the *Ha'amek Sh'eilah*?" I would have been shocked by the question — after all, how could I, a common laborer, produce such a work? But they would have been right, for indeed, I *did* have the potential to write it.

Therefore, this *seudah* is a twofold celebration: to celebrate the completion of this work and to express my gratitude to Hashem that He led me on the path that would bring out my potential, which might have lain dormant forever.

acquire for himself a share in the scholar's Torah, as was the case with Yissachar and Zevulun. Bear in mind, however, that this is true only if he supports the talmid chacham in full, for then he becomes like an actual partner in his learning and has an equal share in it.

If he is unable to support the scholar singlehandedly, he should take with him one or two partners, and together they should support the scholar in full. The greater one's share of the support, the greater one's share in the Torah being studied.[1]

---

1. Even one who has undertaken a "Yissachar-Zevulun" partnership is not exempt from the obligation to study Torah each and every day. *Shulchan Aruch* states: "After leaving the synagogue,

one should go the study hall and set aside time for learning. This time period should be fixed, meaning that one should not miss it even if he thinks that [by missing it] he can earn much profit" (*Orach Chaim* 155:1). Furthermore, the *mitzvah* to study Torah is limitless; whenever one has available time for study, he is obligated to do so (see *Mishnah Berurah* ibid. 4; see also the Chofetz Chaim's closing comment on Day 66).

CONTINUED FROM DAY 66 — PAGE 135

Rabbi Chaim Volozhiner would often stress the point which the Chofetz Chaim makes above, that those who support Torah will be granted knowledge of Torah in the Next World. The Chofetz Chaim once related the following stories involving R' Chaim to butress this very point:

In R' Chaim's time there was a major dispute among the leading Torah authorities concerning some aspects of the laws of *shaatnez* (prohibited mixtures of wool and linen). One night, a former supporter of R' Chaim's yeshivah — who had been known in his lifetime as a simple Jew — appeared to R' Chaim in a dream. R' Chaim asked him what was being said in the Heavenly Academy on that issue, and the man replied with a full discussion of all the sources, as if he had been learning them all his life.

On another occasion, a wealthy man bequeathed to the Volozhiner Yeshivah the majority of his fortune. In return, R' Chaim promised to learn *mishnayos* as a source of merit for the man's soul. Shortly after the man's death, R' Chaim found himself having great difficulty understanding a particular *mishnah*. That night the deceased appeared to him and explained the difficulty. Upon awakening, R' Chaim commented, "I had no idea how quickly things go in Heaven. A Jew who was completely ignorant in Torah learning is able, after a few days in Heaven, to explain even the most complicated *mishnayos*" (from *Reb Chaim of Volozhin*).

CONTINUED FROM DAY 67 — PAGE 137

the person awakened on time but was grossly negligent — he became involved in idle conversation or business talk. For this, one would surely incur severe judgment.

And the same applies to Torah study. A person's free time should be devoted to the study of Torah. If he could be studying many hours each day and instead learns for only an hour, he will have to answer for this. But his judgment will be tempered by the fact that he did set aside fixed time each day for study, and he convinced himself [however wrongfully] that peroccupation with his livelihood did not allow for more learning. His situation does not compare with someone to whom the concept of Torah study is entirely a matter of choice. Such a person might go months without opening a sefer, though he had many opportunities to do so. It is of such a person that the Mishnah states: "Do not be a wicked person before yourself."

CONTINUED FROM DAY 68 — PAGE 139

sage Rava once declared: "When I die, R' Oshaya will come out to greet me [my soul], for I am wont to interpret our Mishnayos in accordance with his teachings" (*Bava Metzia* 62b). How great will be the shame when as these *tzaddikim* come forth in all their radiance, the soul will be met by hordes of accusing angels borne from his many sins.

The G-d-fearing person will take these thoughts to heart and seek to live a life that will produce angels of mercy to defend him on the day of judgment (from *Chofetz Chaim al HaTorah, Parashas Bereishis*).

CONTINUED FROM DAY 69 — PAGE 141

which he sinned. If he was guilty of gazing at immoral sights, he should accustom himself to keeping his eyes cast downward. If he sinned through lashon hara, let him toil in Torah study. With every limb with which he sinned, let him strive to fulfill mitzvos.
(Shaarei Teshuvah 1:35).

Rabbi Yehudah Zev Segal commented: "Sin brings spiritual impurity to the limbs through which it was accomplished. *Mitzvos*, on the other hand, bring sanctity. The impurity of sin can be eradicated only by the sanctity of *mitzvos*. In the words of our Sages, '*Tzaddikim*, through the very means with which they sin, they seek appeasement [before Hashem]' (*Inspiration and Insight*, Vol. II).

On another occasion Rabbi Segal said: "one should never give way to despair, for it is never too late for *teshuvah*. Moreover, through *teshuvah* one can attain awesome spiritual heights, as our Sages state: "The level attained by *baalei teshuvah* cannot be attained even by perfect *tzaddikim*" (*Berachos* 34b). This is alluded to in *Rabbeinu Yonah's* reference to *teshuvah* as a means "to ascend from within the snare of their deeds" (*Shaarei Teshuvah* 1:1).

closet with a magnificent wardrobe and beautifying his home, while according attention to his neshamah (soul) only sporadically. When he departs this world and ascends to Heaven, they will ask him, "So what merchandise have you brought us after being away so long in that faraway land?" How shamed the soul will be if all it has to show for itself is material indulgence, as it pampered the body in which it was clothed, while accomplishing little of substance. The Heavenly Court will declare, "Take what you have brought with you and dispose of it!"

Our parable continues.

this world and endures the suffering of Gehinnom for his sins, he will be ushered into Gan Eden where he will be honored to sit among the Heavenly angels. He will turn to these Heavenly beings and ask, "What's going on? Until now, I've been punished, shamed and subjected to the wrath of other types of angels. But here, it's altogether different. I am honored to dwell among you and I am being treated to pleasures the likes of which I never before experienced!"

The angels will reply: "We searched through your account and found that you had a few merits, from the little Torah study which you accomplished, your answering of "Yehei Shmei Rabbah..." and some other good deeds."

Upon hearing this, the man will burst into tears and cry out, "Woe is me! On the other world, I had tens of thousands of opportunities to study Torah and do other mitzvos. I could have studied thousands of words of Torah each day [and each word would have been a mitzvah in itself]. And there is so much more that I could have accomplished! Instead, I wasted my time and focused on earthly pleasures which lasted but a fleeting moment."

CONTINUED FROM DAY 73 — PAGE 149

"I have set Hashem before me always" is an essential principle for all of the Torah and for achieving lofty heights of the righteous who walk before G-d. For a person does not sit, move and occupy himself when he is alone at home in the same manner which he does when in the presence of a great king. The way in which he speaks and opens his mouth when he is with the people of his household and his relatives, is not the same as when he is at a royal assembly. How much more so when a person takes to heart that the Great King, the Master of the Universe, Whose glory fills the earth, stands over him and sees his every deed, as it is written, "Can a man hide in concealments that I cannot see him? — the word of Hashem" (*Yirmiyahu* 23:24). Immediately, he will attain awe and humility before Hashem, blessed is He, and will feel an ever-present sense of inadequacy before him.

CONTINUED FROM DAY 74 — PAGE 151

under supervision that satisfies even the most observant person. It is indeed possible for someone to be meticulously observant of *kashrus* and yet have at his disposal an abundance of ethnic foods and gourmet delights that enable one to be physically indulgent.

Spiritual achievement and physical delights are at opposite poles. Spirituality requires simplicity, using the goods of the world for survival and optimal function, to enable a person to pursue the ultimate goal in life: service of G-d. A healthy diet which provides adequate nutrition is essential, but titillating the palate with delicacies is not. Thus, if one is seriously interested in the pursuit of spirituality, one should be satisfied with the essentials of life, and forego all unessential excesses and luxuries.

(*Lights Along the Way*, pp. 186-187)

CONTINUED FROM DAY 75 — PAGE 153

Let us follow in the ways of Avraham. When seeing a friend acting in a negative manner, imagine yourself in his position and realize that everyone has his own personal struggles with the *yetzer hara* (evil inclination). Reprove him with gentle words that reflect respect. Show that you truly care and offer your help. This is a *chesed* of great magnitude.

(Inspiration and Insight, Vol. II, pp. 152-153).

CONTINUED FROM DAY 76 — PAGE 155

no cash on hand right now, but if you will return tonight, I will loan you the money." The rich man had a busy agenda that evening, but out of pity for the man, he remained at home waiting for him to come. But the poor man never came. The next morning, the two met in the street. "What happened?" the rich man demanded. "I stayed home last night only because you were so desperate for the money. Why didn't you come?" The poor man assured him that he *was* desperate for the money and said that he would come that night to receive it.

But the night came and went as did the previous night. The next time they met, the rich man lost his temper. "You are a scoundrel!" he thundered. "I wanted to help you but instead you just wasted my time! Don't seek my help ever again."

CONTINUED FROM DAY 78 — PAGE 159

Rabbi Yehudah Zev Segal would often note that the blessings which precede most *mitzvos* begin with, "Blessed are You, Hashem,... Who sanctified us..." Aside from the reward for performing a *mitzvah*, there is a degree of *kedushah* (sanctity) which manifests itself upon a Jew each time that he carries out Hashem's will. Of course, the power of a *mitzvah* is dependent upon a number of factors, especially the *kavanah* (intent) with which one performs a *mitzvah*. Those who were close to Rabbi Segal bear witness that he strove to perform every *mitzvah* with one hundred percent concentration and effort, and purely for the sake of Heaven.

He would preface every *mitzvah*, even those Rabbinically ordained, with a verbal declaration [הִנְנִי מוּכָן וּמְזוּמָן] expressing his intent to perform that *mitzvah*. Even when performing a simple, mundane chore like tying his shoes, Rabbi Segal would bear in mind that he was fulfilling a *halachah* (to tie the left shoe before the right).

Upon learning that one of his students had overslept past the deadline for reciting the morning *Shema*, Rabbi Segal told him, "You must have a strong heart, for you have missed fulfilling a Scriptural *mitzvah*, yet you have not collpased from distress!"

CONTINUED FROM DAY 81 – PAGE 165

attempt to apply the words of *Tanach* to his way of thinking, to propound from them original insights — as many are wont to do. Rather, he always applied his way of thinking to the wisdom of Torah [to understand the plain meaning of each Scriptural verse]. It is not surprising, then, that he was possessed of powerful faith and mighty hope that not one word would remain unfulfilled of the glorious future for our people that the prophets foretell.

CONTINUED FROM DAY 83 – PAGE 169

a time... I did not see anything special in his manner. Suddenly, when he reached נָא רַחֵם (*Have mercy...*) something seemed to happen to him. He cried out: " עַל יִשְׂרָאֵל עַמֶּךְ (*for Your people Israel*), *oy, oy!* וְעַל צִיּוֹן מִשְׁכַּן כְּבוֹדֶךָ (*for Zion, resting place of Your Glory*), *oy, oy!*" He continued in this manner until he reached the end of the fourth and final blessing and stopped (before the *"Harachamons"*). At this point he said, "I see what will be ten years from now. You don't see, but I do. A great conflagration will burn!" In the middle of *Bircas HaMazon*, he suddenly had a vision of future events. "Twelve million is child's play!"

I turned to the person next to me and asked him what the Chofetz Chaim meant with these comments. He replied, "He always talks about it. Twelve million is the sum total of those killed in the [First] World War."

I never forgot this scene and for ten years I repeated it, and waited watchfully, fearfully, for its realization — until ten years later, in 1940, when it started to come true.

This was the Chofetz Chaim.

CONTINUED FROM DAY 84 – PAGE 171

It will tell them what is going to happen and why it is going to happen." It is a very short and concise song, but it has exhaustive information in it. In that song there is a prophecy for everything that is going to happen to the Jewish people.

Hashem tells Moshe that the song is an עֵד. This word has two meanings: *witness* or *warning*. The song of *Haazinu* is both. It is a warning because it explains what the results of certain behavior will be. It is also a witness because we can observe through history that what has been predicted has come true. *Ramban* writes that the song is so accurate that even if we would find it written somewhere other than the Torah, we would have to believe every word of it (from *Reb Simcha Speaks*).

Ramban concludes his commentary to the song by stating:

This song is a clear promise of the future Redemption, contrary to what the heretics claim... Had this song been found in a stargazer's record of his predictions it would be proper to believe it, for all its words have come true to this point. How much more so do we have to believe and anticipate with all our heart the words of G-d which were communicated to His most trustworthy prophet [Moshe], may he rest in peace, who had no equal before him or after him.

(Ramban to *Devarim* 32:40)*

CONTINUED FROM DAY 85 — PAGE 173

...If he is victorious on all fronts, he will then be the "complete man" who will succeed in uniting himself with G-d, and when he leaves the antechamber [this earthly world] to enter the palace [the next world], he will bask in the light of the Divine splendor.

To the extent that one has subdued his evil inclination and desires, avoided those factors which detract from the good, and exerted himself to become united with the good, to that extent he will attain it and rejoice in it.

CONTINUED FROM DAY 86 — PAGE 175

Therefore, when the pride of our nation will be uplifted through the coming of Mashiach, we will attain prophecy and other priceless spiritual rewards without humiliation — for we will have earned it. Then, we will merit the fulfillment of, "...Yaakov will not be ashamed now, and his face will not pale now, when he sees his children, My handiwork, in their midst, who will sanctify My Name, they will sanctify the G-d of Yaakov and revere the G-d of Israel" (Yeshayahu 29:22-23).

Therefore, one who feels overwhelmed by the tribulations of the time should not lose hope, for all of this is a preparation for the glorious days of the future.

CONTINUED FROM DAY 91 — PAGE 185

America and asked to purchase a *Sefer Ketzos HaChoshen*, a work basic to in-depth Talmudic study. The storekeeper climbed a ladder and brought down a volume caked with dust. Wiping it off, he told R' Bloch, "Take good care of this — it's the last *Ketzos HaChoshen* that will be sold in America." He was not joking. With the great yeshivos of Europe gone and few yeshivos elsewhere, the future of Torah scholarship seemed bleak to the average observer.

R' Bloch, however, was not the average observer. He pounded his fist on the store's counter and declared, "And I say that they will yet sell *hundreds* of *Ketzos'en* in America."

Since those words were uttered, *thousands* of *"Ketzos'en"* have been sold in America — and the total number of *sefarim* sold here is probably in the millions. The miracle continues!

CONTINUED FROM DAY 94 — PAGE 191

Hussein, declared his intention to "incinerate the State of Israel." About one month later, Saddam miscalculated and invaded oil-rich Kuwait, which resulted in America and its "coalition" defeating Iraq in the Persian Gulf War. Though a decade later Saddam Hussein seems as dangerous as ever, this does not mitigate the miracle of Eretz Yisrael's salvation at that perilous juncture.

When the war ended on the eve of Purim, Jews around the world rejoiced euphorically. Thirty-nine Scud missiles, with the potential to wreak devastating losses, had been launched by Iraq. Entire housing complexes had been reduced to rubble, yet only one person died as a direct result of the Scuds. In most instances, everyone escaped with nothing more than superficial wounds and with stories of how he or she had left the scene of disaster only moments before the explosion, or how falling debris had missed them by inches.

In an address immediately following the Gulf War, the late Gerrer *Rebbe*, Rabbi Pinchos Menachem Alter, said:

> First and foremost, we are obligated to thank *Hashem Yisbarach* for all the goodness He has bestowed upon us until now. The

miracles that have occurred recently are so obvious that even people far removed from religion must echo the words of *Hallel*, "This emanated from Hashem, it is wondrous in our eyes" (*Tehillim* 118:23).

CONTINUED FROM DAY 95— PAGE 193

For now [in an instant] I could have sent My hand and stricken you and your people with the pestilence and you would have been obliterated from the earth. However, for this I have let you endure, in order to show My strength and so that My Name may be declared throughout the world (Shemos 9:15-16).

And then there are times when Hashem causes the heart of a gentile king to perceive the truth about the Jewish people so that he is inclined to be good to them. This is what happened with King Koresh (Cyrus) who declared: "All the kingdoms of the earth has the L-rd, G-d of Heaven, delivered to me, and He has commanded me to build a Temple for Him in Jerusalem. Among you of His entire people... let him go up to Jerusalem... and build the Temple" (Ezra 1:2-3).

In summation: Hashem has infinite ways of carrying out His will. This is what is meant by, "and with Him is abundant redemption."

(The third reason will be discussed in the following segment.)

CONTINUED FROM DAY 98— PAGE 201

---

his mind, were misdeeds. He found a source for this practice in a Talmudic passage which tells that once, the sage Rabbi Yishmael ben Elisha inadvertently tilted a lamp on Shabbos as he was studying. He recorded in his ledger, "I, Yishmael ben Elisha, studied and tilted the lamp on Shabbos. When the *Beis HaMikdash* is rebuilt, I will bring a choice animal as a sin offering" (*Shabbos* 12b). That he wrote this in a ledger, said the Chofetz Chaim, indicates that Rabbi Yishmael had a system of spiritual accounting.

On at least one occasion, the Chofetz Chaim was seen making a reckoning of every minute of his every waking hour to see if he had been guilty of wasting any time.

When his youngest son-in-law, Rabbi Mendel Zaks, and his wife moved into the Chofetz Chaim's home, he relinquished his attic as his place of study, except for two hours a day, when he would enter the attic alone to study *mussar* (ethical study for self-improvement). With his purity of faith, he regarded the *yetzer hara* (evil inclination) as an armed foe poised for combat who was forever devising schemes against him. From his place in the attic, he could often be heard holding a conversation with his *yetzer hara*, confronting it and rebutting it.

Once, during the *Aseres Yemei Teshuvah* (Ten Days of Repentance), Rabbi Zaks stood on the steps to the attic as he listened to his father-in-law describing himself as being on trial before the Heavenly Court. Graphically, he depicted his *mitzvos* and sins being weighed against each other and found to be equal. The Heavenly Court was merciful: "If he is alive, then let him repent of his sins!"

The Chofetz Chaim then cried out to himself, "Yisrael Meir, don't sleep — repent!"

CONTINUED FROM DAY 101— PAGE 207

the rest of his life, for Mashiach can appear on any given day.

If one truly believes in the possibility of Mashiach's imminent arrival, then he will constantly be in a state of spiritual preparation, through Torah, good deeds and repentance. If, however, such is not the case, then it is apparent that our talk of his imminent coming is mere lip service; in reality, our faith is quite miniscule. This is alluded to in the words told to Sarah, "No, you laughed indeed."

Apparently, Sarah's righteousness protected her from any retribution due to this lapse of faith. We, however, who are far from Sarah's spiritual level, must demonstrate our faith by readying ourselves spiritually so that we will able to greet Mashiach amid a spirit of joy.

CONTINUED FROM DAY 102— PAGE 209

toward helping himself to avoid the sin of lashon hara.

Mesilas Yesharim states (Preface) that it is important to constantly review commonly known truths, for only in this way are they implanted in one's heart and put into practice. Similarly, when one cautions others to avoid *lashon hara*, he himself remains alert to the dangers of forbidden speech and will be more careful to avoid it.

CONTINUED FROM DAY 103– PAGE 211

This sin causes the Jewish people to suffer more than any other nation (as indicated by Rashi to Shemos 2:14).[1]

Talmud Yerushalmi (*Pe'ah* 1:1) states that the reward for studying Torah is equivalent to that of all other *mitzvos* combined, and the punishment for speaking *lashon hara* is equivalent to that of all other sins combined. In *Sefer Shemiras HaLashon*, the Chofetz Chaim explains that Torah study impacts in the Upper Worlds in a way that no other *mitzvah* can. This is because Torah study is performed through the power of speech which essentially is a function of the soul. By contrast, speaking *lashon hara*, which corrupts the power of speech, has a devastating effect in the spiritual realm.

---

1. When Moshe realized that there were informers among the Jews, he said, "Indeed, the matter has become known!" (*Shemos* 2:14). *Rashi* (in his second explanation) interprets, "The matter that I [Moshe] had been puzzled about has been clarified for me. [I used to ask myself,] in what did Israel sin more than the seventy nations that they should be tyrranized with crushing labor? But [now that I see that there are informers among them], I see that they are deserving of such punishment."

CONTINUED FROM DAY 104– PAGE 213

---

hara, it is inconceivable that His glory will be revealed upon us.

Because this sin is widespread among the general populace, it is difficult to implant in their hearts the fact that speaking lashon hara is equivalent to eating ham — literally! The only solution is to assemble many dynamic speakers and other G-d-fearing individuals who will publicize this topic regularly. I have consulted with G-d-fearing men on this matter and it has been decided:

If we cannot rescue the entire generation from this sin, we can at least form a society of those who hearken to the word of Hashem. We shall call this group Agudas HaShomrim (Society of the Watchmen) in keeping with the verse, "One who guards his mouth and tongue, guards his soul from troubles" (Mishlei

21:23). The members of this group will strengthen shemiras halashon, for the honor of Hashem and His Torah.

CONTINUED FROM DAY 105— PAGE 215

Rabbeinu Yonah offers another reason why one should not pride himself for having learned much Torah: no matter how much Torah knowledge one has accumulated, it is miniscule compared to the infinite sea of knowledge which the Torah contains.

CONTINUED FROM DAY 106— PAGE 217

---

donations. The two men were quite pleased with this and took leave of R' Aharon without offering a cent.

R' Aharon's *talmid* was quite upset by this. He said, "I have an idea. The next time such visitors come I will stand behind them and motion to the Rosh Yeshivah as to how much money they should be asked to contribute." R' Aharon did not respond.

The next time such visitors came, the *talmid* did as he had suggested. Much to his dismay, however, R' Aharon ignored him and once again, gave his fiery talk on supporting Torah but did not make a formal request for money. Once again, the people left without leaving a contribution. Exasperated, the *talmid* respectfully asked why the *Rosh Yeshivah* had not solicited a contribution.

R' Aharon replied, "Let me be. It is a *zechus* (privilege) to support Torah. If they will have the *zechus* they will contribute." By this, R' Aharon meant to say that one must be worthy to support Torah study. When one is not worthy, Hashem prevents him from perceiving the immense privilege of participating in this *mitzvah*.

CONTINUED FROM DAY 107— PAGE 219

---

attention to the faults of his neighbor, however, Hashem acts swiftly to punish the guilty person. Therefore, when one speaks against others, he is aiding in the Heavenly prosecution of his fellow Jew, sinking to the level of an informer.

CONTINUED FROM DAY 108— PAGE 221

Some may deny the fact that these inventions came about only because Hashem willed it and instead will attribute their discovery to the great increase in scientific wisdom of recent times. They are like the wicked guest who denies the fact that his host has expended effort on his behalf and therefore feels no appreciation towards him. So too, these people lack a basic principle of faith and instead of recognizing and appreciating Hashem's blessing, they attribute major breakthroughs to nothing more than human intelligence and good fortune.

We who recognize the truth must seek to determine why Hashem has granted us these great gifts.

CONTINUED FROM DAY 109— PAGE 223

---

of advanced technology which has been employed in the service of Torah on a grand scale,[1] but is often used to appeal to man's lowest impulses and has corrupted the world at large to an astonishing degree.[2]

---

1. For example, millions of hours of Torah have been learned via cassete tapes.
2. The television is, of course, a prime example of this.

CONTINUED FROM DAY 112— PAGE 231

---

sinner." It is well known that our Sages have taught (Avos 4:3), "Whether unintentional or intentional regarding chillul Hashem [both are culpable]" and there is no extension of "credit" regarding chillul Hashem [i.e. retribution is swift]. Does not every Jew stand before Hashem each day like a Heavenly angel and declare, "We shall sanctify Your Name in this world just as they sanctify it in the Heavens above...?" Is he then to go and desecrate the Name of G-d and His Torah? Would Hashem's response to this not be, "Who asked that you sanctify My Name? — do not sanctify it and do not desecrate it by transgressing what is clearly written in the Torah!"

CONTINUED FROM DAY 114— PAGE 235

---

viceroy's goblet in Binyamin's sack, he brought the youngest of the tribes back to Yosef, who declared that the "thief" would now serve him as a slave.

But when the viceroy said, "I am Yosef," thus revealing himself as their long-lost brother, the reasons behind all that had transpired became crystal-clear to them. There were no more questions.

So, too, said the Chofetz Chaim, will it be in the days of *Mashiach*, when the One Above will reveal Himself to mankind and say, "I am Hashem." The blinders will be lifted from our eyes and we will fully comprehend all that transpired throughout history.

CONTINUED FROM DAY 116— PAGE 239

> This is a great concept and a wondrous device to remove all outside forces from oneself so that they will not have the slightest effect on him: that a person should establish in his heart, "Hashem is the true G-d and aside from Him there is no power in the world. The entire universe is filled with nothing but the unity of Hashem, Blessed is His Name..."
>
> (*Nefesh HaChaim* 3:12)

CONTINUED FROM DAY 119— PAGE 245

In *Sefer Shemiras HaLashon*, the Chofetz Chaim cites the teaching: "Jerusalem was destroyed only because its inhabitants limited their decisions to [the letter of] the law" (*Bava Metiza* 30b). He comments:

This seems difficult, for Scripture records many sins of which that generation was guilty! The answer to this is, that had the people overlooked the wrong caused to them, then Hashem would have forgiven them as well. However, they were absolutely unrelenting toward each other, demanding from one another whatever they could possibly extract according to the law — and Heaven judged them accordingly.

Let us strive to act towards one another with true *ahavas Yisrael*, and to ignore any hurt that others cause us — and through this may we merit the coming of *Mashiach*, speedily and in our time.

The Chofetz Chaim Heritage Foundation

Since 1989, the Chofetz Chaim Heritage Foundation has successfully launched innovative methods of promoting the Torah's wisdom on human relations and personal development. The foundation utilizes a vast array of effective communication tools including books, tapes, video seminars, telephone classes and a newsletter, designed to heighten one's awareness of such essential values as judging others favorably, speaking with restraint and integrity, and acting with sensitivity and respect. The Chofetz Chaim Heritage Foundation's programs reassert the Torah's timeless recipe for building a world of compassion and harmony.

The following opportunities for learning and personal growth are available through our offices.

BOOKS

Chofetz Chaim: A Lesson A Day and **Chofetz Chaim: A Daily Companion** can be used to participate in Shmiras Haloshon Yomi. Learning the laws of proper speech every day, in small portions, is the method that the Chofetz Chaim recommended for observing this crucial mitzvah. The Torah tells us that Shmiras Haloshon is a limitless source of blessing for ourselves, an essential element in our prayers being accepted, and the most effective way to merit Hashem's mercy.

Daily Learning Calendar

This free daily learning calendar created by the Manchester Rosh Yeshivah, zt"l is already used by thousands to participate in the program by learning the Chofetz Chaim's original work in Hebrew or **Guard your Tongue** in English.

TELEPHONE CLASSES

Our **Chazak Inspiration Line** offers easy-to-listen-to, 10 minute lectures on a wide range of topics such as Shalom Bayis, Shmiras Halashon, Inspiration for Difficult Times and Attaining Happiness. Callers have the opportunity to be inspired by some of today's most dynamic speakers, including Rabbi Yissocher Frand, Rabbi Ezriel Tauber, Rabbi Fishel Schachter and others. This free service is available 24 hours a day at:
718-258-2008 pin # 1234 and **845-356-6665** pin # 3100.

E-MAIL

Our email products offer subscribers a daily dose of inspiration. [Email editorial@chofetzchaimusa.org.]

Shmiras Haloshon Yomi is a daily email, taken from the highly popular **Chofetz Chaim: A Lesson A Day.**

Inspiration Online **offers quotes from the Torah's timeless wisdom that will motivate and inspire.**

THE SHMIRAS HALOSHON SHAILA HOTLINE

This telephone hotline puts callers in contact with expert rabbonim who can answer your halachic questions concerning proper speech. This free service is available at:
718-951-3696 from 9:00 to 10:30 p.m. Monday thru Thursday and Saturday nights.

CHOSEN WORDS NEWSLETTER

This unique biweekly publication is devoted entirely to providing inspiration and practical ways to grow in Avodas Hashem. Available for synagogues and schools and in an email version for individuals, it is filled with advice on effective prayer, better relationships and personal growth. Each issue provides engaging questions for Shabbos table discussions that make self-improvement in Avodas Hashem a lively and important family topic.

THE TORAH HOME SHIUR

Ideal for an organizational program, a yartzheit, Melave Malka or other event, these top-quality, widely-acclaimed videotaped lectures feature the world's most sought-after speakers. Titles include Shalom, The Power of Speech, Kiddush Hashem, and Healing Our World. Presentations are designed to generate meaningful discussion among members of your group.

MACHSOM L'FI

While Shmiras Haloshon is a requirement every day and at all times, focusing specifically on this mitzvah for a set period each day is a proven way to bolster your overall observance. Those who undertake a Machsom L'fi, commit themselves, in conjunction with others, to avoid speaking or hearing loshon hora during a two- hour period each day. This can be done as a powerful merit for someone who is ill, or for anyone that needs Divine mercy. Our office has everything needed to start a Machsom L'fi.

MISHMERES

This program brings 8,300 high-school girls throughout the country exciting programs and learning on shmiras haloshon and character development. For information on how to join, call **732-905-7944**.

B'DRACHOV

The elementary school division of our organization is devoted to creating teaching tools, resource material and programs for making character development an integral part of the classroom. To contact **B'Drachov**, call **732-905-7944**.

For more information about these or any of our other programs, please call us at
   800-867-2482.

Chofetz Chaim Heritage Foundation
6 Melnick Drive
Monsey, NY 10952